Making Gender

Making Gender

The Politics and Erotics of Culture

Sherry B. Ortner

BEACON PRESS • BOSTON

Beacon Press
25 Beacon Street
Boston, Massachusetts 02108-2892

Beacon Press books
are published under the auspices of
the Unitarian Universalist Association of Congregations.

"Is Female to Male as Nature Is to Culture?" was first published in *Feminist Studies* in 1972 and republished in *Woman, Culture, and Society*, ed. Michelle Zimbaist Rosaldo and Louise Lamphere, © 1974 by the Board of Trustees of the Leland Stanford Junior University; reprinted with the permission of the publishers, Stanford University Press. "The Virgin and the State" was first published in *Michigan Discussions in Anthropology* in 1976 and republished in *Feminist Studies* 4(3) (Fall 1978): 19–36; reprinted by permission of the publisher, Feminist Studies, Inc., Women's Studies Program, University of Maryland, College Park, MD 20742. "Rank and Gender" was first published as "Gender and Sexuality in Hierarchical Societies: The Case of Polynesia and Some Comparative Implications," in *Sexual Meanings: The Cultural Construction of Gender and Sexuality*, ed. Sherry B. Ortner and Harriet Whitehead, © 1981 Cambridge University Press; reprinted with the permission of Cambridge University Press. "Gender Hegemonies" was first published in *Cultural Critique* 14 (Winter 1990): 35–80; reprinted by permission of Oxford University Press.

02 01 00 99 98 97 96   8 7 6 5 4 3 2 1

Text design by Christine Taylor
Composition by Wilsted & Taylor Publishing Services

Library of Congress Cataloging-in-Publication Data
Ortner, Sherry B., 1941–
  Making gender : the politics and erotics of gender / Sherry B. Ortner.
    p.   cm.
  Includes bibliographical references and index.
  ISBN 0-8070-4632-9 (cloth)
    1. Sex role.   2. Sex symbolism.   3. Sex role—Political aspects.   4. Feminist anthropology.   I. Title.
  GN479.65.O77   1996
  305.3—dc20   96-12293

For Shelly, who died,

and

to Gwen, who was born,

in the course of all this

Contents

Preface

I find it strange to put together a collection of my own essays. It is not that I do not like to reflect upon them, but there is a sense of packaging the self that makes me uncomfortable. Nonetheless, here it is.

These essays span approximately twenty-five years, a fact that is quite astonishing to me. At one level I think of all of them as very much alive in the present. They embody issues that are still debated, positions that are still held, and a fair number of truths that still seem true. Yet at another level all of the essays exist for me as parts of a history, and this has several implications. First, although I have cleaned up some grammatical errors and the like, I have decided not to tamper with their contents. There are things I probably would not write today, and things I wish I had written differently, but there is something science fiction–like in trying to unwrite and rewrite the essays now, and I could not bring myself to do it.

The historicity of the papers also means that each was embedded in a particular context of writing that is still alive in my memory and consciousness. Each was written at a certain point in time, usually for a particular purpose, and often in the context of particular relationships—of friendship and solidarity, or of antagonism and competition, or both. I have thus added a note for each of the previously published essays detailing a bit of the personal and professional context, and the sometimes quite acrimonious intellectual politics, within which it was written.

Finally, of course, each essay has its own historically situated debts. The acknowledgments must thus for the most part be taken essay by essay. But a few broader thanks need to be expressed here, beginning with Lauren Bryant, formerly of Beacon Press, who urged me gently over the years to put this book together, and Marya Van't Hul, now of Beacon Press, who shepherded it through reviews and production with a combination of warmth, good will, and effectiveness that I consistently appreciated. Thanks also to Louise Lamphere and several anonymous press readers of the manuscript as a whole, for useful comments and reactions. And a vote of appreciation to Suzanne Calpestri, librarian extraordinaire of the Anthropology Library at the University of California, Berkeley.

On a more personal level, I have dedicated the book to Michelle Zimbalist Rosaldo, who first drew me into feminist anthropology. Shelly and I were at once personally close and professionally competitive, and when she died in a fieldwork accident in 1981 I mourned the loss not only of an intense and compelling friend, but of a sharp critic who kept me on my toes intellectually. I have also dedicated the book to my daughter, Gwen, now a maddening teenager and a wonderful human being, who keeps me on my toes in ever so many other ways.

Finally, for extraordinary friendship at every level—personal, political, intellectual—over the years I thank Abigail Stewart; for warm friendship as well as generosity in providing extensive and astute intellectual feedback, I thank Nancy Chodorow and Judith Stacey; and for daily backup and love, as well as always kind but insightful criticisms, I thank Timothy D. Taylor.

Making Gender

Toward a Feminist, Minority, Postcolonial, Subaltern, etc., Theory of Practice

With the title phrase "Making Gender," I point to the double meaning of "making" that operates in contemporary social and cultural studies. On the one hand we have a variety of "constructionisms" in which cultural categories, or historical subjects, or forms of subjectivity are—passive voice—made. The guiding theoretical frameworks here derive from a number of strands of French theory as represented by, among others, Louis Althusser, Jacques Derrida, and Michel Foucault. Despite significant differences between these figures, all have in their own ways directed us to see subjects as constructed by, and subjected to, the cultural and historical discourses within which they must operate. The usual terminology in this context is the heavier "construct" rather than the lighter "make." Within this perspective, the methodology is textual analysis in a broad sense—asking what forms of difference, what kinds of identities and subject positions are constructed within the framework of a given cultural, ideological, or discursive formation.

On the other hand we have "making" from the actor's point of view. The question is how actors "enact," "resist," or "negotiate" the world as given, and in so doing "make" the world. This making may turn out to produce the same old social and cultural thing—"reproduction." Or it may turn out to produce something new, although not necessarily what the actors intended. Indeed intention plays a complex role in the process, for while intention is central to what the actor seeks to accomplish—and therefore must be understood very carefully—its relationship to the outcome is often quite oblique. In any event, the terminology here is more from the language of craft than from heavy industry, "making" rather than "construction," as in E. P. Thompson's *The Making of the English Working Class*. And the methodology is fundamentally ethnographic rather than textual, descriptive and analytic rather than interpretive or deconstructionist—looking at and listening to real people doing real things in a given historical moment, past or present, and trying to figure out how what they are doing or have done will or will not reconfigure the world they live in.

The anthropological project in the fullest sense, as I see it, must always comprise both kinds of work. Studies of the ways in which some set of "texts"—media productions, literary creations, medical writings, religious discourses, and so on—"constructs" categories, identities, or subject positions, are incomplete and misleading unless they ask to what degree those texts successfully impose themselves on real people (and *which people*) in real time. Similarly, studies of the ways in which people resist, negotiate, or appropriate some feature of their world are also inadequate and misleading without careful analysis of the cultural meanings and structural arrangements that construct and constrain their "agency," and that limit the transformative potential of all such intentionalized activity.

There is by now an important body of theory that ideally unites these two forms of analysis—a range of loosely interrelated work that I have elsewhere pulled together under the rubric of "practice theory" (Ortner 1984, 1989). Practice theory represents one of several kinds of theoretical response to earlier structural determinisms—Parsonian systems theory and related functionalisms, Lévi-Straussian structuralism, certain kinds of mechanistic Marxism. Within a practice framework, there is an insistence, as in earlier structural-determinist models, that human action is constrained by the given social and cultural order (often condensed in the term "structure"); but there is also an insistence that human action *makes* "structure"—reproduces or transforms it, or both. Despite the label, practice theory is not really "a theory," in part because it does not pretend to some sort of formal unity, and in part because it lacks two key characteristics of classic social theory: an underlying narrative (for example, the march of modernization), and an underlying norm of the social order (as in functionalism's assumed norms of homeostasis and integration). There is only as it were an argument—that human action is made by "structure," and at the same time always makes and potentially unmakes it.

The first round of formal work articulating various aspects of this theoretical framework was done in the late 1970s and early 1980s—the key texts were Pierre Bourdieu's *Outline of a Theory of Practice* (1977), Anthony Giddens's *Central Problems in Social Theory* (1979), Marshall Sahlins's *Historical Metaphors and Mythical Realities* (1981), and Michel de Certeau's *The Practice of Everyday Life* (1984). Together this work offers one of the potentially most powerful and comprehensive frameworks available for the understanding of cultural and social life. Yet in some ways it seems by now to have stalled out. Although its earlier theorists positioned themselves, and the theory, broadly on the side of the subaltern—the underlying question was always how relations of power and inequality tend to get reproduced but can be changed through practice—yet in fact (with the partial exception of de Certeau) they made little effort to link up with the exciting body of work emerging from feminist and other forms of engaged scholarship in that same era.[1] Explorations of the multiple and contradictory forms of power and of resistance; of the multiple forms and degrees of "agency"; of the relationship of the private and intimate to large-scale structural change; of identity in a world carved up by race, ethnicity, class, and gender; of the adequacy of the very concept of structure—these and other issues have remained relatively marginal to practice theorizing, thereby jeopardizing its relevance to large areas of contemporary social thought.

In turn, although feminist anthropologists and others working in "engaged scholarship" have by no means ignored this work,[2] my sense is that there has been a fairly deep divide between the two arenas of scholarship. For one example, take a recent panel on "Agency" at the American Anthropological Association meetings (1995). This panel was concerned with theorizing agency for women and other subaltern subjects. While it seemed self-evident to me that the question of "agency" had been put on the table precisely as part of the development of practice theories beginning in the 1970s, in fact there was very little reference to that body of literature in the panel. Similarly, in the introduction to their important collection of essays, *Feminists Theorize the Political* (1992), Judith Butler and Joan Scott specifically raised (partly in order to challenge) a range of questions surrounding the absence of an intentional subject, or a notion of "agency," in poststructuralist feminist theory. The contributors to the collection included philosophers, literary critics, legal theorists, political theorists, historians, and an anthropologist. Yet none of them addressed either the gen-

eral theoretical arguments of practice theory, or (with the exception of one
footnote on Bourdieu) its specific theorists. Even in my own writings I have
unintentionally tended to segregate the two perspectives. In the work in
which I have most explicitly addressed practice theories (1984, 1989) I have
not incorporated gender or feminist issues (as commented on by Collier and
Yanagisako 1989 and Lutz 1990), while my feminist work has fairly consistently worked from some form of practice perspective without invoking the
intellectual genealogies or articulating the theoretical issues at stake.[3]

My purpose in this essay, then, which may both stand in itself and be
taken to introduce the essays that follow, is to critique practice theory from
a feminist and more generally subaltern perspective. The purpose of this exercise in turn is to attempt to draw practice theory more fully into the orbit
of feminist and other subaltern theorizing, in part because these perspectives themselves often fall into one or the other trap with which I opened the
essay: too much construction (textual, discursive, etc.) on the one hand, too
much making (decontextualized "resistance") on the other. Since I see practice theory as the only framework that theorizes a necessary dialectic between the two extremes, this strikes me as a useful, and even urgent,
endeavor.

Losing Power

I begin with the problem of the peculiar status of power in theories of practice.[4] None of the major theorists of practice ignores power, yet it is always
in some sense offstage.[5] For Bourdieu (e.g., 1990), for example, there are
structures of inequality and of domination, and various practices reproduce
these structures (or more specifically, reproduce the categories that underlie
them, and the mechanisms that render them unrecognizable). But the practices themselves are largely utilitarian and economistic, with actors seeking
to maximize various forms of capital to enhance their own positions within
these structures. Practices in Bourdieu are not practices of power as such—
acts of domination, control, violence; exercises of authority and claims of
truth; performances of strutting, boasting, humiliating. Or the other side:
rage, impotence, pain, humiliation; collaboration and sleeping with the enemy; struggle, resistance, revolution. This is not to say that such relationships and practices exhaust the totality of social life. But the argument
within feminist, minority, etc., theorizing is to say, let us move these
things—for a change—to the center of the theory and see what happens.

Of the three main practice theorists, Giddens is actually the strongest in foregrounding issues of power. He argues that "orthodox sociology lacked a theory of action [and] . . . this was directly linked to a failure to make questions of power central to social theory" (1979: 253). Yet his work, too, often seems detached from the concerns of feminist, minority, postcolonial, and subaltern theorists. One can tease out a number of possible reasons for this: that he is primarily concerned with social reproduction rather than change; that issues of power are locked into the formalist language of "structure" and "agency"; that his primary model of power is drawn from capitalist class relations and bureaucratic structures, which operate differently than relations of gender, race, and colonial domination.

Finally, let us look at Marshall Sahlins's handling of power in *Historical Metaphors and Mythical Realities* (1981), a gem of a book from which I take a great deal of inspiration. In this book, Sahlins lays out his original formulation of a practice-theoretical framework. He illustrates the arguments sketchily (it is a short book) but persuasively with material from eighteenth-century Hawaii pertaining to the arrival and eventual death of Captain James Cook in the islands.

Sahlins organizes his theoretical framework around what he calls "structures of the conjuncture," historical moments in which different systems of thought and practice—different cultures in this case, but Sahlins claims that other forms of difference would work just as well—come into engagement with one another, and potentially set in motion radical kinds of conceptual and practical unravellings. The illustrative case is the way in which aspects of traditional Hawaiian culture began to unravel, as Hawaiians—chiefs and commoners, men and women—engaged differentially with a variety of European persons and practices.

Sahlins is attentive to the internal politics of rank and gender among the Hawaiians themselves. Indeed these internal relationships of power and privilege are central to his narrative and his theoretical framework. Yet the engagement *between* the Europeans and the Hawaiians is curiously not treated as a relationship of power—here Sahlins moves into the more abstract language of "event" and "structure of the conjuncture." In the end, within Sahlins's account, Cook was killed not because of anything he or his men did to the Hawaiians, but because he violated a set of Hawaiian cultural expectations.

Sahlins's book became the target of a critique articulated from an explicitly postcolonial perspective: Gananath Obeyesekere's *The Apotheosis of Captain Cook: European Mythmaking in the Pacific* (1992). Obeyesekere did not himself focus on the question of power; he primarily went after Sahlins's assertions that the Hawaiians took Captain Cook to be a god, arguing that such a claim is a projection of European orientalist fantasies rather than a representation of Hawaiian realities. Sahlins responded vigorously in a 1995 book, *How "Natives" Think: About Captain Cook, for Example.* Most commentators have considered that Sahlins effectively demolished this particular part of Obeyesekere's argument at multiple levels—in terms of greater control of the data and greater plausibility of its interpretation, and in terms of the ironic reversal of positions wherein the scholar writing from the postcolonial position was forced to deny the authenticity of native Hawaiian culture in favor of a universalized "common sense."

Yet there is a strand of Obeyesekere's book that I found very compelling, and that—unless I missed something in the extraordinary detail of Sahlins's response—Sahlins never refuted. Obeyesekere foregrounded incidents in which Cook, the other British captains, and the crewmen all regularly committed acts of humiliation and violence vis-à-vis the Hawaiians, including an ambiguous incident in which a wooden fence around a ritual compound was taken away by them for firewood; severe and excessive floggings of Hawaiians who stole goods from the ships; and Cook's own increasing moodiness, rage, and violent reprisals in the face of the Hawaiians' increasing "insolence."[6] Although this strand of Obeyesekere's argument got lost in the tangle of trying to prove whether or not the Hawaiians took Cook to be a god, it provides the launching point for re-reading the British-Hawaiian encounter in terms of its fundamental inequality. It forces a recognition of the systematic practices of power and domination, and small and large acts of resistance, that shadowed the economic, sexual, and cultural exchanges that comprised the "structure of the conjuncture." I am inclined to take this piece of Obeyesekere's critique quite seriously, not only because Obeyesekere supports it well and the almost indomitable Sahlins is unable to blow it away, but because it takes shape precisely in the gap that I am pointing to here, the displacement of power and struggle in some of the most influential works of practice theory.

Recovering Agency

If practice theory is somewhat problematic on issues of power, it is nonetheless important for its contributions to questions of agency. Indeed it is precisely for this reason that I am arguing for a greater rapprochement between feminist, minority, postcolonial, and subaltern scholarship, on the one hand, and practice theory on the other. Before launching on this discussion, however, it must be emphasized that the practice-theoretical perspective on agency is in no way a form of voluntarism, does not presume that agents are free individuals, does not construct the agent as a bourgeois subject, and so forth. Rather, practice theory is a site—perhaps the only site—in which there is an effort to theorize human agency without falling into any of those traps.

THE EXCLUSION OF THE SUBJECT AND OF AGENCY

Earlier forms of social theory—British-American structural-functionalism, certain kinds of deterministic/mechanical Marxism, French structuralism—were specifically elaborated without an intentional subject. For both theoretical and real-world reasons, there was a commitment to a view of society and history as machines or organisms, operating according to their own laws and logics, quite apart from the desires and intentions of social actors. The 1970s saw a variety of reactions against these models, including practice theories, but also a range of work gathered under the rubric of poststructuralism. Poststructuralisms also saw themselves as reacting against the mechanism and determinism of the earlier structural(ist) frameworks, yet in contrast to practice-oriented approaches, these schools sustained the position that the intentional subject or "agent" must be excluded from the theoretical model.

For specific historical reasons, in turn, this anti-subject or anti-agent poststructuralism had what many felt to be a surprising impact on certain strands of feminist and postcolonial scholarship. Feminist theorists who take the poststructuralist position clearly assume that the deconstruction of the subject is a radical act, and that leaving any notion of the subject intact poses grave dangers, both intellectual and political: "What are the political consequences for feminism of embracing the subject? What kinds of racial and class privileges remain intact when the humanist subject remains unchallenged?" (Butler and Scott 1992: xvi). The entire theoretical apparatus is often directed toward showing the ways in which the (apparent) subject is actually an ideological effect, a discursively constructed position that cannot recognize its own constructedness.

The anti-subject position has taken a related, but slightly different turn within discussions of postmodernity (as a historical era) and postmodernism (as a theoretical position). Recent accounts of postmodernity have emphasized among other things the fragmentation of the postmodern subject, its depthlessness and lack of coherence. Some (e.g., Baudrillard 1988, Lyotard 1984) have celebrated this development, while others (especially Jameson 1984) have lamented it, but all have agreed that the era in which subjects sought coherence, meaning, and purpose in life, and experienced alienation in the absence of such meaning and purpose, was over.

In response to these positions that omit, exclude, or bid farewell to the intentional subject, there has been a good deal of critical reaction across a broad front of feminist, minority, postcolonial, and subaltern theorizing. The general point across these various responses is that the denial of the intentional subject, and of "agency," both misreads and works against the intellectual and political interests of women, minorities, postcolonial, and other subaltern subjects. In a powerful recent paper, for example, José Limón considers some of the arguments about the postmodern subject in relation to his experiences with and observations of barroom dancing and brawling among poor, working-class Mexican Americans of south Texas (1991). Limón argues eloquently that, while life for these people is indeed full of discontinuity, disruption, and fragmentation, the forms and patterns of their dancing represent a struggle *against* these things, an effort, however momentary and inadequate, to construct a world of meaning and coherence. Similarly, in a discussion of minority and postcolonial discourse, Abdul JanMohamed and David Lloyd address the poststructuralist rather than postmodernist variant of the problem:

> But where the point of departure of poststructuralism lies within the Western tradition and works to deconstruct its identity formations "from within," the critical difference is that minorities, by virtue of their very social being, must begin from a position of objective *non-identity* which is rooted in their economic and cultural marginalization vis-à-vis the "West." The non-identity which the critical Western intellectual seeks to (re)produce discursively is for minorities a given of their social existence. But as such a given it is not yet by any means an index of liberation. . . . On the contrary, the non-identity of minorities remains the sign of material damage to which the only coherent response is struggle, not ironic distanciation. (1987: 16)

THE UNMAKING OF FEMALE AGENCY

Before considering the ways in which practice theory can restore agency without reproducing the bourgeois subject. I want to explore briefly, and through a concrete example, the notion of identity "damage" raised by Jan-

Mohamed and Lloyd (see also Ortner 1995a). I once spent some time analyzing *Grimms' Fairy Tales*, with an interest in seeing the ways in which female agency was constructed differently from male agency, the ways in which heroines were different from heroes.[7] I suppose I expected to find the usual binaries: passive/active, weak/strong, timorous/brave, etc. What I had not quite expected to see was a recognition in the tales that female characters had to be *made* to be passive, weak, and timorous, that is, a recognition that agency in girls had to be *unmade*. Most of the Grimms' heroines are in the mode of what the folklorist Propp (1968) calls "victim heroes": although they are the protagonists, the action of the story is moved along by virtue of bad things happening to them, rather than their initiating actions as in the case of the majority of male heroes. Thus non-agency, passivity, is to some extent built into most of them from the outset. Yet in many cases even these victim heroines take roles of active agency in the early parts of the story. Though their initial misfortunes may have happened to them through outside agency, they sometimes seize the action and carry it along themselves, becoming—briefly—heroines in the active questing sense usually reserved for male heroes.

The structure of virtually all the tales is one of "passage," of moving from childhood to adulthood. For the boy heroes, passage generally involves the successful enactment of agency—solving a problem, finding a lost object, slaying the dragon. For all of the female protagonists, on the other hand, passage almost exclusively involves the *renunciation* of agency. Agentic girls, girls who seize the action too much, even for altruistic reasons, are punished in one of two ways. The less common form of punishment, first, is the denial of passage to adulthood. Five of the tales have heroines who are fully active and fully successful in enacting their projects.[8] To take the most familiar example among these, in "Hansel and Gretel" it is Gretel who tricks the witch and pushes her into the oven. But at the end of the story Gretel returns to her natal home, still in the status of child. She does not achieve what the vast majority of the Grimms' heroines achieve—the mark of female adulthood, marriage.

In the more common female tale, the heroine gets married at the end. But if she has been at all active in the early part of the tale, she must invariably pass through severe trials before being worthy of marrying the prince, or indeed being worthy of any man at all. These trials always involve symbols and practices of utter passivity and/or total inactivity, as well as practices of humility and subordination. For example, in "Sweetheart Roland" she cleverly saves her skin at the beginning, and then saves both herself and her lover, but for her pains her lover betroths another woman. In response, the heroine turns herself first into a stone, then into a flower, and finally cleans house for some time for a shepherd before marrying her sweetheart in the end.[9] The renunciation of agency here is quite painful. To be a stone is to be utterly inert and identityless; to be a flower is to hope to be crushed: "'Somebody at least will tread upon me,' she thought" (*Grimms'* ... 1945: 65).

If any sort of agency must be punished, even for "good" girls, the punishment is even worse for "bad" female characters, witches and wicked stepmothers. These women are highly agentic—they have projects, plans, plots. Needless to say, they all come to terrible ends. After trying and failing to kill Snow White, for example, the stepmother/witch is invited to the wedding of Snow White and the Prince, but once there she is forced to dance in red-hot slippers until she falls down dead. Since she and similar characters have done wicked things, their punishments seem justified on moral grounds, yet within the general pattern of punishing any sort of female agency, it seems fair to suggest that they are punished as much for their excessive agency as for its moral content.[10]

This detour through *Grimms' Fairy Tales* was meant to make a number of points. At one level I am in agreement with poststructuralist and other constructionist positions: the forms and distributions of "agency" are always culturally and politically constructed. Thus *Grimms' Fairy Tales*, like any other cultural texts, must be treated as elements of a larger discourse, a universe of politically inflected meanings through which (among other things) agency is culturally shaped and organized. At the same time, however, we must assume that "agency"—defined minimally as a sense that the self is an authorized social being—is part of simply being human, and thus that its absence or denial is as much of a problem as its construction. Here the tales have been treated as parables of a certain failure in poststructuralist and other anti-subject positions, a failure to recognize that the absence of agency and legitimate intentionality must be seen very critically as effects of power.

This argument is not new; the debates about the political and epistemological adequacy of both poststructuralism and postmodernism, specifically with respect to the agency question, have been going on for some time (see, e.g., Alcoff 1994 [1988]). But that is just the problem. The debates tend to be posed in such a way that one appears to have to choose between

total constructionism and total voluntarism, between the Foucauldian discursively constructed (and subjected) subject, or the free agent of Western
fantasy. It is the argument of a practice theory framework, however, that
this choice is both unnecessary and wrong, which brings us back, finally, to
the point of departure: the construction of agency within practice theory,
and its potential for resolving this problem.

PRACTICE THEORY AND THE RECOVERY OF THE SUBJECT

If poststructuralism was one response to earlier mechanistic and deter-
ministic frameworks, practice theory was another. But whereas poststructuralism, like earlier theories, excluded the intentional subject, practice-
oriented theories offered a way to put human intention and desire back into
the picture. Ironically enough, one of the chief architects of practice theory,
Pierre Bourdieu, nonetheless held out against the idea of the intentional
subject: for Bourdieu there are practices, there are actors, but there are no
significant intentionalities: actors strategize, but their strategies are drawn
from an internalized *habitus* that is itself a virtual mirror of external limits and possibilities. Actions are thus "intelligible and coherent without
springing from an intention of coherence and a deliberate decision; [they
are] adjusted to the future without being the product of a project or plan"
(1990: 50–51).[11]

On this particular point, then, we must set Bourdieu aside. But both Giddens and Sahlins are, in different ways, quite strong on issues of agency, and
specifically on the ways in which agency is both a product and a producer
of society and history. Giddens theorizes knowledgeable and intentional
agents who have the capacity to reflect on their own actions and the ability
to see, to some extent, into the workings of the larger forces that are imping-
ing upon them. At the same time he recognizes, and theorizes, the always
complex relationship between subjects' intentionality and knowledgeabil-
ity, on the one hand, and, on the other, the actual shape ("structure") of a
world which is never a direct outcome of those intentions.

Sahlins works from the same basic assumptions, but handles them differently. Whereas Giddens takes questions of "agency" at the generic level,
Sahlins's discussions are always embedded within the interpretation of ethnographic and historical cases. He is thus able to show in quite nuanced
ways the cultural construction of subjects and agents, and the ways in which
those varying constructions both inflect the historical process, and are
themselves transformed over time (see especially Sahlins 1985 as well as

1981). Moreover, Sahlins's actors are always enmeshed within complex social and political processes, and we are never able to imagine (as sometimes happens with Giddens's abstract modeling) a pure "agent" standing apart from some larger, and constantly shifting, set of relationships.

At this point, we must begin to start pulling the pieces of the discussion together. The problem is in many ways one of representation. Writing in terms of the old binaries—structure/event, structure/agency, habitus/practice—is, I think, a dead end. The challenge is to picture indissoluble formations of structurally embedded agency and intention-filled structures, to recognize the ways in which the subject is part of larger social and cultural webs, and in which social and cultural "systems" are predicated upon human desires and projects. Giddens and Sahlins point us in the right direction, but we need to go further.

Serious Games

Drawing on the essays in this volume, I want to propose a model of practice that embodies agency but does not begin with, or pivot upon, the agent, actor, or individual. While there are very definitely in this view actors and agents, desires and intentions, plans and plots, these are embedded within—what shall we call them? games? projects? dramas? stories?—in any event, motivated, organized, and socially complex ways of going about life in particular times and places. Of the terms just noted, and for reasons that I hope will become clear in the discussion to follow, I find "games" to be the most broadly useful image. But because the idea of the game in English connotes something relatively light and playful, I modify the term: "serious games."[12] The idea of the "game" is meant to capture simultaneously the following dimensions: that social life is culturally organized and constructed, in terms of defining categories of actors, rules and goals of the games, and so forth; that social life is precisely social, consisting of webs of relationship and interaction between multiple, shiftingly interrelated subject positions, none of which can be extracted as autonomous "agents"; and yet at the same time there is "agency," that is, actors play with skill, intention, wit, knowledge, intelligence. The idea that the game is "serious" is meant to add into the equation the idea that power and inequality pervade the games of life in multiple ways, and that, while there may be playfulness and pleasure in the process, the stakes of these games are often very high. It follows in turn that the games of life must be played with intensity and sometimes deadly earnestness. As a final note there is an assumption that there is never only one game, a point that will take on some importance as the discussion proceeds.

Other terms could be used to represent these forms of embedded agency, or what might be called "structures of agency." "Project," for example, is useful in emphasizing the purposiveness of the enterprises of life, but perhaps carries overtones of too conscious a level of intentionality, and at the same time does not conjure up a picture of an intensely social process, with multiple players. "Drama" come closer in this respect—there are multiple interacting characters—but the term seems to put too much weight on the prior "scripting" of the play.[13] "Stories" and "narratives" can be powerful frames for this kind of discussion, yet they may also seem too exclusively linguistic or discursive, and carry overtones of inappropriate fictionality as well.[14] Nonetheless, I have used all of these terms in certain contexts, and have found all of them analytically and interpretively effective for certain purposes. I do not mean to exclude them but have settled for the moment on "serious games" as the most comprehensive theoretical category.

At the same time I do not want to fetishize "games" any more than "structure," "agency," and the like. Any such freezing of categories is itself usually a mistake. The idea of the game is on the one hand drawn from a variety of past social theories (including practice theory; Bourdieu [1990] uses it extensively) as a way of getting past the free agency question, and theorizing a picture of people-in-(power)-relationships-in-projects as the relatively irreducible unit of "practice." At the same time, a feminist/minority/postcolonial/subaltern perspective forces one—forced me, at any rate —to push the usage of the game idea in various directions, and to put relatively novel kinds of pressures on the concept. As a way of seeing its heuristic twists and turns, then, I turn to the papers in this collection.

We may start, as I once started, with de Beauvoir and the existentialists. One of the central terms of existentialist philosophy is the "project," the intentionalized vision of purpose, of making or constructing the self and the world:

> The most rudimentary behavior must be determined both in relation to the real and present factors which condition it and in relation to a certain object, still to come, which it is trying to bring into being. This is what we call *the project*. (Sartre 1968:91)

In *The Second Sex* (1953 [1949]), Simone de Beauvoir derives an entire semiotics of gender from placing a particular project at the center of her

analysis. She says, in effect, that one of the central projects of human existence is the attempt to transcend the natural limits of being human—the in-
evitable and irreducible bodily vulnerability to illness, injury, and death.
Both men and women, as human beings, share this project, but they have
different relationships to it. From this basic starting point, de Beauvoir is
able to develop a very powerful account of the logic of gender in Western
cultural thought, and of the system of representations through which it is
realized.

In "Is Female to Male as Nature Is to Culture?" I took this argument and
did little more than translate it and update it in relation to some feminist anthropological questions of the 1970s. There were a number of things right
and wrong with that paper, which I discuss in several other essays in this
volume ("Gender Hegemonies," and "So, *Is* Female to Male . . ."). Here I
simply point to the methodology, the idea that an understanding of the project, the underlying game, will allow one to unravel extensive aspects of the
semiotics of the situation. Thus I began with de Beauvoir's point that one of
the important games underlying gender ideologies is the game of transcendence of nature, of bodily vulnerability and bodily limits. Given women's
bodily hostage to pregnancy, childbirth, and nursing, in turn, a situation is
created in which women seem to stand for everything that humanity (both
men and women) is trying to escape and transcend. For de Beauvoir's analytic purposes, this situation is what allows men to construct themselves as
subjects vis-à-vis women as objects, Selves vis-à-vis women as Others. I was
less interested in the construction of subjects and objects, and more in the
construction and justification of certain social arrangements, but the basic
point was the same.

If, in these arguments, the game is transcendence, the "structure" that
frames and produces the game is the organization of human existence itself,
the fact that vulnerable bodily beings are also bearers of reflective consciousness who can always imagine or fantasize escapes and alternatives.
On a smaller scale than the organization of human existence, but still on a
fairly large scale of "structure," we may look at the emergence in human social evolution of those large-scale formations of organized inequality called
"states," as I did in a paper called "The Virgin and the State." The official
problem of that paper was, under what conditions did ideas of the protection of female purity and virginity, largely absent in "simple" and "tribal"
societies, emerge? The short answer was, "the rise of the state."[15] I have
some ambivalence today about this sort of social-evolutionary argument,

but the paper seems to work on another level as well, relevant for the present discussion. That is, one can reread the paper as an exercise in the structural production of new games.

States seem to generate at least two new games that have relevance for questions of gender. One is the game of power and authority we would call patriarchy, in which the role of father as an essentially political role emerges. Fathers are constructed as disciplined positions within a hierarchy, made responsible to the state as "heads of household"; at the same time fathers are accorded tremendous power and authority over the subordinates within their households, the women and the junior males; and finally fathers are highly fetishized within the symbolic order, as ancestors, gods, or God.

The other new game is that of social mobility, the newly conjured desire to move up, now that there is an up to move to. This game intersects with gender in an almost endless variety of ways, but I call attention particularly to the newly emergent practice of hypergamy, of women marrying up the social ladder as part of their fathers' and brothers' dreams of mobility. The enforcement of female purity, I argued, is a corollary of this, a way of constructing the woman as worthy of the hoped-for higher-status husband. Yet though this is a man's game, women often embrace these desires and restrictions as well, for there is always a chance that the game will work to their benefit, or that of their daughters.

(Male) games of status and power are also at the heart of the paper entitled "Rank and Gender."[16] Here I locate a central "game" in play across a large number of Polynesian societies, and try to show how the analytic grasp of this game illuminates an enormous range of gender and sexual representations and practices in these societies. The game is once again the game of mobility in an ostensibly immobile society, a society with hereditary rankings. It involves a certain kinship strategy in which, among other things, daughters ideally remain attached to their parental households, bring in husbands, and bear children who in turn remain attached. Men's status is, once again, contingent upon the control they can exercise over the sexuality of their sisters and daughters.

Unlike the previous paper, however, this one explicitly attempts to shift around and look at the system from the different positions established by the game. Junior men and senior men, chiefs and commoners play it differently. Both women and junior men are in many ways pawns within senior men's games. But in some parts of Polynesia (especially the Western Polynesian societies), women can be seen to play the game differently as sisters or as wives. As sisters they identify with their brothers' games of status, and they are themselves rewarded in this position with status and respect. In marrying and becoming "wives" however, women often lose both status and power. This contradiction will reappear in other ethnographic contexts as well.

Female Agency?

One of the problems running through the papers discussed so far is a tendency to see women as identified with male games, or as pawns in male games, or as otherwise having no autonomous point of view or intentionality. At the very least it appears that, even if women have their own projects, these do not significantly organize the cultural order of gender representations and practices, which largely embody a male point of view. Thus the question of how to think about women's relationship to a hegemonically masculinist (if not "male dominant") social order must still be addressed.

It is unsatisfactory to assume that women wholly identify with the hegemony, but it is nonetheless difficult to come up with an alternative that does not fall into the opposite trap, casting women as enacting wholly different (and often supposedly morally better—more "nurturant" and so forth) projects. Thus in the paper called "The Problem of 'Women' as an Analytic Category,"[17] I specifically undertake to look at women as agents without—ideally—falling into these various traps. Are there "women's games" as such?" More generally, how is subaltern agency constructed and enacted?

The case in point was the founding of the first Sherpa nunnery by a group of young women. The Sherpas are a Tibetan Buddhist people of northeast Nepal whom I have been studying since the mid-1960s. In the early decades of the twentieth century, they began to upgrade their religion by building monasteries. This was a grass-roots movement on the part of some young men from relatively high-status families. Shortly after the first monasteries were built, a group of young elite women secretly ran away from their homes to take religious vows in Tibet, and then returned to found the first nunnery.

Although from one angle the women had their own gendered motivations, coming from specifically female experiences in the society, the fact that both they and the male monks were from the more elite sectors of the society meant that they shared as many motives as not. Moreover, the men who became monks were often the disadvantaged middle sons in elite families, which rendered them in some ways structurally parallel to the women, who were disadvantaged within elite families by gender. Thus at one level the paper answered the question of these women's intentionalities by saying, once again, that they were not that much different from the men's.

But to say that they shared men's motives is not to say that they lacked (independent) "agency," in the sense of authorization to have one's own point of view and desires. The point is rather that the two forms of agency are differently organized: women's agency may be seen as bound into a contradiction that undermines its possibility for enactment. Sherpa women are in fact culturally constructed as relatively independent and autonomous persons, as many observers have noted. On the other hand they are restricted from enacting their independence because of gender-biased property rules, the normative authority of husbands over wives, and the cultural representations that portray women as weak and excessively self-interested. This contradiction of the simultaneous encouragement and undermining of women's agency appears in other cultural contexts as well. The elite Hawaiian women who will be discussed in a moment seem to have been operating out of a similar contradiction.

Subaltern Practice Theory

In order to discuss the two final essays in this book, I need to return for a moment to the critique of practice theory begun earlier. As R. W. Connell has emphasized (1987), practice theory in the hands of Bourdieu and Giddens in particular tended to emphasize the role of practice in social reproduction rather than change. This was another aspect of its seeming disconnection from, if not opposition to, the bodies of feminist, subaltern, minority, and postcolonial theory also evolving in this period. Of course questions of social reproduction and social transformation can never, and should never, be wholly separated. But there is a difference in the angle of vision and questioning with which one comes at the analysis. One can do practice analysis as a loop, in which "structures" construct subjects and practices, but subjects and practices reproduce "structures." Or one can do—what shall we call it? subaltern practice theory?—and choose to avoid the loop, to look for the slippages in reproduction, the erosions of long-standing patterns, the moments of disorder and of outright "resistance."

One approach to this looser and more disruptive version of practice theory may be seen in the paper called "Gender Hegemonies." Here the point of departure is the lack of totalization of "structure" itself. The paper is primarily concerned with rethinking "universal male dominance" by way of rethinking "culture" or "structure"—seeing these formations not as totalized hypercoherent objects, but as always partial hegemonies. Much of the paper is taken up with looking at ethnographic cases and trying to think about the ways in which they are or are not "male dominant." But the point of the argument is that, whatever the hegemonic order of gender relations may be—whether "egalitarian," or "male dominant," or something else—it never exhausts what is going on. There are always sites, and sometimes large sites, of alternative practices and perspectives available, and these may become the bases of resistance and transformation. Thus in the last part of the paper, I return to Polynesia and look at the famous case of nineteenth-century Hawaii, in which a group of elite women organized what can only be called a cultural coup, and succeeded in overthrowing the gender arrangements and taboos of their society.

At one level the analysis was an enactment of the classic practice theory agenda. I looked at how the Hawaiian women were constructed by their own culture and history (pushed by cultural and historical contradictions, enabled by elite political status, etc.), and how they in turn (re-)made their culture and history. But the emphasis was on the disjunctions in, rather than the coherence of the structure, on the creativity of the women within the limits of their traditional politics, on the transformations rather than the continuities that ensued. This, then, is one aspect of the subaltern version of practice theory, with everything slightly—but not completely—tilted toward incompleteness, instability, and change.

The final paper complexifies the picture in another way, multiplying not so much the sites of practice, and the contradictions of practice, around and within a single cultural game, but the number of games in play. This paper, called "Borderland Politics and Erotics . . . ," looks at the entry of women, both "first world" and Sherpa, into high-altitude Himalayan mountaineering. In it I follow a slow interactive process that takes place over the course of the whole twentieth century. I look at how a set of gendered meanings gets worked out interactively, from about the 1920s to the 1970s, between men from western and/or dominant cultures ("sahibs") and (male) Sherpas in the intimate and dangerous arena of extreme high-altitude mountaineering. I then look at how those meanings get destabilized for both sahibs and Sherpas as women enter the sport from the 1970s on. Both first-world women ("memsahibs") and Sherpa women come in at about the same historical moment. For both it is a relatively radical act, given the till-then overwhelmingly male nature of the sport. But the styles of practice and the meanings at stake are different for the two sets of women, and for the men as well. And in the end, things have changed for all concerned, in desired and undesired ways, by accident as well as by design. Borrowing a phrase from an early feminist manifesto (Firestone 1972), I call this long, multi-stranded and multi-loop process a "dialectic of sex"—the making and re-making of gender over a long duration, through cultural games of both power and (would-be) solidarity.

The story of gender in Himalayan mountaineering is global and transnational; there are many games in play simultaneously—colonial, national, racial, gendered—and they all keep changing over time as well. This multiplicity of games in turn has multiple effects. On the one hand it establishes the limits on any single one of them: within one (historically specific, and now changing) ordering of the games, Sherpas had to play the sahibs' game even if it killed them. On the other hand the sheer multiplicity of games provides a sense of alternatives, a sense that there are other ways of doing the game of life, even if those alternatives are not immediately available or not subjectively desirable. What is important is that they exist, and thus always prevent closure.

Some Brief Conclusions

One of the central games of life in most cultures is the gender game, or more specifically the multiplicity of gender games available in that time and place. The effort to understand the making and unmaking of gender, as well as what gender makes, involves understanding the workings of these games as games, with their inclusions and exclusions, multiple positions, complex rules, forms of bodily activity, structures of feeling and desire, and stakes of winning, losing, or simply playing. It involves as well the question of how gender games themselves collide with, encompass, or are bent to the service of, other games, for gender is never, as they say, the only game in town.

The idea of the game—the serious game—in turn is meant to resolve a number of problems in a broader theory of practice, problems that arise particularly from concerns that animate feminist, minority, postcolonial, and subaltern theorizing. One is the necessity for retaining an active intentional subject without falling into some form of free agency and voluntarism. Here I have argued that, if we take the methodological unit of practice as the game, rather than the "agent," we can never lose sight of the mutual determination(s) of agents and structures: of the fact that players are "agents," skilled and intense strategizers who constantly stretch the game even as they enact it, and the simultaneous fact that players are defined and constructed (though never wholly contained) by the game. One can say about games what Sartre said about projects: they are a "moving unity of subjectivity and objectivity" (1968: 97). A second problem is the necessity for focalizing power relations and struggles within a practice theoretical framework; here the idea of the serious game signals a range of points that every schoolchild knows: that games are always in some sense contests, even if only with the self; that games always entail including some people and excluding others; that in most kinds of games, some people get to be (or are forced to be) "It" and others not; and so forth. Finally, there is the necessity for theorizing ways to break out of the loop of reproduction; here the emphasis is on loosening up (without totally abandoning) the notion of structure—recognizing its incompletely hegemonic character, and recognizing the multiplicity of games in play, both at any given moment, and across time.

A new and improved brand of practice theory, in turn, holds out the hope of mediating the most recent set of unproductive binaries on the theoretical landscape, between textual studies and ethnographically grounded studies, between "lit-crit" and some supposedly objectifying "social science,"[18] between constructionist theories that emphasize the production of subjects, and seemingly voluntarist accounts that emphasize what subjects make. Yet perhaps the final comment needs to be, once again, that this is not "a theory," something that one either signs up for or rejects. Rather it is a project, a way of trying conceptually and representationally to mimic social life itself as a "moving unity of subjectivity and objectivity."

Is Female to Male
as Nature Is to Culture?

Much of the creativity of anthropology derives from the tension between two sets of demands: that we explain human universals, and that we explain cultural particulars. Given this tension, woman provides us with one of the more challenging problems to be dealt with. The secondary status of woman in society is one of the true universals, a pan-cultural fact. Yet within that universal fact, the specific cultural conceptions and symbolizations of woman are extraordinarily diverse and even mutually contradictory. Further, the actual treatment of women and their relative power and contribution vary enormously from culture to culture, and over different periods in the history of particular cultural traditions. Both of these points—the universal fact and the cultural variation—constitute problems to be explained.

My interest in the problem is of course more than academic: I wish to see genuine change come about, the emergence of a social and cultural order in which as much of the range of human potential is open to women as is open to men. The universality of female subordination, the fact that it exists within every type of social and economic arrangement and in societies of every degree of complexity, indicates to me that we are up against something very profound, very stubborn, something we cannot rout out simply by rearranging a few tasks and roles in the social system, or even by reordering the whole economic structure. In this paper I try to expose the underlying logic of cultural thinking that assumes the inferiority of women; I try to

show the highly persuasive nature of the logic, for if it were not so persuasive, people would not keep subscribing to it. But I also try to show the social and cultural sources of that logic, to indicate wherein lies the potential
for change.

It is important to sort out the levels of the problem. The confusion can be
staggering. For example, depending on which aspect of Chinese culture we
look at, we might extrapolate any of several entirely different guesses concerning the status of women in China. In the ideology of Taoism, *yin*, the female principle, and *yang*, the male principle, are given equal weight; "the
opposition, alternation, and interaction of these two forces give rise to all
phenomena in the universe" (Siu 1968: 2). Hence we might guess that maleness and femaleness are equally valued in the general ideology of Chinese
culture.[1] Looking at the social structure, however, we see the strongly emphasized patrilineal descent principle, the importance of sons, and the absolute authority of the father in the family. Thus we might conclude that
China is the archetypal patriarchal society. Next, looking at the actual roles
played, power and influence wielded, and material contributions made by
women in Chinese society—all of which are, upon observation, quite substantial—we would have to say that women are allotted a great deal of (unspoken) status in the system. Or again, we might focus on the fact that a
goddess, Kuan Yin, is the central (most worshiped, most depicted) deity in
Chinese Buddhism, and we might be tempted to say, as many have tried to
say about goddess-worshiping cultures in prehistoric and early historical
societies, that China is actually a sort of matriarchy. In short, we must be
absolutely clear about *what* we are trying to explain before explaining it.

We may differentiate three levels of the problem:

1. The universal fact of culturally attributed second-class status of
woman in every society. Two questions are important here. First, what do
we mean by this; what is our evidence that this is a universal fact? And second, how are we to explain this fact, once having established it?

2. Specific ideologies, symbolizations, and socio-structural arrangements pertaining to women that vary widely from culture to culture. The
problem at this level is to account for any particular cultural complex in
terms of factors specific to that group—the standard level of anthropological analysis.

3. Observable on-the-ground details of women's activities, contributions, powers, influence, etc., often at variance with cultural ideology (although always constrained within the assumption that women may never

be officially preeminent in the total system). This is the level of direct observation, often adopted now by feminist-oriented anthropologists.

This paper is primarily concerned with the first of these levels, the problem of the universal devaluation of women. The analysis thus depends not upon specific cultural data but rather upon an analysis of "culture" taken generically as a special sort of process in the world. A discussion of the second level, the problem of cross-cultural variation in conceptions and relative valuations of women, will entail a great deal of cross-cultural research and must be postponed to another time. As for the third level, it will be obvious from my approach that I would consider it a misguided endeavor to focus only upon women's actual though culturally unrecognized and unvalued powers in any given society, without first understanding the overarching ideology and deeper assumptions of the culture that render such powers trivial.

The Universality of Female Subordination

What do I mean when I say that everywhere, in every known culture, women are considered in some degree inferior to men? First of all, I must stress that I am talking about *cultural* evaluations; I am saying that each culture, in its own way and on its own terms, makes this evaluation. But what would constitute evidence that a particular culture considers women inferior?

Three types of data would suffice: (1) elements of cultural ideology and informants' statements that *explicitly* devalue women, granting them, their roles, their tasks, their products, and their social milieux less prestige than are granted to men and the male correlates; (2) symbolic devices, such as the attribution of defilement, which may be interpreted as *implicitly* making a statement of inferior valuation; and (3) social-structural arrangements that exclude women from participation in or contact with some realm in which the highest powers of the society are felt to reside.[2] These three types of data may all of course be interrelated in any particular system, though they need not necessarily be. Further, any one of them will usually be sufficient to make the point of female inferiority in a given culture. Certainly, female exclusion from the most sacred rite or the highest political council is sufficient evidence. Certainly, explicit cultural ideology devaluing women (and their tasks, roles, products, etc.) is sufficient evidence. Symbolic indicators such as defilement are usually sufficient, although in a few cases in which, say, men and women are equally polluting to one another, a further indicator is required—and is, as far as my investigations have ascertained, always available.

On any or all of these counts, then, I would flatly assert that we find women subordinated to men in every known society. The search for a genuinely egalitarian, let alone matriarchal, culture has proved fruitless. An example from one society that has traditionally been on the credit side of this ledger will suffice. Among the matrilineal Crow, as Lowie (1956) points out, "Women . . . had highly honorific offices in the Sun Dance; they could become directors of the Tobacco Ceremony and played, if anything, a more conspicuous part in it than the men; they sometimes played the hostess in the Cooked Meat Festival; they were not debarred from sweating or doctoring or from seeking a vision" (p. 61). Nonetheless, "Women [during menstruation] formerly rode inferior horses and evidently this loomed as a source of contamination, for they were not allowed to approach either a wounded man or men starting on a war party. A taboo still lingers against their coming near sacred objects at these times" (p. 44). Further, just before enumerating women's rights of participation in the various rituals noted above, Lowie mentions one particular Sun Dance Doll bundle that was not supposed to be unwrapped by a woman (p. 60). Pursuing this trail we find: "According to all Lodge Grass informants and most others, the doll owned by Wrinkled-face took precedence not only of other dolls but of all other Crow medicines whatsoever. . . . This particular doll was not supposed to be handled by a woman" (p. 229).[3]

In sum, the Crow are probably a fairly typical case. Yes, women have certain powers and rights, in this case some that place them in fairly high positions. Yet ultimately the line is drawn: menstruation is a threat to warfare, one of the most valued institutions of the tribe, one that is central to their self-definition; and the most sacred object of the tribe is taboo to the direct sight and touch of women.

Similar examples could be multiplied ad infinitum, but I think the onus is no longer upon us to demonstrate that female subordination is a cultural universal; it is up to those who would argue against the point to bring forth counterexamples. I shall take the universal secondary status of women as a given, and proceed from there.

Nature and Culture[4]

How are we to explain the universal devaluation of women? We could of course rest the case on biological determinism. There is something genetically inherent in the male of the species, so the biological determinists would argue, that makes them the naturally dominant sex; that "something" is lacking in females, and as a result women are not only naturally subordinate but in general quite satisfied with their position, since it affords them protection and the opportunity to maximize maternal pleasures, which to them are the most satisfying experiences of life. Without going into a detailed refutation of this position, I think it fair to say that it has failed to be established to the satisfaction of almost anyone in academic anthropology. This is to say, not that biological facts are irrelevant, or that men and women are not different, but that these facts and differences only take on significance of superior/inferior within the framework of culturally defined value systems.

If we are unwilling to rest the case on genetic determinism, it seems to me that we have only one way to proceed. We must attempt to interpret female subordination in light of other universals, factors built into the structure of the most generalized situation in which all human beings, in whatever culture, find themselves. For example, every human being has a physical body and a sense of nonphysical mind, is part of a society of other individuals and an inheritor of a cultural tradition, and must engage in some relationship, however mediated, with "nature," or the nonhuman realm, in order to survive. Every human being is born (to a mother) and ultimately dies, all are assumed to have an interest in personal survival, and society/culture has its own interest in (or at least momentum toward) continuity and survival, which transcends the lives and deaths of particular individuals. And so forth. It is in the realm of such universals of the human condition that we must seek an explanation for the universal fact of female devaluation.

I translate the problem, in other words, into the following simple question. What could there be in the generalized structure and conditions of existence, common to every culture, that would lead every culture to place a lower value upon women? Specifically, my thesis is that woman is being identified with—or, if you will, seems to be a symbol of—something that every culture devalues, something that every culture defines as being of a lower order of existence than itself. Now it seems that there is only one thing that would fit that description, and that is "nature" in the most generalized sense. Every culture, or, generically, "culture," is engaged in the process of generating and sustaining systems of meaningful forms (symbols, artifacts, etc.) by means of which humanity transcends the givens of natural existence, bends them to its purposes, controls them in its interest. We may thus broadly equate culture with the notion of human consciousness, or with the products of human consciousness (i.e., systems of thought and technology), by means of which humanity attempts to assert control over nature.

Now the categories of "nature" and "culture" are of course conceptual categories—one can find no boundary out in the actual world between the two states or realms of being. And there is no question that some cultures articulate a much stronger opposition between the two categories than others—it has even been argued that primitive peoples (some or all) do not see or intuit any distinction between the human cultural state and the state of nature at all. Yet I would maintain that the universality of ritual betokens an assertion in all human cultures of the specifically human ability to act upon and regulate, rather than passively move with and be moved by, the givens of natural existence. In ritual, the purposive manipulation of given forms toward regulating and sustaining order, every culture asserts that proper relations between human existence and natural forces depend upon culture's employing its special powers to regulate the overall processes of the world and life.

One realm of cultural thought in which these points are often articulated is that of concepts of purity and pollution. Virtually every culture has some such beliefs, which seem in large part (though not, of course, entirely) to be concerned with the relationship between culture and nature (see Ortner 1973a, 1974). A well-known aspect of purity/pollution beliefs cross-culturally is that of the natural "contagion" of pollution; left to its own devices, pollution (for these purposes grossly equated with the unregulated operation of natural energies) spreads and overpowers all that it comes in contact with. Thus a puzzle—if pollution is so strong, how can anything be purified? Why is the purifying agent not itself polluted? The answer, in keeping with the present line of argument, is that purification is effected in a ritual context; purification ritual, as a purposive activity that pits self-conscious (symbolic) action against natural energies, is more powerful than those energies.

In any case, my point is simply that every culture implicitly recognizes and asserts a distinction between the operation of nature and the operation of culture (human consciousness and its products); and further, that the distinctiveness of culture rests precisely on the fact that it can under most circumstances transcend natural conditions and turn them to its purposes. Thus culture (i.e., every culture) at some level of awareness asserts itself to be not only distinct from but superior to nature, and that sense of distinctiveness and superiority rests precisely on the ability to transform—to "so-cialize" and "culturalize"—nature.

Returning now to the issue of women, their pan-cultural second-class status could be accounted for, quite simply, by postulating that women are being identified or symbolically associated with nature, as opposed to men, who are identified with culture. Since it is always culture's project to sub-sume and transcend nature, if women were considered part of nature, then culture would find it "natural" to subordinate, not to say oppress, them. Yet although this argument can be shown to have considerable force, it seems to oversimplify the case. The formulation I would like to defend and elabo-rate on in the following section, then, is that women are seen "merely" as being *closer* to nature than men. That is, culture (still equated relatively un-ambiguously with men) recognizes that women are active participants in its special processes, but at the same time sees them as being more rooted in, or having more direct affinity with, nature.

The revision may seem minor or even trivial, but I think it is a more accu-rate rendering of cultural assumptions. Further, the argument cast in these terms has several analytic advantages over the simpler formulation; I shall discuss these later. It might simply be stressed here that the revised argu-ment would still account for the pan-cultural devaluation of women, for even if women are not equated with nature, they are nonetheless seen as representing a lower order of being, as being less transcendent of nature than men are. The next task of the paper, then, is to consider why they might be viewed in that way.

Why Is Woman Seen as Closer to Nature?

It all begins of course with the body and the natural procreative functions specific to women alone. We can sort out for discussion three levels at which this absolute physiological fact has significance: (1) woman's *body and its functions*, more involved more of the time with "species life," seem to place her closer to nature, in contrast to man's physiology, which frees him more completely to take up the projects of culture; (2) woman's body and its func-tions place her in *social roles* that in turn are considered to be at a lower or-der of the cultural process than man's; and (3) woman's traditional social roles, imposed because of her body and its functions, in turn give her a dif-ferent *psychic structure*, which, like her physiological nature and her social roles, is seen as being closer to nature. I shall discuss each of these points in turn, showing first how in each instance certain factors strongly tend to align woman with nature, then indicating other factors that demonstrate her full alignment with culture, the combined factors thus placing her in a problematic intermediate position. It will become clear in the course of the discussion why men seem by contrast less intermediate, more purely "cultural" than women. And I reiterate that I am dealing only at the level of cultural and human universals. These arguments are intended to apply to generalized humanity; they grow out of the human condition, as humanity has experienced and confronted it up to the present day.

I. WOMAN'S PHYSIOLOGY SEEN AS CLOSER TO NATURE

This part of my argument has been anticipated, with subtlety, cogency, and a great deal of hard data, by de Beauvoir (1953). De Beauvoir reviews the physiological structure, development, and functions of the human female and concludes that "the female, to a greater extent than the male, is the prey of the species" (p. 60). She points out that many major areas and processes of the woman's body serve no apparent function for the health and stability of the individual; on the contrary, as they perform their specific organic functions, they are often sources of discomfort, pain, and danger. The breasts are irrelevant to personal health; they may be excised at any time of a woman's life. "Many of the ovarian secretions function for the benefit of the egg, promoting its maturation and adapting the uterus to its requirements; in respect to the organism as a whole, they make for disequilibrium rather than for regulation—the woman is adapted to the needs of the egg rather than to her own requirements" (p. 24). Menstruation is often uncomfortable, sometimes painful; it frequently has negative emotional correlates and in any case involves bothersome tasks of cleansing and waste disposal; and—a point that de Beauvoir does not mention—in many cultures it interrupts a woman's routine, putting her in a stigmatized state involving various restrictions on her activities and social contacts. In pregnancy many of the woman's vitamin and mineral resources are channeled into nourishing the fetus, depleting her own strength and energies. And finally, childbirth itself is painful and dangerous (pp. 24–27 passim). In sum, de Beauvoir concludes that the female "is more enslaved to the species than the male, her animality is more manifest" (p. 239).

While de Beauvoir's book is ideological, her survey of woman's physiological situation seems fair and accurate. It is simply a fact that proportionately more of woman's body space, for a greater percentage of her lifetime, and at some—sometimes great—cost to her personal health, strength, and general stability, is taken up with the natural processes surrounding the reproduction of the species.

De Beauvoir goes on to discuss the negative implications of woman's "enslavement to the species" in relation to the projects in which humans engage, projects through which culture is generated and defined. She arrives thus at the crux of her argument (pp. 58–59):

> Here we have the key to the whole mystery. On the biological level a species is maintained only by creating itself anew; but this creation results only in repeating the same Life in more individuals. But man assures the repetition of Life while transcending Life through Existence [i.e., goal-oriented, meaningful action]; by this transcendence he creates values that deprive pure repetition of all value. In the animal, the freedom and variety of male activities are vain because no project is involved. Except for his services to the species, what he does is immaterial. Whereas in serving the species, the human male also remodels the face of the earth, he creates new instruments, he invents, he shapes the future.

In other words, woman's body seems to doom her to mere reproduction of life; the male, in contrast, lacking natural creative functions, must (or has the opportunity to) assert his creativity externally, "artificially," through the medium of technology and symbols. In so doing, he creates relatively lasting, eternal, transcendent objects, while the woman creates only perishables—human beings.

This formulation opens up a number of important insights. It speaks, for example, to the great puzzle of why male activities involving the destruction of life (hunting and warfare) are often given more prestige than the female's ability to give birth, to create life. Within de Beauvoir's framework, we realize it is not the killing that is the relevant and valued aspect of hunting and warfare; rather, it is the transcendental (social, cultural) nature of these activities, as opposed to the naturalness of the process of birth: "For it is not in giving life but in risking life that man is raised above the animal; that is why superiority has been accorded in humanity not to the sex that brings forth but to that which kills" (ibid.).

Thus if male is, as I am suggesting, everywhere (unconsciously) associated with culture and female seems closer to nature, the rationale for these associations is not very difficult to grasp, merely from considering the implications of the physiological contrast between male and female. At the same time, however, woman cannot be consigned fully to the category of

nature, for it is perfectly obvious that she is a full-fledged human being endowed with human consciousness just as a man is; she is half of the human
race, without whose cooperation the whole enterprise would collapse. She
may seem more in the possession of nature than man, but having consciousness, she thinks and speaks; she generates, communicates, and manipulates
symbols, categories, and values. She participates in human dialogues not
only with other women but also with men. As Lévi-Strauss says, "Woman
could never become just a sign and nothing more, since even in a man's
world she is still a person, and since insofar as she is defined as a sign she
must [still] be recognized as a generator of signs" (1969a: 496).

Indeed, the fact of woman's full human consciousness, her full involvement in and commitment to culture's project of transcendence over nature,
may ironically explain another of the great puzzles of "the woman problem"—woman's nearly universal unquestioning acceptance of her own
devaluation. For it would seem that, as a conscious human and member
of culture, she has followed out the logic of culture's arguments and has
reached culture's conclusions along with the men. As de Beauvoir puts it
(p. 59):

> For she, too, is an existent, she feels the urge to surpass, and her project
> is not mere repetition but transcendence towards a different future—
> in her heart of hearts she finds confirmation of the masculine preten-
> sions. She joins the men in the festivals that celebrate the successes and
> victories of the males. Her misfortune is to have been biologically des-
> tined for the repetition of Life, when even in her own view Life does
> not carry within itself its reasons for being, reasons that are more im-
> portant than life itself.

In other words, woman's consciousness—her membership, as it were, in
culture—is evidenced in part by the very fact that she accepts her own devaluation and takes culture's point of view.

I have tried here to show one part of the logic of that view, the part that
grows directly from the physiological differences between men and women.
Because of woman's greater bodily involvement with the natural functions
surrounding reproduction, she is seen as more a part of nature than man is.
Yet in part because of her consciousness and participation in human social
dialogue, she is recognized as a participant in culture. Thus she appears as
something intermediate between culture and nature, lower on the scale of
transcendence than man.

2. WOMAN'S SOCIAL ROLE SEEN AS CLOSER TO NATURE

Woman's physiological functions, I have just argued, may tend in themselves to motivate[5] a view of woman as closer to nature, a view she herself, as an observer of herself and the world, would tend to agree with. Woman creates naturally from within her own being, whereas man is free to, or forced to, create artificially, that is, through cultural means, and in such a way as to sustain culture. In addition, I now wish to show how woman's physiological functions have tended universally to limit her social movement, and to confine her universally to certain social contexts which *in turn* are seen as closer to nature. That is, not only her bodily processes but the social situation in which her bodily processes locate her may carry this significance. And insofar as she is permanently associated (in the eyes of culture) with these social milieux, they add weight (perhaps the decisive part of the burden) to the view of woman as closer to nature. I refer here of course to woman's confinement to the domestic family context, a confinement motivated, no doubt, by her lactation processes.

Woman's body, like that of all female mammals, generates milk during and after pregnancy for the feeding of the newborn baby. The baby cannot survive without breast milk or some similar formula at this stage of life. Since the mother's body goes through its lactation processes in direct relation to a pregnancy with a particular child, the relationship of nursing between mother and child is seen as a natural bond, other feeding arrangements being seen in most cases as unnatural and makeshift. Mothers and their children, according to cultural reasoning, belong together. Further, children beyond infancy are not strong enough to engage in major work, yet are mobile and unruly and not capable of understanding various dangers; they thus require supervision and constant care. Mother is the obvious person for this task, as an extension of her natural nursing bond with the children, or because she has a new infant and is already involved with child-oriented activities. Her own activities are thus circumscribed by the limitations and low levels of her children's strengths and skills:[6] she is confined to the domestic family group; "woman's place is in the home."

Woman's association with the domestic circle would contribute to the view of her as closer to nature in several ways. In the first place, the sheer fact of constant association with children plays a role in the issue; one can easily see how infants and children might themselves be considered part of nature. Infants are barely human and utterly unsocialized; like animals they are unable to walk upright, they excrete without control, they do not speak. Even slightly older children are clearly not yet fully under the sway of culture. They do not yet understand social duties, responsibilities, and morals; their vocabulary and their range of learned skills are small. One finds implicit recognition of an association between children and nature in many cultural practices. For example, most cultures have initiation rites for adolescents (primarily for boys; I shall return to this point below), the point of which is to move the child ritually from a less than fully human state into full participation in society and culture; many cultures do not hold funeral rites for children who die at early ages, explicitly because they are not yet fully social beings. Thus children are likely to be categorized with nature, and woman's close association with children may compound her potential for being seen as closer to nature herself. It is ironic that the rationale for boys' initiation rites in many cultures is that the boys must be purged of the defilement accrued from being around mother and other women so much of the time, when in fact much of the woman's defilement may derive from her being around children so much of the time.

The second major problematic implication of women's close association with the domestic context derives from certain structural conflicts between the family and society at large in any social system. The implications of the "domestic/public opposition" in relation to the position of women have been cogently developed by Rosaldo (1974), and I simply wish to show its relevance to the present argument. The notion that the domestic unit—the biological family charged with reproducing and socializing new members of the society—is opposed to the public entity—the superimposed network of alliances and relationships that *is* the society—is also the basis of Lévi-Strauss's argument in *The Elementary Structures of Kinship* (1969a). Lévi-Strauss argues not only that this opposition is present in every social system, but further that it has the significance of the opposition between nature and culture. The universal incest prohibition[7] and its ally, the rule of exogamy (marriage outside the group), ensure that "the risk of seeing a biological family become established as a closed system is definitely eliminated; the biological group can no longer stand apart, and the bond of alliance with another family ensures the dominance of the social over the biological, and of the cultural over the natural" (p. 479). And although not every culture articulates a radical opposition between the domestic and the public as such, it is hardly contestable that the domestic is always subsumed by the public; domestic units are allied with one another through the enactment of rules that are logically at a higher level than the units themselves; this creates an emergent unit—society—that is logically at a higher level than the domestic units of which it is composed.

Now, since women are associated with, and indeed are more or less confined to, the domestic context, they are identified with this lower order of social/cultural organization. What are the implications of this for the way they are viewed? First, if the specifically biological (reproductive) function of the family is stressed, as in Lévi-Strauss's formulation, then the family (and hence woman) is identified with nature pure and simple, as opposed to culture. But this is obviously too simple; the point seems more adequately formulated as follows: the family (and hence woman) represents lower-level, socially fragmenting, particularistic sorts of concerns, as opposed to interfamilial relations representing higher-level, integrative, universalistic sorts of concerns. Since men lack a "natural" basis (nursing, generalized to child care) for a familiar orientation, their sphere of activity is defined at the level of interfamilial relations. And hence, so the cultural reasoning seems to go, men are the "natural" proprietors of religion, ritual, politics, and other realms of cultural thought and action in which universalistic statements of spiritual and social synthesis are made. Thus men are identified not only with culture, in the sense of all human creativity, as opposed to nature; they are identified in particular with culture in the old-fashioned sense of the finer and higher aspects of human thought—art, religion, law, etc.

Here again, the logic of cultural reasoning aligning woman with a lower order of culture than man is clear and, on the surface, quite compelling. At the same time, woman cannot be fully consigned to nature, for there are aspects of her situation, even within the domestic context, that undeniably demonstrate her participation in the cultural process. It goes without saying, of course, that except for nursing newborn infants (and artificial nursing devices can cut even this biological tie), there is no reason why it has to be mother—as opposed to father, or anyone else—who remains identified with child care. But even assuming that other practical and emotional reasons conspire to keep woman in this sphere, it is possible to show that her activities in the domestic context could as logically put her squarely in the category of culture.

In the first place, one must point out that woman not only feeds and cleans up after children in a simple caretaker operation; she in fact is the primary agent of their early socialization. It is she who transforms newborn infants from mere organisms into cultured humans, teaching them manners and the proper ways to behave in order to become full-fledged members of the culture. On the basis of her socializing functions alone, she could not be more a representative of culture. Yet in virtually every society there is a point at which the socialization of boys in transferred to the hands of men. The boys are considered, in one set of terms or another, not yet "really" socialized; their entrée into the realm of fully human (social, cultural) status can be accomplished only by men. We still see this in our own schools, where there is a gradual inversion in the proportion of female to male teachers up through the grades: most kindergarten teachers are female; most university professors are male.[8]

Or again, take cooking. In the overwhelming majority of societies cooking is the woman's work. No doubt this stems from practical considerations—since the woman has to stay home with the baby, it is convenient for her to perform the chores centered in the home. But if it is true, as Lévi-Strauss has argued (1969b), that transforming the raw into the cooked may represent, in many systems of thought, the transition from nature to culture, then here we have woman aligned with this important culturalizing process, which could easily place her in the category of culture, triumphing over nature. Yet it is also interesting to note that when a culture (e.g., France or China) develops a tradition of *haute cuisine*—"real" cooking, as opposed to trivial ordinary domestic cooking—the high chefs are almost always men. Thus the pattern replicates that in the area of socialization—women perform lower-level conversions from nature to culture, but when the culture distinguishes a higher level of the same functions, the higher level is restricted to men.

In short, we see once again some sources of woman's appearing more intermediate than man with respect to the nature/culture dichotomy. Her "natural" association with the domestic context (motivated by her natural lactation functions) tends to compound her potential for being viewed as closer to nature, because of the animal-like nature of children, and because of the infrasocial connotation of the domestic group as against the rest of society. Yet at the same time her socializing and cooking functions within the domestic context show her to be a powerful agent of the cultural process, constantly transforming raw natural resources into cultural products. Belonging to culture, yet appearing to have stronger and more direct connections with nature, she is once again seen as situated between the two realms.

3. WOMAN'S PSYCHE SEEN AS CLOSER TO NATURE

The suggestion that woman has not only a different body and a different social locus from man but also a different psychic structure is most controversial. I will argue that she probably *does* have a different psychic structure, but I will draw heavily on Chodorow's paper (1974) to establish first that her psychic structure need not be assumed to be innate; it can be accounted for, as Chodorow convincingly shows, by the facts of the probably universal female socialization experience. Nonetheless, if we grant the empirical near universality of a "feminine psyche" with certain specific characteristics, these characteristics would add weight to the cultural view of woman as closer to nature.

It is important to specify what we see as the dominant and universal aspects of the feminine psyche. If we postulate emotionality or irrationality, we are confronted with those traditions in various parts of the world in which women functionally are, and are seen as, more practical, pragmatic, and this-worldly than men. One relevant dimension that does seem pan-culturally applicable is that of relative concreteness vs. relative abstractness: the feminine personality tends to be involved with concrete feelings, things, and people, rather than with abstract entities; it tends toward personalism and particularism. A second, closely related, dimension seems to be that of relative subjectivity vs. relative objectivity: Chodorow cites Carlson's study (1971), which concludes that "males represent experiences of self, others, space, and time in individualistic, objective, and distant ways, while females represent experiences in relatively interpersonal, subjective, immediate ways" (Chodorow 1974: 56, quoting Carlson, p. 270). Although this and other studies were done in Western societies, Chodorow sees their findings on the differences between male and female personality—roughly, that men are more objective and inclined to relate in terms of relatively abstract categories, women more subjective and inclined to relate in terms of relatively concrete phenomena—as "general and nearly universal differences" (p. 43).

But the thrust of Chodorow's elegantly argued paper is that these differences are not innate or genetically programmed; they arise from nearly universal features of family structure, namely that "women, universally, are largely responsible for early child care and for (at least) later female socialization" (p. 43) and that "the structural situation of child rearing, reinforced by female and male role training, produces these differences, which are replicated and reproduced in the sexual sociology of adult life" (p. 44). Chodorow argues that, because mother is the early socializer of both boys and girls, both develop "personal identification" with her, i.e., diffuse identification with her general personality, behavior traits, values, and attitudes (p. 51). A son, however, must ultimately shift to a masculine role identity, which involves building an identification with the father. Since father is almost always more remote than mother (he is rarely involved in child care, and perhaps works away from home much of the day), building an identification with father involves a "positional identification," i.e., identification with father's male role as a collection of abstract elements, rather than a personal identification with father as a real individual (p. 49). Further, as the boy enters the larger social world, he finds it in fact organized around more abstract and universalistic criteria (Rosaldo 1974: 28–29; Chodorow, p. 58), as I have indicated in the previous section; thus his earlier socialization prepares him for, and is reinforced by, the type of adult social experience he will have.

For a young girl, in contrast, the personal identification with mother, which was created in early infancy, can persist into the process of learning female role identity. Because mother is immediate and present when the daughter is learning role identity, learning to be a woman involves the continuity and development of a girl's relationship to her mother, and sustains the identification with her as an individual; it does not involve the learning of externally defined role characteristics (Chodorow, p. 51). This pattern prepares the girl for, and is fully reinforced by, her social situation in later life; she will become involved in the world of women, which is characterized by few formal role differences (Rosaldo, p. 29), and which involves again, in motherhood, "personal identification" with *her* children. And so the cycle begins anew.

Chodorow demonstrates to my satisfaction at least that the feminine personality, characterized by personalism and particularism, can be explained as having been generated by social-structural arrangements rather than by innate biological factors. The point need not be belabored further. But insofar as the "feminine personality" has been a nearly universal fact, it can be argued that its characteristics may have contributed further to the view of women as being somehow less cultural than men. That is, women would tend to enter into relationships with the world that culture might see as being more "like nature"—immanent and embedded in things as given—than "like culture"—transcending and transforming things through the superimposition of abstract categories and transpersonal values. Woman's relationships tend to be, like nature, relatively unmediated, more direct, whereas man not only tends to relate in a more mediated way, but in fact ultimately often relates more consistently and strongly to the mediating categories and forms than to the persons or objects themselves.

It is thus not difficult to see how the feminine personality would lend weight to a view of women as being "closer to nature." Yet at the same time, the modes of relating characteristic of women undeniably play a powerful and important role in the cultural process. For just as relatively unmediated relating is in some sense at the lower end of the spectrum of human spiritual functions, embedded and particularizing rather than transcending and synthesizing, yet that mode of relating also stands at the upper end of that spectrum. Consider the mother-child relationship. Mothers tend to be committed to their children as individuals, regardless of sex, age, beauty, clan affiliation, or other categories in which the child might participate. Now any relationship with this quality—not just mother and child but any sort of highly personal, relatively unmediated commitment—may be seen as a challenge to culture and society "from below," insofar as it represents the fragmentary potential of individual loyalties vis-à-vis the solidarity of the group. But it may also be seen as embodying the synthesizing agent for culture and society "from above," in that it represents generalized human values above and beyond loyalties to particular social categories. Every society must have social categories that transcend personal loyalties, but every society must also generate a sense of ultimate moral unity for all its members above and beyond those social categories. Thus that psychic mode seemingly typical of women, which tends to disregard categories and to seek "communion" (Chodorow, p. 55, following Bakan 1966) directly and personally with others, although it may appear infracultural from one point of view, is at the same time associated with the highest levels of the cultural process.

The Implications of Intermediacy

My primary purpose in this paper has been to attempt to explain the universal secondary status of women. Intellectually and personally, I felt strongly challenged by this problem; I felt compelled to deal with it before undertaking an analysis of woman's position in any particular society. Local variables of economy, ecology, history, political and social structure, values, and world view—these could explain variations within this universal, but they could not explain the universal itself. And if we were not to accept the ideology of biological determinism, then explanation, it seemed to me, could only proceed by reference to other universals of the human cultural situation. Thus the general outlines of the approach—although not of course the particular solution offered—were determined by the problem itself, and not by any predilection on my part for global abstract structural analysis.

I argued that the universal devaluation of women could be explained by postulating that women are seen as closer to nature than men, men being seen as more unequivocally occupying the high ground of culture. The culture/nature distinction is itself a product of culture, culture being minimally defined as the transcendence, by means of systems of thought and technology, of the natural givens of existence. This of course is an analytic definition, but I argued that at some level every culture incorporates this notion in one form or other, if only through the performance of ritual as an assertion of the human ability to manipulate those givens. In any case, the core of the paper was concerned with showing why women might tend to be assumed, over and over, in the most diverse sorts of worldviews and in cultures of every degree of complexity, to be closer to nature than men. Woman's physiology, more involved more of the time with "species life"; woman's association with the structurally subordinate domestic context, charged with the crucial function of transforming animal-like infants into cultured beings; "woman's psyche," appropriately molded to mothering functions by her own socialization and tending toward greater personalism and less mediated modes of relating—all these factors make woman appear to be rooted more directly and deeply in nature. At the same time, however, her "membership" and fully necessary participation in culture are recognized by culture and cannot be denied. Thus she is seen to occupy an intermediate position between culture and nature.

This intermediacy has several implications for analysis, depending upon how it is interpreted. First, of course, it answers my primary question of why woman is everywhere seen as lower than man, for even if she is not seen as nature pure and simple, she is still seen as achieving less transcendence of nature than man. Here intermediate simply means "middle status" on a hierarchy of being from culture to nature.

Second, intermediate may have the significance of "mediating," i.e., performing some sort of synthesizing or converting function between nature and culture, here seen (by culture) not as two ends of a continuum but as two radically different sorts of processes in the world. The domestic unit—and hence woman, who in virtually every case appears as its primary representative—is one of culture's crucial agencies for the conversion of nature into culture, especially with reference to the socialization of children. Any culture's continued viability depends upon properly socialized individuals who will see the world in that culture's terms and adhere more or less unquestioningly to its moral precepts. The functions of the domestic unit must be closely controlled in order to ensure this outcome; the stability of the domestic unit as an institution must be placed as far as possible beyond question. (We see some aspects of the protection of the integrity and stability of the domestic group in the powerful taboos against incest, matricide, patricide, and fratricide.[9]) Insofar as woman is universally the primary agent of early socialization and is seen as virtually the embodiment of the functions of the domestic group, she will tend to come under the heavier restrictions and circumscriptions surrounding that unit. Her (culturally defined) intermediate position between nature and culture, here having the significance of her *mediation* (i.e., performing conversion functions) between nature and culture, would thus account not only for her lower status but for the greater restrictions placed upon her activities. In virtually every culture her permissible sexual activities are more closely circumscribed than man's, she is offered a much smaller range of role choices, and she is afforded direct access to a far more limited range of its social institutions. Further, she is almost universally socialized to have a narrower and generally more conservative set of attitudes and views than man, and the limited social contexts of her adult life reinforce this situation. This socially engendered conservatism and traditionalism of woman's thinking is another—perhaps the worst, certainly the most insidious—mode of social restriction, and would clearly be related to her traditional function of producing well-socialized members of the group.

Finally, woman's intermediate position may have the implication of greater symbolic ambiguity (see also Rosaldo 1974). Shifting our image of the culture/nature relationship once again, we may envision culture in this case as a small clearing within the forest of the larger natural system. From this point of view, that which is intermediate between culture and nature is located on the continuous periphery of culture's clearing; and though it may thus appear to stand both above and below culture, it is simply outside and around it. We can begin to understand then how a single system of cultural thought can often assign to woman completely polarized and apparently contradictory meanings, since extremes, as we say, meet. That she often represents both life and death is only the simplest example one could mention.

For another perspective on the same point, it will be recalled that the psychic mode associated with women seems to stand at both the bottom and the top of the scale of human modes of relating. The tendency in that mode is to get involved more directly with people as individuals and not as representatives of one social category or another; this mode can be seen as either "ignoring" (and thus subverting) or "transcending" (and thus achieving a higher synthesis of) those social categories, depending upon the cultural view for any given purpose. Thus we can account easily for both the subversive feminine symbols (witches, evil eye, menstrual pollution, castrating mothers) and the feminine symbols of transcendence (mother goddesses, merciful dispensers of salvation, female symbols of justice, and the strong presence of feminine symbolism in the realms of art, religion, ritual, and law). Feminine symbolism, far more often than masculine symbolism, manifests this propensity toward polarized ambiguity—sometimes utterly exalted, sometimes utterly debased, rarely within the normal range of human possibilities.

If woman's (culturally viewed) intermediacy between culture and nature has this implication of generalized ambiguity of meaning characteristic of marginal phenomena, then we are also in a better position to account for those cultural and historical "inversions" in which women are in some way or other symbolically aligned with culture and men with nature. A number of cases come to mind: the Sirionó of Brazil, among whom, according to Ingham (1971: 1098), "nature, the raw, and maleness" are opposed to "culture, the cooked, the femaleness";[10] Nazi Germany, in which women were said to be the guardians of culture and morals; European courtly love, in which man considered himself the beast and woman the pristine exalted object—a pattern of thinking that persists, for example, among modern Spanish peasants (see Pitt-Rivers 1961; Rosaldo 1974). And there are no doubt other cases of this sort, including some aspects of our own culture's view of women. Each such instance of an alignment of women with culture rather than nature requires detailed analysis of specific historical and ethnographic data. But in indicating how nature in general, and the feminine mode of interpersonal relations in particular, can appear from certain points of view to stand both under and over (but really simply outside of) the sphere of culture's hegemony, we have at least laid the groundwork for such analyses.

In short, the postulate that woman is viewed as closer to nature than man has several implications for further analysis, and can be interpreted in several different ways. If it is viewed simply as a *middle* position on a scale from culture down to nature, then it is still seen as lower than culture and thus accounts for the pan-cultural assumption that woman is lower than man in the order of things. If it is read as a *mediating* element in the culture-nature relationship, then it may account in part for the cultural tendency not merely to devalue woman but to circumscribe and restrict her functions, since culture must maintain control over its (pragmatic and symbolic) mechanisms for the conversion of nature into culture. And if it is read as an *ambiguous* status between culture and nature, it may help account for the fact that, in specific cultural ideologies and symbolizations, woman can occasionally be aligned with culture, and in any event is often assigned polarized and contradictory meanings within a single symbolic system. Middle status, mediating functions, ambiguous meaning—all are different readings, for different contextual purposes, of woman's being seen as intermediate between nature and culture.

Conclusions

Ultimately, it must be stressed again that the whole scheme is a construct of culture rather than a fact of nature. Woman is not "in reality" any closer to (or further from) nature than man—both have consciousness, both are mortal. But there are certainly reasons why she appears that way, which is what I have tried to show in this paper. The result is a (sadly) efficient feedback system: various aspects of woman's situation (physical, social, psychological) contribute to her being seen as closer to nature, while the view of her as closer to nature is in turn embodied in institutional forms that reproduce her situation. The implications for social change are similarly circular: a different cultural view can only grow out of a different social actuality; a different social actuality can only grow out of a different cultural view.

It is clear, then, that the situation must be attacked from both sides. Efforts directed solely at changing the social institutions—through setting quotas on hiring, for example, or through passing equal-pay-for-equal-work laws—cannot have far-reaching effects if cultural language and imagery continue to purvey a relatively devalued view of women. But at the same time efforts directed solely at changing cultural assumptions—through male and female consciousness-raising groups, for example, or through revision of educational materials and mass-media imagery—cannot be successful unless the institutional base of the society is changed to support and reinforce the changed cultural view. Ultimately, both men and women can and must be equally involved in projects of creativity and transcendence. Only then will women be seen as aligned with culture, in culture's ongoing dialectic with nature.

The Virgin
and the State

I n an extraordinarily wide range of societies in the world one finds a peculiar "complex": ideologically it is held that the purity of the women reflects on the honor and status of their families; and the ideology is enforced by systematic and often quite severe control of women's social and especially sexual behavior. One sees this pattern manifested among peasant societies in Latin America and around the entire Mediterranean area, among pastoral nomadic tribes of the Middle East and southwest Asia, among the castes of India, and among the elites of China. In extreme cases, such as classical Athens or among Brahmins of India, women were confined to the house for life. In imperial Turkey, the sultan had vast numbers of wives and daughters "in an elaborately organized harem, or seraglio, with disciplinary and administrative officers, ruled over by [his] mother" (Encyclopaedia Britannica 1974, 4: 907). Among poorer peasants and nomads, a variety of other devices—veils; rules of body-disguising dress and of modest demeanor; restrictions on expression, communication, and movement; all overseen by the family in particular and the gossip of the community in general—serve to restrict women's social and sexual behavior as effectively as if they were locked up.[1]

Reviewing the variety of cases, one tends to get involved in particular cultural symbolizations and practices, and to lose sight of the broad similarities of pattern. Further, the pattern does not seem to be confined to any particular type of society, or to any consistent stratum: peasants and elites, agriculturalists and pastoral nomads, all seem to embrace some version of the female purity ethic with equal intensity and commitment. It seems difficult to imagine that there might be a single interpretation that would cover, or at least interrelate, all the cases.

In fact, in the anthropological analyses of particular cases, a variety of interpretive frameworks have been used: psychoanalytic, structural, functional, ecological, political, or some mixture of several of these. Let me begin to situate the question of why the control of female sexual purity is such a widespread and virulent phenomenon by reviewing briefly some of the major attempts at interpretation in the anthropological literature.[2]

In an early essay from a psychoanalytic perspective, Kathleen Gough (1955) analyzed the female initiation rites among the Nayar and other groups of the Malabar region of India. Gough interpreted the rituals as signifying the formal renunciation by the girl's consanguineal kinsmen of rights to her sexuality, in a social context in which there is evidently strong incest temptation. Further, during these rites the young girl was actually or symbolically deflowered by a person other than her prospective husband, and Gough interpreted this point as representing male fear of the defloration of virgins in the course of normal sexuality. Although Nayar women do not seem to fit our model in that, following their initiation they had great sexual freedom, we must not forget that their freedom was gained at the expense of Nambudiri Brahmin women, who were subject to virtually total seclusion and control. Untold numbers of Nambudiri women died virgins, while Nambudiri men mated with the conveniently available Nayar.

In a subsequent counteressay, Nur Yalman (1963) challenged (and ridiculed) Gough's interpretation and recast the whole argument in terms of the control of female purity. He stressed that the rites establish the purity of the women in their own castes and serve to define and regulate the women's subsequent choices of mates, who must always be of equal or higher caste status. The issue, he argued, is control of caste purity and status as a whole, which must be maintained by regulation of female sexuality, because regardless of the descent principles operating within intracaste kinship groupings, caste as opposed to kin affiliation is always inherited bilaterally. Further, if caste membership is defined as coming only through one parent, that parent is always the mother. Thus for purposes of sustaining caste purity, the woman's purity in particular must be controlled, protected against pollution by lower-caste mates. Men, on the other hand, are free to have sexual relations with anyone, "high or low" as Yalman says, and he then explains this in both cultural and natural terms. Culturally, Indians distinguish between internal and external pollution. Women are subject to internal pollution in sexual intercourse, which is very hard if not impossible to cleanse, but men are subject only to external pollution in intercourse and can be cleansed by a simple ritual bath. Yet Yalman goes further than this cultural point, and relates the ideology to natural factors: "the bond between the genitor and the child is tenuous; it can always be denied or minimized; the children can always be repudiated by the father" (1963: 41).

More recent studies have tended to get away from elusive unconscious factors and symbolic cultural notions of pure and impure, and to stress the brass tacks of economics and politics. Lawrence Watson (1972) describes the practices of the Guajiro of Venezuela, among whom the virginity of a girl upon marriage is absolutely demanded, the result being assured by a combination of psychological terrorism and physical punishment, mostly enacted by mothers on their daughters. For a serious offense, "the mother may place the tip of a hot branding iron on the girl's vagina to make the punishment a convincing object lesson" (1972: 151).[3] Watson casts his interpretation of this system in terms of the political structure of the society, in which every group is concerned about maintaining its status in a rigid class system; the group's status depends in part upon the quality of the women it can deliver in the marriage alliance process. Especially among the upper classes, influential chiefs overtly use marriage alliances of daughters and sisters as a way of building up followings for political and military backing. "If . . . a woman causes her father or uncle to lose valuable political allies because of deficiencies in her sexual behavior, she becomes a liability and she can seriously impede her lineage's chances of building up a secure base of political support (1972: 154). In this interpretation, the sadistic control of female purity is simply a form of *realpolitik*.

And finally, Jane Schneider (1971) presents an argument in terms of ecological and economic factors, and the politics thereof. In her important paper "Of Vigilance and Virgins . . . ," she begins with the general point that "honor can be thought of as the ideology of a property holding group which struggles to define, enlarge, and protect its patrimony in a competitive arena" (1971: 2). She then goes on to argue that both pastoral and peasant societies tend to be highly socially fragmented and "unsolidary," although the reasons for this social fragmentation are different in the two cases. And according to Schneider, honor is the code that keeps this "centrifugal" situation together: it "helps shore up the identity of a group (a family or a lineage) and commit to it the loyalties of otherwise doubtful members. [It] defines the group's social boundaries, contributing to its defense against the claims of equivalent competing groups. [It] is also important as a substitute for physical violence in the defense of economic interests. . . . Honor regulates affairs among men" (1971: 17). But why the honor of the *women*? Why should the women's honor represent the honor of the group as a whole? Because, says Schneider, resolutely practical to the end, among the pastoralists concerned with lineage continuity, female reproductive capacity is valuable, and women are "contested resources much like pastures and water" (1971: 18). As for the agrarian peasants, the problem seems primarily to be the potential fragmentation of the family of procreation, with fathers, sons, and brothers set off against one another because of inheritance rules; here the daughters/sisters provide the one shared focus of concern that can hold the group together (1971: 21).

I will restrain my temptation to dissect the circularities and self-contradictions of many of these arguments and will simply say that, with the exception of the psychoanalytic argument, all of them share common functionalist orientations: the purity of women is seen as adaptive for the social coherence, economic viability, or cultural reputation of the group, regardless of whether the group is a caste, lineage, or family. When the theorists try to explain why women in particular should represent the coherence and integrity of the group, rather than, say, a totemic bird or a sacred flute, the answers are more variable—in terms of women's natural childbearing abilities, women's physical structure (internal pollution), women's function as tokens of alliance, or women's symbolic roles in the family. None of these answers is very satisfactory; all use as explanations the very things that need explaining. We are still left with the paradox that male-defined structures represent themselves and conceptualize their unity and status through the purity of their women.

I would argue then that all of these explanations can be lumped together and that they share a set of common failings. First, all are static functional accounts, and lack time depth. Second, all share the common functionalist fallacy of reifying the unit under study and treating it as closed, exclusive, and isolated from a larger social context—the family, lineage, or caste is treated almost as a society in itself. And finally, all explanations, with the exception of the psychoanalytic discussion, take the point of view that the problem is one of male/male relations, in which the women are intermediaries, rather than the problem being, as it at least equally is, a problem of male/female relations. Although each of the arguments contains some useful kernel of truth, none provides a framework for encompassing and accounting for the phenomenon as a whole in cross-cultural, cross-class, and cross-sex perspective.

What I should like to do in this paper, then, is to offer some observations, thoughts, suggestions, and hypotheses for exploring this problem more systematically, and in a way that will illuminate problems of social and cultural process in general, as well as male/female relations in particular.

I would begin by noting that all of the modern cases of societies concerned with female purity are in fact of a certain type, namely, that all are part of, or have historically been part of, states, or at least systems with fairly highly developed stratification.[4] Thus hyperpure Brahmins and hyperpoor Mediterranean peasants share the status of being part-structures, elements in larger stratified political structures. Even when the larger state structures in which they originally developed are no longer organically intact, all of the modern groups in question bear the cultural ideologies, and particularly the religions, which were part of the organic emergence of their ancestral states in the first place. Most of the societies concerned with female purity are involved in so-called great traditions, especially Christianity, Islam, and Hinduism. And these religions evolved in conjunction with the emergence of states (or "civilizations," or empires) which, although most are no longer intact, nonetheless shaped the societies and cultures of the groups that bear their cultural heritages. And most of the peasants whose ancient states have decayed are now involved with modern states in ways that are structurally similar to their places in the original ones.

It is true that there are pre-state societies which, for example, require the virginity of women at marriage, and probably the majority of human societies expect relative sexual faithfulness of women after marriage. But no pre-state societies, as far as I have been able to ascertain, evince the sort of pattern I am concerned with here—the ideological linkage of female virginity and chastity to the social honor of the group, such chastity being secured by the exertion of direct control over women's mobility to the point of lifetime seclusion, and/or through severe socialization of fear and shame concerning sex.[5] What I am suggesting, then, is that this sort of concern with the purity of women was part of, and somehow structurally, functionally, and symbolically bound up with, the historical emergence of systematically stratified state-type structures, in the evolution of human society.[6]

Before examining what the purity of women might have to do with the emergence of states, however, let me sketch very briefly what I see as the patterns and tendencies of female/male relations in pre-state societies, or rather in contemporary societies that have historically been outside of known state systems, and that have not themselves evolved the social, political, and economic characteristics of states. I would begin with the point that there is always, even in the most primitive of known societies, some sort of asymmetry between the sexes. Even the most manifestly egalitarian of band [hunting/gathering] societies accords some edge of authority or charisma or status to men, if only on the view that the big game that the men bring home is superior as food to the women's gathered produce. In slightly more complex band societies, it seems that there is always some sacred center or ritual from which women are excluded. And although women may have their sacred ceremonies, from which men are excluded, the male ceremonies are considered to be for the welfare of the group as a whole, while the women's ceremonies are specific to the welfare of women. Finally, in the most complex of the known band societies, primarily in Australia, male authority is asserted through, and reinforced by, systematic control of the marriage system, the exchange of women and goods. Control of the marriage system, always in the hands of men, transforms diffuse authority or charisma into the beginnings of real power and control. Nonetheless, being bartered about in a system of marriage exchange is not the same thing as having one's day-to-day behavior and freedom of movement directly controlled, and in fact women in band societies evidently have a great deal of autonomy of action, as long as they comply with the legal rules of the game. There is also no ideology in these societies about protecting female purity.

If anything, the ideology is just the reverse, and women are often seen as, to some degree, dangerous and polluting. According to Mary Douglas (1966), pollution beliefs are systematically related to cultural category ambiguities and anomalies; the danger and pollution of women would seem to derive in large part from the fact that women systematically appear as ambiguous vis-à-vis two very important, and partly related, category distinctions that may be common to all human societies. The first distinction is the nature/culture dichotomy, and I have discussed at length elsewhere woman's ambiguity vis-à-vis this opposition (Ortner 1972, this volume). The second is the structure/antistructure, or order/disorder dichotomy, in which men and male groups are identified with structure, order, social organization itself. Insofar as women are moved around in marriage, in a social exchange system controlled by, and culturally seen as composed of, structured groups of men, women appear interstitial within the fundamental kinship architecture of society (Rosaldo 1974). Further, the ambiguity of women would derive not only from a marriage perspective; insofar as there is descent ideology, whether patrilineal or matrilineal, women are seen as "in between" in these sorts of systems as well, for descent groups (such as clans) see themselves as groups of males, with women as their reproductive agents. With respect to either or both of these oppositions—nature/culture, structure/antistructure—women may appear ambiguous, and hence potentially polluting and dangerous. And although none of the simplest hunting/gathering societies manifest the phobia about female pollution and danger that appears among, for example, New Guinea horticulturalists, most have a variety of taboos and avoidance rules that seem concerned with keeping at least some of the boundaries drawn.

Now between hunting/gathering band societies on the one hand, and states on the other, there is obviously a vast range of types of societies, of widely varying structure and complexity. I have yet to find or devise a classification scheme that organizes all of them in some satisfactory evolutionary sequence. I will plow right through all this complexity, however, and simply say that through all the types of pre-state societies, female/male relations stay broadly within the pattern established over the range of band societies—from relatively mutualistic and balanced, to the extreme cases of sex antagonism, with male self-segregation, and strong expressions of fear of women as dangerous. But again the expression of and reaction to fear of women in those extreme cases, and here I am thinking largely of New Guinea and South America, involves *exclusion* of women, or attempts thereof, rather than systematic domination and control. My image here is the New Guinea or South American village, with the men huddled in men's houses in the center off-limits to the women, and the women strung out around the periphery in their individual huts with their uterine families. Even in North America, a much less extreme area on this score, we find the male sweat lodges, the kivas into which women are not allowed, and so forth. But as long as the women do not trespass on the off-limits areas, they have considerable autonomy of action, and indeed a certain edge of power insofar as they can appropriate and judiciously imply control of some of the powers with which the male culture endows them. As in band societies, the one area in which men do exercise systematic control over women is the marriage system. Again, however, there is no ideology that the women exchanged in marriage must be virginal, sexually naive, and mystically pure; nor is seclusion of women practiced as a means of controlling their sexuality.

Finally, however, we get to the great divide: the rise of the state. Here there is a radical shift of both ideology and practice. On the ground, we have the emergence of the patriarchal extended family. Indeed here for the first time the term patriarchy becomes applicable, because the structure involves the absolute authority of the father or other senior male over everyone in the household—all junior males and all females. And now women are for the first time brought under direct and systematic control, first by their natal families, and then by their husbands and their affinal kin. Among elites, one has the image of women being rounded up in great numbers and confined in harems and analogous arrangements elsewhere. Among the Brahmins of India, they are locked in great purdah palaces and never emerge into the world. The notion develops that men are directly responsible for the behavior of their women, rendering it part of every man's definition of self and manliness that "his" women never escape his control; his honor, and the honor of his group, are at stake.

At the same time, there is a great shift in the ideology concerning women. Before they were dangerous, but now they are said to be *in danger*, justifying male protection and guardianship. Before they were polluting, and this had to be defended against, but now they are said to be pure, and to need defending. At the same time, one finds for the first time symbolic idealization of woman in the mother-aspect, rather than in the sexual-reproductive aspect. Eventually, as the symbol system gets itself together in one part of the world with which we are all familiar, the ideal woman emerges as all the best things at once, mother and virgin.

Now the way in which I've described the pattern, and the way in which it might, at first glance, be viewed, is in terms of the domestication of women, a sort of Neolithic of the sexes wherein women, like plants and animals, were brought under control in the service of the race. Actually, however, my thinking is to envision the process in terms of the beginnings of the domestication of *men*, as part of a larger pattern of systematization of hierarchy and control in the evolution of state structures. I will return to this point later.

In any case, the whole business is terribly complex. What I shall do here is simply offer a brief checklist of points that I think would be important to consider in trying systematically to account for the changes in sex-role relations and ideology that seem to be associated with the emergence of the state. The checklist consists of the following items, in no particular order:

the question of diffusion, the question of changes in the division of labor, changes in religious thought, changes in family structure, and changes in marriage patterns. I shall only be able to say a few words about each, merely pointing in the direction I think investigation should go.

Diffusion, first, is something that cannot be entirely ruled out. It is possible that the pattern I have described—idealization of female chastity; ideology of protection, control, and seclusion of the women—developed in one area of the ancient old world, and reached other early states through trade and other diffusionary mechanisms. Most of the known contemporary societies with this pattern are geographically contiguous, in a broad band from the circum-Mediterranean area, across the Middle East and southwest Asia, across India, and up into China.[7] The new world indigenous states would thus have to be investigated for independent evolution of the pattern.[8] Even if indicated, however, we know that diffusion in itself never explains very much, for peoples hear of many peculiar customs practiced by their neighbors, yet those practices will only be adopted if the social structural and ideological conditions are ripe for their reception. That is, the diffusion would only have taken hold as independently developing societies evolved the sorts of structures within which such a pattern of sex-role relations would be functional and meaningful.

The second point, very briefly, is the question of whether changes in the division of labor may have motivated changes in sex-role relations and ideologies. One standard view has it that, with the rise of plow agriculture and/or systematic irrigation systems associated with the rise of states, women were excluded from major roles in the sphere of production, while their reproductive value in the family was more strongly emphasized. My own reading of the data is quite different. It is probably true that men became associated with plowing as a specific activity, and with the engineering and control of irrigation systems, and both of these points are quite important in the symbolics of male prestige. Nonetheless it seems that women continued to be fully productive, and if anything worked even harder than they did before, in both grain production in the western old world and rice production in the east. The gradual withdrawal of women from production (where it happened) was, I think, a very late development. It will thus not account for the emergence of the female purity pattern, although it will have repercussions for that pattern later.

In the domain of religion, next, I would stress the point that an elaborated notion of purity *in general* only comes in systematically with the emergence of state structures. In pre-state societies, including the simplest that we know, one of course finds the notion that exceptional purity, often including temporary celibacy, is required for specific important purposes. Generally, it is associated with some major male undertaking—a hunt, a raid, or a ritual—and is conceived in terms of purifying or at least not polluting male energies, so that they will be strong and focused for the big event. Nonetheless, there is no notion that it would be good for some people, female or male, to strive for permanent exceptional purity, including permanent celibacy. Such notions probably come in with permanent standing priesthoods of some kind, and these of course are standard, virtually diagnostic, features of early states.

If the chastity of priests was the first application of the notion of chastity to a social group, its rationale was probably similar to that for the episodic demands for purity in pre-state societies: the priest is charged with protection of sacred objects and activities, and he (or sometimes she) must be in a permanent state of non-pollution for the job. But it would seem that there is more to it than this. In particular I would suggest that in state religions and cosmologies, what seems to happen is that the whole purity ceiling is raised, so to speak. That is, one finds systematic elaboration of higher realms of purity and sacredness than existed before, with more exacting demands upon the laity for conforming to religious ideals. Thus it may be a matter of the religion postulating higher, more sacred, and more demanding gods (e.g., the Aztec gods who required human sacrifice), and/or a more articulated after-death state (as, for example, in *The Egyptian Book of the Dead*). Transcendental power, divinity, sacredness, and purity are all more articulated than previously.

It is not at all difficult to account for the emergence of such ideologies in state structures, in relation to the overall increased complexity of society—for example, more complex divine hierarchies may reflect more complex social hierarchies; or more demanding gods may reflect the greater demands of the state and the dominant classes; or more elaborated notions of afterlife may be interpreted as promising the newly emergent masses their rewards later rather than now, and so forth. The situation is of course infinitely more complex than this, but cannot be explored here. My point is simply that one would begin to investigate the elaboration of the notion of female purity by contextualizing it in the emergence of systematic views of transcendental purity in state cosmologies in general. Purity as something that whole categories of people might intrinsically possess, or might systematically be required to sustain, is itself, I think, a product of state-related religious thought. Mind/body dualisms (reflecting, among other things, new divisions of labor between intellectual/artistic/political elites and producing masses), and the control of sexuality, sensuality, and materialism (part of, among other things, a delayed-gratification, reduced-material-expectations ideology for the masses) would be aspects of this general pattern.

Coming down from the cosmological heights to ground-level social structure, the fourth item covers changes in the structure of the family. Again I will be very brief, although the problem requires detailed scrutiny. The key point is undoubtedly the emergence of the patriarchal family structure, and probably ideally the patriarchal extended family. But the way in which I would look at this phenomenon, as I noted earlier, is in terms of the domestication of men, both as husbands/fathers, and as sons. Probably the catalyst around which the whole thing crystallized was property holding in one form or another, although it was certainly not yet "private" property. Be that as it may, what I think was at issue was the gradual deepening of involvement of individual males in responsibility, as husbands/fathers, for their specific family units—not just economic responsibility, for that was always accepted, but also what might be called political accountability. The family became in a sense an administrative unit, the base unit in the political-economic structure of the state. The husband/father was no longer simply responsible *to* his family, but also *for* his family vis-à-vis the larger system. It became the base, and often the only base of his jural status.

Now, judging from contemporary cases, I imagine that such deepening involvement of men in families was accepted only reluctantly, and as part of a tradeoff for patterns of deference and respect from wives and children. The reluctance of males to be involved with their families except on terms of distance, respect, and submission on the part of the other members is still I think to be seen in most of the world today, and the domestication of men is still largely incomplete. Nonetheless, the notion that males are not only economically but also legally and politically responsible for the proper functioning of the family unit seems to be part of the systematic extension of principles of hierarchy, domination, and order in the evolution of states as a whole. Responsible husbands/fathers are more systematically incorporated into the system.

Responsible husbands/fathers, which is to say in this context patriarchal husbands/fathers, in turn keep everyone else in line—the women, of course, but also the sons. Indeed, perhaps the most striking characteristic of the patriarchal family is the prolongation of dependence and subjugation of sons. This is such an overdetermined phenomenon that one can hardly begin to sort out its sources and components. However, let it suffice to say that sons are held back from the acquisition of property, wives, and emotional maturity by such a powerful combination of forces, emanating from both father and mother, that it is certainly one of the key changes that we see in family structure, regardless of household composition (that is, regardless of whether the family is "extended" or not). Male initiation rites virtually disappear in state societies; far from fathers and other senior males facilitating, however frighteningly, a young male's passage to adulthood, the young adult male in the patriarchal family remains in a jurally dependent status at least until he is married, and often beyond. In many cases marriage itself becomes the only rite of passage, and thus manhood becomes equated with responsibility for wife and children, part of the pattern described above.

This pattern is likely to have certain psychodynamic implications. One may wish to go the Freudian route, in terms of deep unconscious factors, and I am not immune to the persuasions of a well-done Freudian analysis. Kathleen Gough's paper on female initiation rites, mentioned earlier, is an excellent and very convincing Freudian discussion of the sorts of fears and ideals of women produced in such family situations in the Indian case. However, one can probably account for a lot without recourse to unconscious factors, through careful symbolic analysis of cultural notions of mothers and wives in such systems. The pivotal point of such analysis would be that men were not only "domesticated" as part of the crystallization of authority structures of the state; they were also juvenilized—vis-à-vis women, senior men, and the rulers and overclasses of the system.

Note that I have not tried to postulate motives for either women or men in this process. I have suggested that men were "reluctant" about being domesticated, but I would imagine that women had equally mixed feelings about the greater presence of male authority in the family unit. I do not think it is useful to view this process in terms of (in Engels's famous phrase) "the world historical defeat of women" by men, or other such motivated formulations. The crystallization of patriarchal family corporations was doubtless a precipitate of larger political and economic processes. Nonetheless, once it got going, it became a social force in its own right, affecting not only the further evolution of gender relations, but also the economic and political evolution of the larger system itself.

The final item on the present checklist is the question of changes in marriage systems. I noted earlier that concern for the purity of women is found, in contemporary societies, among both elites and lower strata. In southern Europe, the peasants seem much more concerned about the issue than the upper classes; for elites the relative freedom of their women is a symbol of their modernity, or else simply a symbol of their being above the codes. In India or China, on the other hand, the Brahmins and upper classes were far stricter about the purity of their women than the lower castes and the peasants. In trying to account for the emergence of a code of female purity as part of the emergence of the state, one would perhaps want to begin with the question of which stratum started the whole thing. Thus some might argue that it was probably originally an elite conceit, in that elite women (if not other women) did not need to engage in productive labor, and could be secluded and protected from the pollutions of work and people as a mark of upper-class status. One could argue with equal logic, however, that there are aspects of peasant social life and social structure that would generate a concern for the purity of women, as in Jane Schneider's discussion previously noted.

The way out of the puzzle, I would suggest, lies in stressing the stratified nature of the state as a totality, and seeking the dynamics of the process in the *interaction* between elites and lower strata. In particular, my analytic instinct is to look at patterns of hypergamy (up-status marriage, virtually always between upper men and lower women) in state systems, and to consider very centrally the possibility that one of the significant developments in stratified societies was the shifting of marriage from an essentially lateral transaction, between essentially equal groups, to at least a potentially vertical transaction, wherein one's sister or daughter is potentially a wife or consort of a king or nobleman, or could be dedicated to the temple and the services of the priesthood.

I think it is fairly safe to expect to find patterns and ideals of hypergamy, or what might be called vertical alliance, in stratified societies. Vertical alliance would constitute one of several sorts of paternalistic ties between the strata. But what analytic consequences flow from putting this point at the center of the analysis?

In the first place, as has been noted by others for India (e.g., Tambiah 1973), the assumption of systematic hypergamy as an ideal and to some extent as a practice will account for the phenomenon of women accumulating at the top of the system. Because lower-status families are eager to marry their women upwards for political reasons, the elites would accumulate wives. At the same time, the elites would often be unable to get rid of their own sisters and daughters, for there is nowhere further up for those women to go. Thus the emergence of harems, purdah palaces, and so forth, would partly be a structural precipitate of the hypergamy system, rather than an indication of (among other possibilities) the extraordinary lust of sultans. At the same time, the accumulation of wives by polygynous royalty and nobility would certainly have value in the symbolics of power, for it would suggest their potency in everything from sex to politics to the fertility of the land. Thus the image of herds of penned-up women that is projected in these sorts of systems flows partly from the dynamics of the marriage system, and not from men rounding up and controlling women as such.

Second, hypergamy may provide the strongest explanation for the purity of women ideal and for certain peculiarities of this ideal. The context of hypergamy is a context of orientation toward upward mobility, through manipulation of marriages. We know that the *economic* value of women becomes a focus in these contexts, for it is here that we find the emergence of dowry (Goody 1973), enhancing the girl's value for a higher-status spouse. In addition, however, there is the question of her mystical or spiritual value, her inner worthiness for such an alliance. The notions of virginity and chastity may be particularly apt for symbolizing such value, rather than, for example, external beauty, because virginity is a symbol of exclusiveness and inaccessibility, nonavailability to the general masses, something, in short, that is elite. A virgin is an elite female among females, withheld, untouched, exclusive.

The assumption of hypergamy would also account for one of the major puzzles of the female purity phenomenon, namely, that the women of a given group are expected to be purer than the men, that upon their higher purity hinges the honor of the group. I would argue that the women are *not*, contrary to native ideology, representing and maintaining the group's *actual* status, but are oriented upwards and represent the ideal higher status of the group. One of the problems with the purity literature, I think, has been a failure to get beneath native ideology; the natives justify female purity in terms of maintaining the group's actual status, as a holding action for that status in the system, when in fact it is oriented toward an ideal and generally unattainable status. The unattainability may in turn account for some of the sadism and anger toward women expressed in these purity patterns, for the women are representing the over-classes themselves.

And finally, the hypergamy assumption gives us at least one clue about a girl's (or woman's) motivation for cooperation in her own subordination and control. For if she is a good girl, she has the potential for personal status mobility which in fact exceeds that of most of the men of her group. Here it becomes intelligible that it is often women themselves who actively reproduce the patterns of female purity, socializing their daughters in fear of and shame about sex, telling them that it is for their own good (which in a way it is), and spying on and gossiping about one another's daughters as part of an overall deep internalization of and loyalty to the system. Again the point is the future orientation of the ideology, toward some often quite illusory but nonetheless remotely imaginable status mobility, which the girl herself internalizes as the "someday my prince will come" theme. It is no wonder too that women later may resent their husbands as deeply as husbands resent their wives—not only or even necessarily because of the husbands' direct domination, but for what their husbands represent in status terms. For if the husband is of one's own status level, then one has saved all that purity for nothing, while if he is of the ideal higher status level, he is likely to be an undesirable mate who is willing to take a lower-class wife because of some personal or social defect—some lecherous old Molièrian widower, or someone of noble credentials but no money.

A final point about hypergamy leads me to my brief conclusions. Note that, once again, women are crossing boundaries, in this case boundaries separating classes or castes or status groups in vertical stratification systems. Thus the ambiguity of femaleness vis-à-vis social categories remains at the core of the problem, and views of women remain bound in the purity/pollution idiom. Perhaps partly because the boundary crossing is in an upward direction, however, the symbolization of ambiguity shifts from danger to purity, although the deep structure, if one may use that phrase, remains the same.

At the ideological level, then, one may say that there has been a fairly simple structural transformation, and nothing much has changed in male attitudes toward and mistrust of women. It is clear in contemporary cultures with female purity ideologies that women are still feared as ambiguous and dangerous creatures. Nonetheless I wish to close on an optimistic note.

Lévi-Strauss (1960) has suggested that there is no reason to assume that women and men would, if left to their own devices, form durable bonds of mutual interdependence. The phase of social evolution that I have been discussing may perhaps least depressingly be viewed as a long, painful, and unfinished moment in the dialectic of the evolution of such bonds.[9]

Rank and Gender

Introduction

Since the days of the early voyagers, Polynesia has been famed for its distinctive culture of gender and sexuality. Sensualism, eroticism, and a high level of sexual activity are actively cultivated throughout the area. Homosexuality is unstigmatized. Relations between men and women are relatively harmonious and mutually respectful. Women achieve high public office with some regularity. From a western point of view, the area has appeared as a "paradise" of "liberation," liberation of sex and of women.

This picture is surprisingly accurate as far as it goes, but it is only a partial picture. A more thorough excursion into the ethnographic literature reveals some more problematic features: enforced virginity of unmarried girls, a relatively high frequency of rape, a very marked subordination of wives to husbands within the domestic context.

The purpose of this essay[1] is to develop a general and systematic interpretation of Polynesian society that will account for as many as possible of the salient (and apparently contradictory) features of Polynesian gender culture. I will argue that the sex/gender system (as Rubin [1975] calls it) can be best understood in relation to the workings of the "prestige system," the system within which personal status is ascribed, achieved, advanced, and lost.

For Polynesia the "prestige system" is a system of hereditary ranking.[2] People are born into certain statuses, high or low, that are theoretically unchangeable for life, and that in turn are passed on to their offspring. Polynesia thus belongs to that large class of societies labeled "hierarchical" in Louis Dumont's (1970) classic formulation. In modern times the most famous exemplar of the category is India, organized as a system of ranked castes. Dumont argues for the uniqueness of the Indian case, but the organizational principles he identifies for India may be seen as central to a wide range of well-known societies—feudal Europe, feudal Japan, pre-modern China, much of Southeast Asia, and probably the "archaic states" of Egypt, Mesopotamia, and Central and South America. Most recently Irving Goldman has (independently) discussed Polynesia in much the same terms in which Dumont discusses India, and Goldman's superb (in my view) *Ancient Polynesian Society* (1970) inspired much of my thinking in developing the present essay.

The characteristic features of "hierarchical" societies may be very briefly summarized here. The first is what Dumont calls the "encompassing" status of prestige criteria vis-à-vis other principles of social organization. This means, very simply, that persons and/or categories of persons are ranked or graded according to criteria of social or religious value that theoretically transcend immediate political and economic "realities." Neither great wealth nor great power necessarily generates great prestige, which derives rather from intangible qualities like "purity" (in India) or "mana" (in Polynesia), considered to be largely innate and inherited. The highest social status in the system is the one highest on the scale of such qualities, regardless of actual political or economic power. To put the point slightly differently, doctrines of hereditary purity or heredity mana are ideologies of aristocratic superiority, and these are the hegemonic ideologies of the society. The Brahmins of India, and the highest-ranking aristocrats of Polynesia, may not in fact be the most powerful group in terms of "real" politics, but it is their values that order society as a whole from high to low, and that must be drawn upon to legitimate more mundane political and economic power.

The second distinctive feature of hierarchical organization is what Dumont calls "holism," which has two interrelated aspects. First, rather than the "strata" being seen as independent units that are then "linked" in various ways, they are seen as differentiated, functionally specialized precipitates of a prior whole. In terms of social practice this means in turn—the second aspect of holism—that social relations between members of the different strata are organized in terms of mutual reciprocities and obligations. Inferiors owe goods and services to superiors, but superiors also have reciprocal obligations to inferiors: *noblesse oblige*. Thus notions of "exploitation" appropriate to the analysis of "class" societies are only partially and imperfectly applicable to the analysis of hierarchies.

In the present essay I will attempt to account for features of Polynesian gender and sexual culture by relating them to various aspects of the hierarchical social organization, or in other words, to aspects of the workings of "the prestige system." I must thus begin by justifying the decision to draw this particular set of connections.

The decision partly derives from the fact that, as just discussed, prestige criteria are in fact "encompassing": They provide the largest framework and the ultimate reference point for the organization of almost every aspect of social life. Further, my reading of the general literature on sex and gender over a wide variety of ethnographic cases—and not only in hierarchical societies—suggests that, empirically, the prestige system virtually always seems to have powerful interactions with the gender system. Thus in New Guinea the system of achieving "big man" status seems "key" to the organization of gender (see, for example, Strathern 1981); in India it appears to be caste ranking (see Gough 1955; Yalman 1963; Leach 1970; Tambiah 1973); and in the Mediterranean it appears to be the system by which men gain and lose "honor" (see Pitt-Rivers 1966, 1977; J. Schneider 1971).

Finally, and perhaps most importantly, there is a more general theoretical reason for looking to prestige. The prestige system of any society is the system that defines the ultimate goals and purposes of life for actors in that society. It defines what men and women are, as well as what they are (or should be) trying to accomplish or to become, and it defines how they can and cannot go about that project. To anchor the analysis in the prestige system, in other words, is to anchor it in *cultural* definitions of personal and social value, rather than in externally defined criteria. This does not mean that we confine ourselves analytically to explicit cultural notions and values; on the contrary, as will be evident in this essay, we must be aware that cultural categories and values themselves constitute interpretations and even distortions of other configurations, which must be brought to light through the application of our own ("external") analytic tools. But we must *start* with the cultural categories, or we will distort the data from the outset.

I begin the discussion then by describing the formal characteristics of the Polynesian prestige ("rank") system. I then move on to a discussion of the primary goals of social action in such a system. Briefly, these include the *maintenance* of status position, which is legitimate, and the *advancement* of status position, which is not legitimate (and theoretically not even possible). I then consider the structurally available means (or, in the jargon, the "strategies") for achieving these goals, and specifically those strategies with the maximum number and widest range of implications for gender relations. Put very simply, I ask first what men (for it is usually their prestige system) are trying to do in these societies, and then how that project hinges on the organization of their relations with women.

The approach I utilize thus entails identifying a particular pattern of action that systematically links male–female relations on the one hand with the largest culturally defined orders of prestige relations on the other. The pattern or strategy in question is often (but not always) "hidden"; identifying it properly is in many ways the hardest part of performing the analysis. Parenthetically it might be noted that, whereas the analysis of "egalitarian" systems entails identifying the hidden *constraints* on prestige-oriented action, the analysis of hierarchies entails locating the hidden *possibilities* for such action.

Finally, in the conclusion, I turn to the implications of the Polynesian analysis for understanding sex and gender patterning in hierarchical societies in general. I try to establish that there is in fact something like a "complex," a coherent set of sex/gender patterns characteristic of such societies, and that this "complex" is best interpreted in relation to certain general structural features of hierarchical social organization. I base the comparative discussion on Goody's and Tambiah's essays in *Bridewealth and Dowry*, covering large areas of Europe and Asia. In making manifest the empirical parallels between Polynesia and these more well-known areas, and in critiquing Goody's and Tambiah's interpretations of their data from the point of view of the Polynesian analysis, I try to show that the interpretation developed in the present essay for one fairly exotic corner of the world is in fact of quite wide applicability.

The Rank System

STRUCTURE AND FUNCTIONING

Polynesia is the designation for a large number of islands in the south Pacific, including (to mention a few that are familiar to non-specialists) Hawaii, Tahiti, and Samoa. The populations of the islands are historically related to one another, although all of the historical links have not been fully established. The languages of the various islands are also closely related, and the peoples are racially very similar. Furthermore, there are both general and specific similarities of social and cultural patterning over the whole of the area.

Among the many social and cultural patterns shared, with variations, by all Polynesian societies, perhaps the most prominent is the system of hereditary ranking. I argued earlier that Polynesian rank systems fit Dumont's definition of "hierarchical" societies, and must be kept conceptually distinct from societies organized in terms of "class." It may be noted here, however, that in some Polynesian societies the social organization is more classlike, while in others it is more "hierarchical" in the Dumontian sense. I will use Goldman's terminology to tag the different types, "traditional" being the more hierarchical, "stratified" being the more classlike.[3] In a future essay I hope to look into variations of gender patterning in relation to variations of social organization along the hierarchy-versus-class axis, but such comparative questions are beyond the scope of the present essay.

Rank in Polynesia operates through the kinship system.[4] The primary units of social, economic, and political organization are (internally stratified) descent groups, at the apex of which stand the "chiefs" who collectively constitute the "aristocracy" of the society. Such descent groups are sometimes ranked in relation to one another, with some sort of supreme or paramount chief at the top of this ranking, but such meta-organization is not present in all cases.

Within descent groups all subunits and individuals are ranked through the application of two simple rules. These are: (a) that siblings (I confine myself to males unless otherwise stated) are ranked by birth order, and (b) that descendants of siblings are ranked collectively by the birth order of their respective ancestors. Hence the elder brother is senior to his younger brother, and all the descendants of the elder brother are senior (and socially superior) to all the descendants of the younger brother. An elder and a younger brother thus theoretically produce two related descent lines that are ranked as superior and inferior, respectively, within a single descent group. Within the respective lines, in turn, the same rules continue to apply, and ranking is systematically applied down to every individual, the eldest son of the eldest son (of the eldest son, etc.) being highest in the group, the youngest son of the youngest son (of the youngest son, etc.) being lowest.

Ranking is thus continuous from top to bottom, the principles of seniority of descent producing a gradation of superiority and inferiority that encompasses all members of the group. In addition, however, all Polynesian societies make a categorical distinction between "aristocracy" and one or more nonaristocratic classes. The terminological distinction is clear enough, but the question of who falls into which category is extremely variable from one Polynesian society to the next, and is often rather hazy at the border even within any given society. Best's comment about the Maori is applicable to most Polynesian societies: "Inasmuch as all members of a tribe are connected with well-born families, then it becomes a difficult matter to define the *ware* or *tutua* class, the people of low degree. Never have I met a native who would admit that he was a member of that class" (Best I 1924: 346).

But the difficulty of stating authoritatively who is "in" the aristocracy, and the vagueness of the border between aristocrats and everyone else, will not affect the arguments in the present essay. A fairly junior member of the descent group as a whole may well be the senior figure in his locality, style himself as a member of the aristocracy, and be treated as such in the local framework of social relations. Insofar as this is the case his family would exhibit the same behavioral tendencies and patterns characteristic of the "aristocracy" in other localities or at higher levels of the structure.

Within the descent group, "the aristocracy" consists of the senior line— the "chief," his senior son, *his* senior son, and so on. From a perspective external to any given descent group, the aristocracy of the society as a whole consists of all the senior lines of all the descent groups. The extent to which they form a society-wide self-conscious "class" is one of the major axes of variation between the most "traditional" (or ranklike) and the most "stratified" (or classlike) Polynesian societies. Even in the simplest, most "traditional" cases, tendencies toward class formation are present, particularly with respect to marriage—senior lines of different descent groups tend to intermarry with one another, across the groups, whereas the remainder of the descent group tends to be endogamous, the members marrying within the unit. In the more complex "stratified" systems, this tendency hardens into fixed rules and practices of class endogamy. Tendencies toward aristocratic class formation are also seen in visiting and feasting patterns—aristocrats travel to visit one another, and host one another to lavish hospitality, with the produce supplied by the host's descent group, eager to have their chief put on a good show.

In some of the "stratified" societies, the ruling class is in effect a single kin group, unrelated to the commoners of the society. In most Polynesian societies, however, the aristocrats are senior kin to their own commoners, and this fact places important constraints on true class formation, as well as on class conflict. Chiefs and aristocrats share at least as many interests with their own commoners as they do with other members of their status class. Thus the Maori, a "traditional" Polynesian society organized along lines quite close to the ideal state of affairs outlined here, say that it is impossible for chiefly and commoner interests to diverge (Mishkin 1961: 433). This is surely an overstatement even in a traditional system, but it refers to the fact that although all chiefs belong to "the aristocracy," each is there only by virtue of his kinship position in his own descent group. He is more like a representative of his group within the aristocratic circle, than a member of an exclusive "class" with interests divergent from those of the "class" of commoners.

Polynesian politics, religion, and economics are all best understood with reference to the descent group organization and class tendencies just outlined. Considering politics first, power and authority are fairly directly ordered by the nesting structure of the ranked units within the descent group. Chiefs have both more power and wider power; lesser aristocrats (such as heads of junior lineages) have less power, and over smaller units; and so on down to household heads. Power is a direct function of status position. It is not primarily a function of wealth per se (though chiefs are generally a little richer than everyone else); and it is not, except in the most complex, "stratified" societies, a direct function of control over economic production.

Access to supernatural power (*mana*), and degree of personal sacredness (*tapu*), closely follow the same lines, although tapu tends to be graded along the continuum of graded rank, whereas access to and control of mana tends to be binary—aristocracy has it and commoners do not. The tapu/mana distinction is thus partly intelligible in relation to the contrast between continuously graded kinship rank on the one hand, and the (incipient or overt) class distinction between aristocrats and commoners on the other. The aristocracy's exclusive direct access to or possession of mana is in some cases the most important basis of the class distinction (e.g., in Tikopia [Firth 1963: 314]). The significance of the chief's control of mana for his political authority cannot be overstated: Throughout much of the area the chiefs are believed to control the forces of nature critical to life and death, even where their worldly power over their subjects is quite minimal and circumscribed.

As for economic organization, most observers agree that the key to understanding the system in Polynesia lies in distribution rather than production. Although chiefs have certain regulatory functions in production, and are the ultimate titular "owners" of all the land, they, and the aristocracy in general, do not have actual control over the distribution of the means of production (primarily land), or over the actual execution of production, except in the "stratified" systems. Within the distribution structure, on the other hand, the chief is focal: Surplus in the form of gifts, tribute, first fruits, and the like is channeled up to him from his kinsmen, and he in turn redistributes most of it back down through the structure of the kin group. Redistribution is one of the most fundamental obligations and privileges of chiefship; it displays both his "power," in terms of his ability to command resources from a wide group, and his qualities of leadership, in the sense that his wide distributions appear as generosity, and as concern for the welfare of the whole.

As the chief's political authority is in the simplest cases a function of his kinship seniority, so are his economic functions and capacities. In the absence of taxation and other force-sanctioned surplus extraction mechanisms, which only appear in the "stratified" societies, his capacity to draw resources to himself depends upon normal mechanisms of kinship prestations and exchanges. And by virtue of being at the pinnacle of the kin group, the chief simply has more kinsmen (that is, more active kin ties with more people) than other members of the group (Firth 1975: 235).

I have thus far been using the terms "chiefs" and "aristocrats" somewhat interchangeably. But whereas all chiefs are aristocrats, all aristocrats are not chiefs. The chiefship is an office occupied by a single individual, whereas the aristocracy is a category and, in some cases, a social class. Thus, succession to the chiefship is a somewhat distinct issue. In a large number of cases the seniority principle of prestige ranking is the same principle that produces the chief—the chief is the senior son of the last chief. In other cases, however, this does not apply, and succession to high office operates on different principles. The succession principle must be separately determined for each society.

It is also important to distinguish between principles, or rules, of succession, descent, and inheritance. Throughout Polynesia, succession to high office passes patrilineally (through the male line), whether to the first-born son (primogeniture) or to some other patrilineally related male chosen by some other criterion. In exceptional cases it passes to a daughter or some other patrilineally related female, but always "in trust" for the next patrilineally related male when he becomes available, or after the death of the woman.

Descent, however, passes cognatically, that is, membership in a descent group passes through both men and women. Throughout Polynesia descent groups are preferentially endogamous, that is, it is both normal and preferred for one to marry a member of one's own descent group beyond a certain prohibited degree of kinship. Given these points, a child normally belongs to the descent group of both of its parents. When the parents belong to two different groups, the child's affiliation seems largely determined by residence—by whether the family resides with the wife's or husband's group. Given cognatic descent, however, the child also retains claims of membership in the other parent's group, and can activate that tie if he or she desires, for whatever reason.

Inheritance patterns are similar to descent patterns. By and large, inheritance is bilateral, that is, both sons and daughters inherit rights in their family's real property, mostly land. But a daughter's rights in land are largely usufructory—she and her husband and children can work it and enjoy its produce during her lifetime, but it reverts to her brothers or their children when she dies. Only the brothers can continue to pass land down to their children, unless again the woman's children reside and affiliate with her kin rather than her husband's. There is a general preference for virilocal residence, for the wife to reside with her husband's people, but in fact the rates of uxorilocality, of husbands residing with the wife's people, are quite high throughout Polynesia. Where the rate is reported it seems to be between 30 percent and 40 percent of all postmarital residence (Hecht 1977: 193; Loeb 1926: 80; Mead 1930: 23). Even in cases of virilocal residence, however, women commonly send one or more sons back to be adopted into households of their immediate kin, and thus to retain a stake in the property.[5]

Finally, one should also mention rules of what might be called "breeding." Throughout Polynesia these are somewhat variable. In general, however, it appears that the father is seen as the fixed point of reference, while the mother acts as the variable, that is, all things being equal, one inherits one's father's rank or status, but if there are major divergences of status between mother and father in either direction, the mother exerts the greater pull on the child's status, up or down. Normally marriages are between persons relatively equal in rank, but both hypergamy (women marrying up) and hypogamy (women marrying down) are possible and not uncommon.

WHAT DO ACTORS WANT AND HOW CAN THEY GET IT?

Within the structure and rule system just described, Polynesian men and women pursue lives informed by the values and ideals built into the system, and constrained by its structural constraints. The supreme cultural values are implicit in the claim that issues of status and prestige are culturally encompassing. What every Polynesian wants is, minimally, to maintain the status and prestige given by the position into which he or she was born, and maximally, to improve position and hence gain more prestige.

In theory, of course, status is fixed by birth. Advancement or rise (as opposed to simple maintenance) is theoretically not possible, although some Polynesian societies (those Goldman labels "open") allow for the legitimate rise of exceptional individuals by virtue of extraordinary deeds in special circumstances. In fact, however, there is a hidden mechanism of status advancement available, with only minor variations, in *all* Polynesian societies, including the "open" ones, which does not depend on extraordinary personal characteristics or deeds at all. It depends simply on systematically manipulating the descent system in a certain way, and it serves as well for maintaining position (which accounts for its legitimacy) as for advancing or rising. This mechanism, moreover, hinges centrally on the manipulation of women, and on the manipulation of men *through* women, by senior males in positions of authority. The mechanism thus links the organization of gender relations to ultimate cultural goals, and as such it will play a major role in subsequent discussions. I will sketch it briefly here, and return to it in more detail at various points throughout the essay.

We may begin by taking the point of view of a junior aristocrat seeking to rise in the system. It will be recalled that a descent group consists of senior/ superior and junior/inferior "lines," theoretically descended from senior and junior siblings. If a junior line can build itself up in size, strength, and wealth, it may arrive at the possibility of either fissioning off and establishing a full-fledged independent group of its own, or of making a bid for the leadership and dominant position in its own group. (This latter is only possible if the senior line is very impoverished in membership, and/or has no appropriate candidate to succeed to the chiefship. But this state of affairs may itself be the result of the building process of the junior line, during which it attracts many members of the senior line to its ranks [see also Biersack 1974].)

Status advancement through descent-line building is explicitly recognized among the Maori (Best II 1924: 24), but something like it must take place in all Polynesian societies. Thus even where it is not explicitly described, there are references throughout the literature to the importance of maintaining large group size, as well as an interest in weakening other groups by thinning their membership (for example, Buck 1932: 29; Linton 1939: 157; Gifford 1929: 30; Mariner I 1827: 82). Even in those (many) Polynesian societies in which warfare is the more visible (if illegitimate) route to mobility, it may be presumed that descent line and/or descent group building is necessarily operating, for a group would have to attain relatively large size before it could undertake a major military campaign.

Descent line growth, as well as decline and deterioration, must often happen "naturally," as a consequence of demographic fluctuations in different lines. It is also, however, highly manipulable, and in ways that are particularly significant for issues of gender. Specifically, it appears that a father may utilize the bilateral inheritance system, the flexibility of cognatic descent line affiliation, and the flexibility of residence rules, to bring new members and even additional land into his orbit. Because daughters can inherit, sons-in-law with less substantial property stakes in their own lines may be attracted into their wives' lines, while at the same time, given the patrilineal bias in the inheritance structure, they can hold on to their own land and bring it into their affinal line's orbit. And perhaps even more important for this process, the children of an uxorilocal marriage would be more likely to affiliate with their mother's than their father's kin, thus adding significant numbers of people to the line. People, even more than land, are the basis of descent line strength.

We have thus far viewed the process primarily from the point of view of an upwardly mobile junior aristocrat, for whom building up a large descent line could result in major status advancement. With a large group there is the possibility of either fission, in which case the leader becomes the top man in the newly independent unit, or of direct takeover of leadership within the natal unit as the senior line withers and wanes. The process is not all that different for commoners. A commoner cannot actually envision becoming a chief in his lifetime, because he is not by birth a member of the aristocracy from which chiefs are drawn. But on a smaller scale a commoner might build his line to a point at which it behooves a chief to take notice of its strength, and thus to make special efforts to retain its loyalty to himself rather than, say, to his presuming younger brother. Thus the chief might marry one of his daughters into the line, and/or give the line special land grants, and/or appoint its leader to special office, and so forth, all of which (but particularly the first) begins a process of "aristocratization" of the line.

Indeed, even for an individual with no personal ambitions for mobility, there is value in playing the same game, in maintaining the size and strength of the unit, however small and low, of which he is the head. Headship of any significance only exists when there is membership of any significance. There is a sense then in which even the littlest man is actually or potentially engaged in this process.

And finally we must consider the high chiefs themselves, who pursue a slightly different though closely related set of strategies. A chief, like everyone else, would hope to attract uxorilocal sons-in-law, and ultimately to retain children of daughters as well as sons, to maintain or augment the strength of his own particular line. But he also has an interest in the well-being of the descent group as a whole—in its internal cohesiveness and its external relations—because the group, and not just his own line, is his political base. Hence at least some chiefly daughters are exported from the group to forge strategic alliances with other groups, while yet others, as previously noted, might be married down into lower internal lines, to reward them for past services and/or to bind them more closely to the chiefly line. Beneath these varying strategies, however, lies the same thread: enriching, enlarging, and solidifying the descent group through retention of female as well as male kin, the females in turn "binding in" additional members or potentially schismatic existing members.

It should be noted for future reference that even the export of chiefly daughters to other groups for purposes of forging political alliances has a significance different from that of the exogamy typically practiced in unilineal systems. Given the cultural emphasis on descent group endogamy in Polynesia, even exogamous marriages are viewed as "incorporative," or at least centripetal. A Maori "tribe," for example, viewed such marriages as "cords" to "pull" other tribes its way when assistance was needed in war (Best II 1924: 235). Thus the retention of the daughter's or sister's loyalty, if not her actual residential presence, remains crucial to the strategies of status maintenance among chiefs, as it is to strategies of both maintenance and advancement at other levels of the system.

Another way of visualizing this process is to realize that, from the point of view of heads of social units (whether of households, descent lines, or full descent groups) cognatic kinship reckoning creates an in-built problem: The units always have the potential for evaporating out from under the top.

Given the fact that everyone has dual affiliation, everyone could theoretically disperse to his or her other set of kin, leaving the head as head of nothing. There is thus great cultural emphasis on centripetal processes, on "pulling," "binding," and "concentrating," accounting among other things for the preference for descent group endogamy, and even in some cases for (chiefly) brother-sister marriage, which "concentrates" the "mana" of the line in which it occurs (see Kirkpatrick 1979). Kinswomen—especially daughters and sisters—are crucial to this "pulling in" process, in ways we have already indicated, and on which we will elaborate more fully in later sections.

Before moving on to a consideration of the treatment of kinswomen, however, it is important to reemphasize that manipulations of descent, marriage, and residence are not ends in themselves. They serve the purpose of maintaining or enhancing status, which are the supreme goals of the system. Much of the ensuing analysis will concentrate on the relationship between descent and marriage manipulations on the one hand, and patterns of gender relations on the other, but such manipulations are means, not ends. The significant analytic relationship remains that between status or prestige on the one hand, and gender and sexuality on the other.

Gender Relations

SISTERS AND DAUGHTERS

The emphasis on descent for the reproduction of status; the descent group as the most important social, economic, and political unit; and finally the cognatic and endogamous nature of Polynesian descent groups, all combine to make kin relations the most important relations in society. Within the general domain of kin relations, in turn, the cultural emphasis falls upon siblingship. The sibling axis is both the axis of unity and the axis of division in the system. A solidary group of brothers (we will come to the role of sisters in a moment) is the cultural ideal, forming the structural backbone of a solidary kin group. But there is also incipient division in this group: The question of succession to headship of the unit divides one brother (usually the eldest) from all the others. Given high rates of divorce and remarriage, as well as polygyny among chiefs, there are half-brothers as well, whose claims to succession, like those of junior full brothers, are weaker, but who may well have such designs nonetheless. Sibling unity is the ideal, but sibling rivalry, sometimes violent, is documented throughout the area

(Best I 1924: 100, 413; Firth 1963: 166, 330; Buck 1938: 155; G. Rogers 1977: 172; Mariner I 1827: 137; Mariner II 1827: 112; Oliver 1974: 644, 727, 742).[6]

The respect for sisters, also documented throughout Polynesia, "fits" with the general emphasis on the sibling axis, but is not fully explained by it, and must be explored more fully. The sister is in some sense a "key symbol" (Ortner 1973b; D. Schneider 1968; Turner 1967) in Polynesian culture, and like all good key symbols she opens many doors and guides us to important insights into the inner workings of the system.

Brother–sister and father–daughter relations. Goldman points out that the terms of address for opposite-sex siblings (sister, brother speaking; brother, sister speaking) are throughout the area, and with very few exceptions, built on a stem term that is related to the term for "deity": "Throughout all of the area this one concept of the godlike quality of brother and sister to each other stands as a formidable constant" (1970: 460; see also Firth 1970: 272 and passim). Goldman cautions us against reasoning from terminology to behavior, and indeed the brother–sister relationship has a markedly different character in Western and Eastern Polynesia (see Goldman's chart on the distribution of brother–sister "respects" [1970: 579]).[7] In the West the brother–sister relationship is one of great formality of interaction, or of complete formal avoidance. Cross-siblings in such avoidance relationships do not speak to one another, eat together, sleep under the same roof, or even (in some cases) remain in the room when the other one is present. Above all, the subject of sex must never be raised when an opposite sex sibling is about (Huntsman and Hooper 1975: 425; Mead 1949: 34; Gifford 1929: 21; Goldman 1970: 579).

In the East on the other hand the relationship is close and even intimate. In some cases brothers and sisters are active in facilitating the love affairs of their opposite-sex siblings. In Mangaia, for example, "a brother and sister may ease the way for a sibling's partner of whom they approve" (Marshall 1971: 128; see also Loeb 1926: 65 for Niue, and Firth 1957: 180 for Tikopia. [Tikopia is a western Polynesian society with "eastern" brother–sister relational patterns.]). And in Hawaii, "The most suitable partner" for the king was his sister; their offspring were "sacred" and "divine" (Malo 1903: 80).[8] Thus where, as in these examples, the brother–sister relationship is not marked with formal respect and avoidance, it often appears as having particular intimacy.

The Western Polynesian pattern of formal respect between brother and sister has implications for intergenerational kinship relations. Throughout this part of Polynesia, the father's sister stands in a relationship of exceptional authority over her brother's children (in Tonga, an even higher authority than their father), and the mother's brother stands in a relationship of exceptional indulgence to his sister's children (Huntsman and Hooper 1975: 424; Firth 1957: 196, 199; Mead 1930: 18, 136–45; Gifford 1929: 17, 18, 23–5; Kaeppler 1971: passim; G. Rogers 1977: passim). Father's sisters and mother's brothers also often have important ritual responsibilities vis-à-vis their cross nieces and nephews, from which the mother and father may be excluded (Huntsman and Hooper 1975: 424; Mead 1930: 27, 29. See also Handy 1923: 71 and Suggs 1966: 127 for an Eastern case of this).

Concerning the complementary issue of great intimacy between brother and sister carrying into the succeeding generation, it should be noted that although brother-sister marriage is rare, and is restricted to high aristocracy, first cousin marriage is not uncommon throughout the area. Mostly it takes place between cross-cousins, that is, between children of opposite-sex siblings, and so carries the theme of the special relationship between opposite-sex siblings further. In the Marquesas it is the preferred form of marriage, at all levels of the society (Suggs 1966: 127; Handy 1923: 71), but in most cases it is preferred and prevalent primarily among the aristocracy, and optional for members of other strata (Buck 1938: 130–3; Gifford 1929: 16; Oliver 1974: 764; Handy and Pukui 1958: 109). Because cross-cousins are classed with siblings in many Polynesian societies (Goldman 1970: 464), cross-cousin marriage is sometimes culturally recognized as marriage between "brothers" and "sisters," and hence as a violation of the incest taboo (Gifford 1929: 22; Goldman 1970: 464)—which is nonetheless culturally rationalized in various ways.[9]

It will be useful before pursuing the discussion further to expand our sense of the sister, and to see her as, at the same time, the daughter of her and her brothers' father. The cultural emphasis on her as sister makes sense in terms of the overall emphasis on the sibling unit, as the unit of both necessary solidarity and potential division over time. In fact however the treatment of daughters is virtually constant throughout the area, even where (mostly in Eastern Polynesia) the special respects, avoidances, and obligations of the brother–sister relationship are not culturally elaborated. It may be tentatively suggested that the sister avoidance complex is a particular variant on the more general pattern of special treatment of daughters. But we need not decide whether the daughter or the sister is the more basic figure in this drama. It will simply be useful to be able to shift flexibly between her two aspects as the occasion arises.

It will be recalled that daughters as well as sons normally inherit at least usufructory rights to real property throughout the area.[10] Although there is a general preference for, or at least a tendency toward, virilocal residence, there is also a high rate of uxorilocal residence, mostly for reasons of the wife's property. Uxorilocal residence appears to carry no shame or social disability for the in-marrying husband, nor is he placed in a subordinate or dependent position vis-à-vis his affines, because affinal relations, unlike kin relations, are not inherently hierarchical. Thus uxorilocal residence may often have attractions for the individual male, especially a junior son/ brother with no particular prospects of succession in his own line, who can at least better his economic situation if not his status prospects.

From the point of view of his wife's kin, in turn, in-marrying sons-in-law are also highly attractive. Not only do such sons-in-law themselves add strength to their affinal descent lines. They also probably add their children who, because of residing with the mother's kin and working their land, will tend to affiliate with their mother's line rather than their father's. Moreover, the in-marrying sons-in-law may also add land. A woman's land rights generally revert to her kinsmen after she dies and cannot be passed on to her children, unless she and the children remain on the land and affiliate with her father's and brothers' line. Men's rights, on the other hand, are "real" and heritable; even if they move away their claims are stronger on retaining the land and passing it on to their children. The uxorilocal son-in-law may thus add himself, his children, and his land to his wife's group. Virilocal residence, the "normal" pattern, maintains the status quo; it neither adds nor subtracts much of significance for the wife's or husband's line. Uxorilocal residence, on the other hand, has very strong building power for the wife's line.

It is thus clear that enlarging a descent line by means other than, or in addition to, natural increase entails holding on to daughters (or, from the brothers' point of view, sisters) and using them to bring in men as in-marrying sons-in-law.[11] It is this dynamic that provides the basis for understanding the peculiar treatment of Polynesian daughters: enforcing their virginity while at the same time beautifying them and making them more sexually attractive. This pattern makes sense if we see the first part, control of virginity, as a symbolic "holding on" to the daughter through close regulation of her sexual behavior, and the second part, the enhancement of her sexual attractions, as an expression of her function as "bait" for her descent line. The two practices, in other words, are really two sides of the same coin, the coin of her role in the descent line building game. Let us now explore some of the ramifications of controlling and beautifying Polynesian daughters.

Virginity. "Holding on" to daughters may begin early, with special affection and indulgence accorded them in childhood by their fathers (see Firth 1963: 154; Kaeppler 1971: 191). But the fullest manifestation of this tendency is seen in the guarding of unmarried daughters' virginity. The most fully elaborated form of the sexually controlled daughter/sister in turn is to be seen in the institutionalized "sacred maid," found throughout the aristocracy of Western Polynesia. I will begin with her, and then show how the principles of her role, minus the full institutional paraphernalia, are to be seen operating throughout the entire area, and through all levels of society.

The "sacred maid" complex has been described by Mead for Samoa. The Samoan sacred maid, or *taupo*, is supposed to be the chief's sisters' daughter, but often in fact it is his daughter (Mead 1930: 26).[12] The *taupo* position is one of ritual responsibility and honor. She heads the organization of unmarried girls and untitled men's wives that has the responsibility of hosting and entertaining visiting parties that come to the village. Her position is actually ritually superior to that of the chiefly heir and successor, the *manaia*, who heads the organization of unmarried and untitled men (Mead 1930: 14). She even receives more respect than the wives of high chiefs (Mead 1930: 184).[13] Her marriage is a village affair (Mead 1930: 27) and all the women of the village make mats and tapa for her dowry (Mead 1930: 70). In a real sense she is symbolically the daughter/sister of the entire village, and its prestige is tied up with her prestige (Mead 1949: 65). *But*: The *taupo* is under strictest sexual constraint. She has to retain her virginity until marriage, and if she is seduced, it is dealt with by the *fono*, the governing council, as a public crime punishable by the drowning or beating to death of her seducer (Mead 1930: 17). Her marriage may be publicly consummated (Mead 1949: 63), but even if it is not, there is public display of the proof of her virginity in the form of a bloodstained mat, after the consummation. If she is found not to be a virgin, she is beaten by her (female) relatives (Mead 1949: 56).

A similar institution is reported for pre-sixteenth-century Tonga (G. Rogers 1977); in modern Tonga all the chief's unmarried daughters are called *taupo* (the term borrowed from Samoa) and must be chaste (Gifford 1929: 129), but the specially favored figure is the *tamaha*, the chief's sister's daughter (Gifford 1929: 74, 79, 80). A *taupo*-type institution is mentioned for Mangaia (Mead 1930: 93), and one observer notes in modern times that the only virgins and/or "old maids" in the Mangaian village he studied were from a high chiefly family (Marshall 1971: 130). In Mangareva, if the first born of the first wife of a high aristocrat is a female, she is given the special status of *tepeiru*, with very high social rank. She often receives "exaltation by the people of her district, and some *tepeiru* went on to become de facto rulers of their groups" (Buck 1938: 156). Among the (ancient) Maori the institution closely resembled that in Samoa. The *puhi*, or sacred maid, was usually the eldest daughter of a chief of high rank "who was elected or chosen as a person of consequence and made tapu in the sense of prohibited. She had to remain a virgin until marriage" (Best I 1924: 450). She often had ceremonial functions, and was highly respected, even "petted" and deferred to (1924: 351). "Some famous *puhi* became renowned chieftainesses in later life, and commanded respect of their own and other tribes" (1924: 453). But they were "sometimes late marrying because their families were so particular about the choice of mate" (1924: 450). And finally, in Pukapuka, the sacred maid—"an eldest daughter, eldest sister, or even father's sister"—is initiated with special rites and never marries at all, "remaining a guarded virgin for life." She is a fully sacred figure who links the chief to the gods (Hecht 1977: 196–98).

It is important to note first that the sacred maid position is one of high—sometimes very high—honor. This may be taken as, among other things, an expression of the genuine value of the daughter or sister who remains affiliated with her natal group, in line with the arguments presented earlier.

In addition to great public honor, the most obvious aspect of the sacred maid's situation is her virginity, which is culturally stressed and forcefully protected. What is symbolized by her virginity is not her own self-control (as in occasional, usually religious, male celibacy) but the control by her kinsmen over her behavior (see especially Shore 1981). As a symbol of the structure discussed earlier, the daughter's virginity thus represents the kinsmen's "hold" on her, necessary for the process of building or simply maintaining descent line size and strength.

The process of descent line maintenance is particularly important for chiefs, whose very position depends upon heading a large, internally cohesive, and externally well-connected group that is his economic and political base. We said earlier that chiefs may deploy their daughters in a variety of ways to achieve this end, including retaining them in uxorilocal marriages, marrying them down into lower lines of the descent group, or sending them out in geographically exogamous marriages. But we also noted that all of these methods (including exogamy) assume the notion of the daughter as a centripetal force. It is vital that she be "held" symbolically even when sent out in marriage for strategic purposes.

Not surprisingly, then, the virginity of chiefly daughters is nearly *universally* required throughout Polynesia, and backed by physical force, even where there is no sacred maid complex at all (Goldman 1970: 564). Among commoners, however, there is also a generally reported tendency to oversee daughters' sex lives more closely than sons' (e.g., Buck 1932: 34; Suggs 1966: 64; Gifford 1929: 21, 191). This would be consistent with the point that status mobility through descent line building is an avenue potentially open to all. In general however, commoner control of daughters' sexual behavior is far less strict than among the aristocracy, because the chances of mobility for commoners are clearly more remote (Goldman 1970: 564).

Sex as theft. Although high-status girls are heavily controlled, and lower-status girls are at least more closely watched than boys, this does not mean that there is little premarital sexual activity in Polynesia—far from it. Boys, as we shall see, are encouraged to be as sexually active as possible, and most of their sexual activity takes place precisely with these same girls. Paternal/ fraternal control thus does not actually block premarital sexual activity, but it does mean that sex with an unmarried girl is in some sense "stolen" from her father and/or her brothers. It is in the context of a view of much of premarital sex as "theft" in turn that a fairly wide range of Polynesian sexual practices becomes intelligible: the semi-institutionalized form of (quasi) rape called "sleep crawling"; the general interest in deflowering virgins; institutionalized elopement and marriage by capture; and the displays of hymeneal blood and other signals of "triumph" at weddings. Not all premarital sex in Polynesia is construed by the parties involved as "theft," but the proliferation of sexual *patterns* with theft connotations requires explanation. I will say a few words about each.

Sleep crawling, first, entails stealthily and unexpectedly entering a girl's house at night and having sex with her, usually over her protest and resistance. In Mangaia it is called *motoro*, and is seen as a sign of masculinity. A man who gains sexual access to a girl through formal engagement is seen as a weakling. The important thing is to sweet-talk her, rather than to use force, so that she will not scream and wake up her family (Marshall 1971: 129). In Rakahanga *motoro* is said to be noncoercive, but the emphasis again is on not waking the father, who will beat the boy if he discovers him (Vayda 1961: 204). Sleep crawling is also common in Mangareva (*motoro*—Buck 1938: 120), in Samoa (*moetotolo*—Mead 1930: 61; Shore 1981),[14] and in Tahiti (*mafera*—Oliver 1974: 365),[15] in the latter two cases apparently coercive. The institution expresses well the fact that, because unmarried girls are under the control of their fathers and brothers, sex with them must be "stolen." This is the case even when they are consenting, as they sometimes are in sleep crawling, and usually are in other contexts. Indeed the fact that coercion in sleep crawling might range from none to total shows that the girl's personal interest or lack of it is irrelevant, for the practice has more to do with her structural position than with her sentiments. On the other hand, the fact that there *is* often strong coercion, that sleep crawling often approximates rape, will require further discussion, and I will return to this aspect of it later.

The other great sport of adolescent sexual activities is deflowering virgins, the interest in which is nearly universal throughout Polynesia. Deflowering a virgin is a major event for a boy, and boys "count coup" as to how many virgins they have deflowered (see Firth 1957: 519; Marshall 1971: 151; Mead 1930: 95–96). In Tikopia a boy might undergo a private religious ritual for success in deflowering virgins (Firth 1957: 523). Most men also claim to want virgin wives, or at least girls who were virgins when they first got to them (Firth 1957: 514; Loeb 1926: 75). Because girls in fact do not make much effort to retain their virginity, the interest in the conquest of virgins has again less to do with conquering the girl, than in succeeding in taking something that "belongs" to her kinsmen.[16]

Elopement and marriage by capture again carry the same message. In Samoa the great thing is to elope with the *taupo* of the next village, stealing her out from under the collective nose of her kin (Mead 1930: 95). More generally, elopement is the standard form of marriage in Samoa, modern

Tonga, and among Tikopian commoners (Mead 1930: 95; 1949: 64–67; G. Rogers 1977; Beaglehole 1941: 98; Firth 1957: 439). Among the Tikopian aristocracy, on the other hand, virtually all marriage is by capture. The woman is selected by the groom's kin, forcibly taken from her household to the waiting bridegroom, and held down for her first (rape) intercourse with her husband (Firth 1957: 442, 450). It is considered a shame for the bridegroom if the girl is not a virgin (Firth 1957: 451). The capture is often resisted violently, in a more or less pitched battle, by the girl's family (as well as by the girl herself), and later often retaliated in a countercapture (1963: 470).

Finally, in this cluster of patterns expressing the notion of sex as theft from the girl's kin, I would also include the pattern of public display of tokens of virginity at marriage, reported from Samoa (Mead 1930: 95–96), and for Tikopia (Firth 1963: 464). Tongans too expect their women to be virgins at marriage, although they dispense with the public display of hymeneal blood as "indelicate" (Mariner I 1827: 141). Note however that at one Tui Tonga's wedding, a man at the door of the nuptial chamber announced the bedding down of the bride and groom with "three hideous yells (similar to the war-whoop) . . . followed up immediately by the loud and repeated sound of the conch" (Mariner I 1827: 124). In all three cases the demonstrations appear as "triumphal," expressing *both* the boy's triumph in "getting" the girl, *and* her kinsmen's triumph in having successfully guarded her virginity until then.[17]

To recapitulate: A girl has real value to her descent line, particularly if she sustains her affiliation with it and brings in her husband, his land, and their children. There is thus structural motivation for "holding on" to a daughter/sister. This "holding on" is symbolically expressed through control of her virginity. The virgin both displays her kinsmen's symbolic retention of her and, because virginity is defined as highly honorable, expresses her genuine value to her group. At the same time the control structure means that sex with her must be "taken," "stolen," or otherwise forcefully appropriated, even when she presents herself, as she often does, as a consenting party. Hence the prevalence of various forms of sexual theft—sleep crawling, marriage by capture, triumphal defloration of virgins, and the like.

We have seen that some of these sexual forms are violent, not only vis-à-vis the girl's family, but vis-à-vis the girl herself. In fact the full range of sexual violence has yet to be explored and accounted for. In addition to the various forms already discussed, there is a fairly high incidence of plain rape, both by individual males, and by gangs. In order to understand this, as well as to understand the full significance of the daughter/sister in general, we must explore further the symbolic treatment of this figure.

Beautification. For the full process of building or even sustaining a descent line to work itself out, the girl must not only be retained by her kin but must also bring in a husband. The Pukapukan sacred maid who remains celibate for her entire life is an extreme symbol of the first part of the process, but most sacred maids, and indeed most daughters, however closely guarded they may have been, eventually marry. If one side of the symbolic coin is strong control of the girl's sexual behavior, rendering her remote if not wholly inaccessible, the other side entails enhancing her attractions and her value. Hence the apparently contradictory practice of elaborately beautifying the girl while keeping her under surveillance and control. The daughter/sister is clearly being used as "bait."

It should be remembered that her value is already high. Economically she has her inheritance that, if the boy is willing to join her group, becomes more "real" and transmissible to her and her husband's children. Ritually too her status is high. Sacred maids have formal status superiority, but all virgins have the honor that derives from virginity itself. In other words the guarding of her virginity is also part of her general social enhancement.

Beyond all of this, however, there are direct and systematic efforts aimed at enhancing a girl's beauty and sexual desirability. In most cases the beautification practices are combined with the restraint and/or seclusion of the girl, thus showing rather conclusively the link between retaining her as a virgin, and treating her as sexual "bait." In Tonga, "special care [is] taken of the complexion of a girl of rank." Her skin is lightened through the use of various preparations, and she is kept sitting in the shade as much as possible. She sits on soft cushions to keep her buttocks and thighs soft and smooth, and sits in such a way as to keep her ankles from being marred, all of which both beautifies and immobilizes her simultaneously. A daughter of a very high chief is bathed and oiled every evening, after which her knees are tied together and she is laid down on her side. The position is said to serve the dual function of keeping her elbows smooth and securing her against sexual attack (Gifford 1929: 129–30). In Mangaia the upper ranks seclude young people (why both sexes are included will be explained shortly) for bleaching and fattening. Mangaian girls also have their clitorises lengthened, and are given instruction by older women in achieving orgasm (Marshall 1971: 110, 124, 122). Tahiti too has both fattening and skin bleaching, and girls are "trained" to be pleasing and charming to men (Oliver 1974: 257, 431, 783; Henry 1928: 274). In the Marquesas adolescent girls are kept at home for skin bleaching (and in some cases tattooing) and for vaginal treatments aimed at beautifying their sexual organs (Suggs 1966: 88, 39–42, 65–66; Handy 1923: 75. See also Hecht 1977: 190 on Pukapuka, and Handy and Pukui 1958: 94 on Hawaii.).

The girl in these cases is almost wholly turned into a symbolic object by her kin. The result is sometimes formally displayed for the appreciation of the young males who are its targets. In the Marquesas there is "ritual display" of the girls' bodies and genitalia (Suggs 1966: 88). In Mangareva there are "beauty shows" at which secluded children are brought out and displayed (Buck 1938: 127–28). And although these cases are somewhat extreme (the Marquesas in particular appear extreme in many aspects of their sexual culture, although clearly within the Polynesian range) the principle of displaying daughters and sisters as passive objectified attractors of men is seen in other cases as well. Among the Maori the sacred maids (*puhi*) attract "young men, singly or in parties, [who come] from distant parts to see them and try to find favor in their eyes" (Best I 1924: 450). And in Mangaia, according to hearsay information Best picked up among the Maori, "girls of good family stayed in a collective house before marriage. At the age of marriage they were lined up against the wall of the house, and young men of rank would come in and line up and look them over. Each man then picked out one and if she were agreeable . . . they were . . . married" (Best I 1924: 453; she also Handy and Pukui 1958: 102 on Hawaii).

Elucidating the consistent cultural tendency to use a daughter or sister as sexual bait to "pull in" (desirable) men also allows us to account for what would otherwise be some rather discordant reports concerning postcontact Polynesian prostitution. In the Marquesas, Tahiti, and Mangaia, girls are reported to be prostituted, mainly to Europeans, by their fathers and/or brothers (Suggs 1966: 64; Oliver 1974: 356; Marshall 1971: 152). Given the overall Polynesian respect for sisters, and the special protection of daughters, this pattern would make no sense at all unless it were realized that the special protection of these girls relates in part precisely to their value as centripetal forces, used to attract men and/or their valuables into the women's families. In the case of European men what is apparently being "drawn in" is the men's superior *mana*, via their insemination of the women (Sahlins 1981).

Rape. The discussion developed thus far also provides us with most of the pieces necessary to account for the prevalence of rape in Polynesia. I include here ordinary individual rape, gang rape, sleep crawling where it is reported to be typically coercive, and marriage by capture and/or abduction. Rape and gang rape are reported for Tahiti (Oliver 1974: 363, 607), Mangaia (Marshall 1971: 152), Samoa (Shore 1981), and the Marquesas (Suggs 1966: 63, 96, 120). Samoa, Tahiti, and Mangaia are all reported to have sleep crawling with fairly strong coercion (Mead 1949: 61; Oliver 1974: 365; Marshall 1971: 129). Tikopia has marriage by capture, with rape consummation, and even the reportedly less libidinous (Best I 1924: 450) Maori occasionally forcibly abduct unwilling brides (Best I 1924: 462).[18]

Reported motives for rape include anger at, and retaliation for, rejection, and/or an intention to "tame" a woman who gets out of line. Mead reports anger over rejection as a motive for coercive sleep crawling in Samoa (1949: 61), and it is generally a rejected Maori suitor who forcibly abducts his bride (Best I 1924: 462). In the Marquesas girls "who do not receive the advances of men" are often raped (Suggs 1966: 63). Jealous and "difficult" Marquesan wives may also be raped by their husbands to bring them into line (Suggs 1966: 120). And in Mangaia gang rape is said to be perpetrated "to tame a haughty girl" (Marshall 1971: 152). It should be noted that the cultures treat these actions as semiacceptable and, as it were, understandable. Although a girl's kinsmen may avenge her honor (or their own) by beating up the boy—*if* she reports the incident to them—the *public* sanctions range from light to nil. In Mangaia the penalty is less than that for stealing a pig (Marshall 1971: 152).[19]

In light of our earlier discussions, much of this information is now explicable. Rape presupposes the resistance of the girl (or woman), and it seems reasonable to suggest that girls accept the symbolic value placed by their kin on their virginity, their sexuality, and indeed their persons. They would tend to consider themselves sought-after and valuable objects who may voluntarily withhold sex altogether, and who always at least retain the right to pick and choose their lovers. Because girls and women are in fact genuinely valued by their kin, and in some sense "by society," their stance is consistent with their status, but to men it may appear "stuck-up" and haughty. Hence the "taming" aspects of rape motivation. But a girl's haughty stance might not in itself provoke sexual assault, were it not for the other message the girl is transmitting, a message *also* consistent with her self-perception as encouraged by her treatment in her kin group: enhanced sexual attractiveness. I suggest that it is the combined and contradictory message transmitted by the girl—"come hither/go away"—that is so provoking to the men. The permissive cultural attitude toward rape would moreover seem to recognize the "legitimacy," as it were, of this sort of reaction to this sort of bind.[20]

This discussion of the (non-kin) male reaction to the young woman's presentation and self-presentation now brings us to the question of what young men are up to themselves at this stage of life. As we turn to a consideration of adolescent males, it is important to keep in mind that girls, although more closely watched than boys, are hardly sexually unavailable. Whereas sacred maids and high chiefs' daughters exhibit the extremes of both control and enhancement, other girls are treated with somewhat less of both. Indeed as one moves down the social ladder, the control appreciably diminishes and the availability correspondingly increases. On the other hand, boys and men of all classes are subject to virtually no constraints. On the contrary, they are expected by society—by their seniors, their peers, and the girls themselves—to be as sexually active, skilled, and successful as possible. We must now consider some of the sources and consequences of this pattern.

BROTHERS

Let us return once again to the dynamics of status maintenance and mobility, this time from the point of view of male siblings. We must first distinguish between the select individual who will succeed to the headship (whether of household, descent line, or kin group as a whole), and all the rest of the siblings who will not. The successor is usually, but not always, the first born; I will refer to him as the senior sibling whether he is typically the eldest or not, and to all the rest as juniors. Whereas there is only one senior son per father, there are potentially a large number of juniors, including not only the full brothers of the senior son, but also the sons of secondary wives and/or concubines, and of other marriages of the father. The senior sibling is sometimes the metaphoric "chief" of his juniors, who are his metaphoric "commoners" (Buck 1932: 45; Handy and Pukui 1958: 199); in Tonga junior siblings become "virtual servants" of senior siblings (Gifford 1929: 112), and in Hawaii the junior siblings are metaphorically their senior siblings' "slaves" (Malo 1903: 96).

The structural possibilities of, and constraints upon, the life careers of senior and junior siblings are as different as their statuses. The senior son/brother has an unambiguous position as heir to the headship, and an unambiguous duty to marry and reproduce the line. The junior siblings' situation, on the other hand, is much more ambiguous, both with respect to their prospects for succession, and with respect to their obligation to marry and reproduce. It is these ambiguities that we shall explore in this section.

We have seen that there is a tendency to try to hold onto sisters, for the enrichment of the group and hence for the (potential) advancement of its status. If a sister stays and brings in resources, both human and material, this represents a gain for her kin. However, given the status superiority of husband to wife (which will be explored later), it is considered "normal" for daughters/sisters to reside virilocally, and to merge themselves and their children with their husbands' lines. Thus, if they stay with their kin it is a gain, but if they leave, it is not seen as a loss. Brothers, on the other hand, are the backbone of the group, and their unity is essential. A brother who fissions off with his descendants and followers is taking the very stuff of the group with him. By and large, it appears that full brothers, particularly in families of any substance, normally do stay together and share a concern for the welfare of the unit as a whole, but this outcome is never assured.

The potential for split is obviously situated at the point of marriage and reproduction. An unmarried junior brother has no wife and children dividing his interests between his paternal/fraternal group and his own. He works the paternal land, participates in the work projects of the paternal household, and is simply a contributing member of the group. We thus begin to see some of the systemic "interest" in delaying, if not prohibiting, the marriage of junior brothers. In fact, in Tikopia, the marriage of junior brothers is discouraged altogether. They are expected to remain single (though not celibate) for life, and to form a cohesive body of "executive officials" for the senior brother who has the position of leadership, and who marries and reproduces the next leader and his fraternal executives (Firth 1975: 188). The Maori show the same pattern in less extreme form: "Males seem to have awaited more mature age until marrying. They often took wives when middle aged, sometimes slave-class women, or a widow of a brother . . ." (Best I 1924: 450). And in Tahiti too, as we shall see, junior siblings could join a "society" with a positive ethic in favor of singleness and against reproduction.

Normally however there is an important counterforce that favors eventual marriage and reproduction by junior siblings: the reproduction of the hierarchical structure itself. For it is the junior siblings who produce the junior descent lines, ranked collectively below the senior descent lines, and forming the commoners of whom the chiefs are chiefs. The notion of commoners as descendants of junior siblings of chiefs is culturally articulated. The Tongarevans call the younger brother "the link with the people" (Buck 1932: 45), and the same idea is expressed in most other Polynesian societies (see Mishkin 1961: 434; Firth 1963: 312; Buck 1938: 145; Malo 1903: 96; Gifford 1929: 112; Mariner II 1827: 90). Junior siblings should thus ultimately marry and reproduce not only for the maintenance of the size and "weight" of their descent line, but for the reproduction of the hierarchical structure of "classes" within the group and within society as a whole.

At the same time they (and their descendants) must remain subordinate and loyal to the senior brother and/or the senior line of the group. The actual incidence of junior full siblings fissioning off and making war on senior brothers for the headship is nearly impossible to determine, but was probably, in fact, rare. The incidence of half-brother and cousin "treason" was probably somewhat higher (see Mariner I 1827: 137; Oliver 1974: 742; G. Rogers 1977: 172). Most commonly, a junior brother might simply replace the senior brother at the head of the unit if the senior appears less competent. This is always open as a possibility, even in the strictest primogeniturial systems (Goldman 1970: 26). In theory the junior brother should simply hold the headship until a more competent member of the senior line comes of age, but in practice a strong junior can probably arrange things so that succession passes to his own descendants.

All of which explains the fact that sibling rivalry, in the form of suspicion and mistrust, seems to go from senior to junior sibling rather than the other way around as one might have expected. In the hierarchical society, it is "ungrammatical" for a junior to envy a senior; the privileges accorded to the senior are based on a superiority seen as "natural." Seniors, on the other hand, may well suspect the loyalty and subordinate solidarity of juniors, given the juniors' potential for ascent just outlined. Thus both Tonga and Tahiti have legends of older brothers killing their younger siblings (Mariner II 1827: 112; Oliver 1974: 727). Elder-to-younger sibling rivalry is also documented for Tikopia, where it is apparently encouraged by the fact that fathers tend to favor, sentimentally and materially, their young sons (Firth 1963: 166). A similar pattern is seen among the Maori, where the youngest son is often spoiled and petted by the father, and tends to be seen as more intrinsically clever and talented than the eldest (Mishkin 1961: 455n.; see also Handy and Pukui 1958: 46 on Hawaii).

Junior siblings then are in a peculiar and ambiguous position within the structure. Particularly in high-ranking families, they are both high (by parentage) and potentially low (as progenitors of subordinate lines), but also low (by birth order) and potentially high (by replacing the senior or by heading their own independent groups). They are, we begin to see, a liminal category in the social structure, and it is the varying and contradictory aspects of their position that provide the key to many features of male adolescent sexual culture.

Polynesian adolescence may be characterized as a period in which boys form cohorts, the primary focus of which, and the primary topic of interest of which, is sex: having a wide range and a large number of sexual relations with girls. Because elite girls are, for the most part, well watched and controlled, it appears that they participate in adolescent activities, if at all, only on a very reduced scale. Similarly, there is good evidence that, in many cases, the most senior elite males, those who will actually succeed to the titles and headships, are often de facto removed from participation. In some cases they, like elite girls, are secluded for fattening, tattooing, or skin bleaching. In other cases they are betrothed in early childhood, or forced as youths into early marriage (see Firth 1957: 440; Best I 1924: 454–55; Malo 1903: 80; Handy and Pukui 1958: 105). The social composition of adolescent cohorts thus primarily includes (a) *junior* elite males, (b) commoner males, and (c) commoner females.

Adolescent social activities include making assignations, having a large number of sexual affairs, and exchanging information on such affairs as well as sexual folklore in general. In addition, boys and girls spend time in same-sex and/or cross-sex groups beautifying themselves, composing songs, poems, and entertainments, and engaging in pleasant sports, games, and amusements. For the most part they do little productive work. In many Polynesian societies they live apart from their parents, either in sex-segregated "dormitories," or in individual separate residences in their parents' compounds; in other cases there are collective houses where young people may congregate and sleep when they wish to be away from home. (See Suggs [1966: 175] for a list of ten cases, in addition to the Marquesas which are his primary focus. See also Firth [1963: 82].)

We may now consider this "complex" of institutionalized sexual activeness for adolescent males in relation to the structural problems of the male sibling bond already discussed. From a purely functional point of view, Polynesian adolescence may be seen as both solidifying the sibling bond *and* contributing to the slight downward mobility of junior siblings, thus reproducing correct united-but-hierarchical relations between brothers and their descendants.

In the first place, the marriage and (legitimate) reproduction of the junior sibling is simply delayed, with his happy and voluntary compliance. The junior brother thus remains longer in his subordinate and dependent role in his paternal/fraternal household (although the behavioral freedom and independence masks this dependency to some extent). At the same time, Polynesian adolescent culture emphasizes the importance of large numbers of affairs with a range of girls. Adolescent boys should play the field. Strong attachment to any one girl is antithetical to a proper adolescence, and may have the unfortunate effect of leading to marriage. The pattern of low emotional involvement, particularly with members of the opposite sex, but more generally with any individual, has been reported by some observers to begin in early childhood (Mead 1949: 118; Levy 1973: 496), and is both expressed and reinforced during the adolescent period of playing the field. The effect of this emotional detachment is not only to leave the sibling bond relatively unthreatened by competing attachments during adolescence, but possibly also to establish (or reinforce) a pattern that will continue after marriage as well. As we shall see in the next section, the husband-wife bond is relatively "weak," and there is a sense in which husbands (and wives) remain Polynesian-style adolescents for life, with frequent adultery, divorce, and serial monogamy.

Both delay of marriage and encouragement of a wide range of noninvolving affairs support the cohesiveness of the sibling bond and of kin (as against sexual/marital) relations in general. At the same time the social organization of adolescence encourages the downward social identification and even downward mobility of junior siblings. As already noted, male adolescent cohorts contain both junior elites and commoners. The elite boy is often the leader, formal or informal, of the group, and its social focus (Suggs 1966: 91, 95; Mead 1930: 14; Gifford 1929: 128; Firth 1963: 392; Oliver 1974: 961). As such he gains a sense of prestige and leadership in relation to *his* structural juniors, shifting his sense of himself from one of junior elite to, in a sense, senior commoner, which is precisely the shift that must take place in his orientation in order for him fully to accept his mediating place in the hierarchy, as "link with the people."

There is an analogous effect in his heterosexual relations. Because elite girls are largely kept from participating in the assignations and affairs (which does not fully prevent the young men from trying to court and seduce them, but which makes it all somewhat more difficult), it is the lower-status girls who are more sexually available. The chances are thus reasonably good that a boy will eventually marry a girl of slightly lower status than himself (radical differences in status between husband and wife are generally frowned upon). The slightly lower status of the wife is important for not contradicting the normative domestic superiority of the husband, which will be discussed later.[21] More important for the present argument, lower status of the wife will generally insure lower status of the children because, as noted earlier, the social status of the children appears to be determined more by the mother than the father in the case of status discrepancies between the two. Thus the greater availability of lower-status girls in adolescent activities increases the possibility of a junior elite boy marrying and reproducing in a slight downward direction, which is desirable for the reproduction of correct hierarchical relations between his and his elder brother's descendants.[22]

But enough of functions. There is also a sense in which adolescence is *formally*, as well as functionally, appropriate to the structural situation of junior male siblings. The organization of the cohorts and their typical behavioral patterns, as well as the patterning of the sexual relations themselves, may be seen to encode and express the structural features of the junior sibling position already discussed. Sons and brothers, like daughters and sisters, are simultaneously symbols and actors within their structural positions.

Specifically, just as the junior sibling position may be seen as a liminal one, so too the organization of adolescent activity has typical "liminal" qualities (Turner 1967; van Gennep 1960). First, adolescent sexual activity, or even hints thereof, has to be invisible to society at large. It takes place in special houses or dormitories, or else in the bush or on the beach, and properly at night in the dark (see, for example, Shore 1981). In many Polynesian societies opposite-sex adolescents, particularly individuals who are having sexual relations with one another, do not mix at all in public and/or during the day (Marshall 1971: 127; Loeb 1926: 88; Buck 1938: 183; Handy and Pukui 1958: 171; Oliver 1974: 613).[23]

In addition to being "outside" the structure, adolescent activity typically has certain *anti*structural qualities. Maori young men show off by "violating minor tapus" (Mishkin 1961: 453). Marquesan and Tongan young men raid people's food storehouses (Handy 1923: 97; Mariner I 1827: 78). Sleep crawling, in which the boy both "steals" the daughter under the father's nose, and has illicit sexual intercourse *inside* the house, surely has the same antistructural quality, as does dramatically eloping with the *taupo* in Samoa, and perhaps eloping with any girl. Modern Tahitian youths even risk "a little incest" for the excitement and virility of it all (Hooper 1976: 235–36). But the fullest development of antistructural forms and symbols is seen in the most fully institutionalized adolescent organization, the (now defunct) Tahitian *arioi*. Its members were "communalistic" with respect to property, they went about giving "lewd plays and performances," during which they might "snatch the tapa clothing off the women in the audience." Their plays involved social satire, including "making jokes of high personages." In some contexts "they broke all the tabus" (Oliver 1974: 225, 913–62 passim; Henry 1928: 230–40 passim).

But it is important to emphasize that, despite the many extrastructural and antistructural qualities of adolescent cohorts throughout Polynesia, *rank is always maintained*. In most, as noted, the elite boys are the groups' informal leaders. And in the Tahitian *arioi*, which had a formal structure of ranks and offices, only elite boys could occupy the upper ranks and higher offices (Oliver 1974: 961). The combination of both structure and antistructure in these cohorts thus expresses faithfully the double aspect of the junior sibling's position, as both (ideally) committed to his hierarchical relations and (potentially) schismatic from them.

Why sex? It could be argued that adolescent male sexual activity functions, socially and psychologically, as a cathartic mechanism for potentially disruptive junior siblings. All but the most elite individuals are encouraged to waste themselves in socially inconsequential but personally absorbing sexual activity, as well as in games and sports that may be seen as having many of the same effects. The Samoans, in fact, classify sex with other forms of "play" (Mead 1930: 84), and Tongans liken it to the sport of pigeon snaring (Gifford 1929: 117). Furthermore, in both sex and sports, with their aspects of "winning" and "triumphing," young men get to play at power and status in ways that have few real-world effects, but yet presumably satisfy desires for prestige felt by all in these status-conscious societies.

The catharsis argument may well be appropriate but hardly tells the whole story. Junior males are potentially disruptive, for various structural reasons, in many societies, but there are alternative ways of controlling them. It must be recalled at this point that the "problem" of junior males centers about their marriage and reproduction, which are both socially motivated (for maintaining the size and strength of the kin group, and for reproducing heirarchical organization) and countermotivated (as potentially schismatic). The "solution" to the problem of junior siblings would thus intrinsically tend to focus, at least in part, on sexual and reproductive behavior. In other words, the first answer to the question "why sex?" is that sex is in fact central to the problem at hand.

It is, however, possible to carry the argument further, through an exploration of the cultural meanings of sex and reproduction. Both sex and reproduction in Polynesia were, in the past, deeply involved in religious notions of the original creation of the cosmos, of ongoing creation and creative power, and of the ongoing fertility of the land.[24] The gods were born from the sexual union between (male) Sky and (female) Earth. All of the gods were male. Humans were begat by a god fashioning a physical female form from (nondivine) earth, then vivifying her with his breath and mating with her. The process of cosmic creation is a continuing process: ". . . creation was not believed to be one series of events accomplished in a distant past, but to proceed continuously in all time through fertilization" (Handy 1927: 24). The *mana*, the "natural" energy or power upon which success and efficacy in all human enterprises depends, was itself in its original essence procreative power (1927: 27). "*Mana* was primarily associated with nature's superior, divine aspect, with male procreative energy, with light, . . . [and with] life" (1927: 35). The Polynesians "made generation, operative through sexual union, a universal principle of their natural philosophy" (1927: 143).

The gods were responsible in an ongoing way for the fertility of the land. It was apparently thought that their divine libido needed to be stimulated and aroused in order to get them to perform their fertilizing function. This was the rationale for the extensive use of erotic chanting and dancing in religious ritual, as well as for sexual orgies in ritual contexts, especially during "the season of abundance" surrounding harvest: "The erotic dancing . . . which was in its origin a form of worship, was designed to stimulate and bring into action the *mana* of the gods who were believed to be animated by the same emotions as men, and on whose procreative activities the fecundity of human beings, the earth and sea depended" (Handy 1927: 210; see also 307–8). The idea that sexual arousal raises productivity is also seen in modern times in the Mangaian practice of telling obscene jokes to get people to work harder on collective projects (Marshall 1971: 109).

The specific channel of divine *mana* on earth was the chief. "As the first born male of the tribe, he stood for land and people as the prime embodiment of generative power in nature" (Handy 1927: 138). "He was the channel or medium through which the land was nourished," and was believed to have "close rapport" with the natural elements (Handy 1927: 141, 142; see also Firth 1975: 171 and passim; Hocart 1915: 637; Loeb 1926: 55). Given the chief's association with divine procreation and fertility, "the generative organs . . . of the divine chief were thought to be particularly potent" (Handy 1927: 145). Certain sacred and esoteric words, which give power to certain Marquesan spells, "all had reference to the virile organ of the chief" (1927: 143), and one modern Marquesan euphemism for the penis is "chief" (Suggs 1966: 81). In the past, Hawaii and Tahiti had rituals centering on the loincloths of the "kings" and of the god-images (Handy 1927: 146–49).

Beyond the sphere of religion, it may be noted that chiefs are associated with exaggerated sexual activity and prowess in ordinary life. Chiefs are typically polygynous (Goldman 1970: 564) and are expected to have more affairs and conquests (e.g., Gifford 1929: 21), as well as to perpetrate more rape (see note 18). They are probably also more visibly fertile, in that with multiple wives, concubines, and passing affairs they probably produce more children than other men. Furthermore, chiefly reproduction is much more highly ritualized—their first matings, and/or the birth of their first children are everywhere surrounded with elaborate rites celebrating the continuation of their lines (Goldman 1970: 522–36 passim).

Several generalizations about cultural notions of sex and reproduction may be drawn from this sketch. First, and most clearly, both sex and reproduction are basically masculine activities. The female principle is conceived as passive (Handy 1927: 12), a receptacle for and a vehicle of male sexual and procreative energy. It is partly no doubt because of these associations that masculine pride in Polynesia is tied up with sexual success in a way that is less true of feminine pride (see Goldman 1970: 564; Best II 1924: 532; Mead 1949: 30, 19; Marshall 1971: 24, 126, 151; Gifford 1929: 21, 117). In Mangaia it is said that "the name of the island travels on its penis" (Marshall 1971: 26).

As for fertility and reproduction, the original responsibility of (male) gods for cosmic creation, and the ongoing responsibility of both gods and chiefs for the fertility of nature, mean that fertility too is basically the doing of men.[25] These beliefs thus probably contribute to the notion prevalent in at least some Polynesian societies that the male contribution to human conception is greater than that of the female. Both Maori and Tikopia claim that the woman is merely the "haven" for the development of the fetus, which is made from the male contribution (Best I 1924: 406; Firth 1957: 479). Tahitians also attribute at least greater, if not exclusive, reproductive influence to the male than to the female (see Oliver 1974: 410; see also Handy and Pukui 1958: 54 for Hawaii; Handy 1923: 73 for the Marquesas).

Both sex and reproduction are thus male in general, and chiefly in particular. It may also be noted that married men are metaphoric chiefs, the metaphor referring primarily to their status superiority vis-à-vis their wives, but also clearly describing their sexual situation, as both sexually active and reproductive. It now remains to point out that adolescent males are normatively sexually active *but not reproductive*. The norm against adolescent reproduction is implicit in a variety of cultural rules and practices. Illegitimacy is culturally frowned upon in many parts of the area (see Best I 1924: 474; Loeb 1926: 84; Buck 1938: 120). This fact is surprising in light of the encouragement of active adolescent sex, the absence of indigenous contraceptive methods, and the actual high rate of illegitimate births. But the cultural view makes sense in terms of the unspoken rule that adolescents must not be reproductive. The combination of encouraging intensive sexual activity for the unmarried while prohibiting their reproduction reaches formal expression in the Tahitian *arioi* society, in which many of the implicit norms of adolescence in other Polynesian societies were here formally codified as rules. In the *arioi* society sexual promiscuity of the members was required, but reproduction was specifically banned. A woman (and/or a couple) who bore a child and did not kill it was expelled from the society (Oliver 1974: 940; Henry 1928: 235).

I suggested earlier that the general focus on sexuality and (negative) reproduction is symbolically (as well as functionally) consistent with the nature of the "problem" of junior siblings in Polynesian hierarchical society. The more detailed exploration of the norms of adolescent sexual behavior now allows us to see even more specific symbolic consonances. The active sexual behavior of junior males aligns them with maleness in general, including the maleness of gods and chiefs, as the restraints on girls' participation aligns them with the cultural view of femaleness as passive. But the normative nonreproductiveness or infertility of junior males distinguishes them sharply from gods and chiefs (and married men who are metaphoric chiefs). Once again then junior males are symbolically "in between," affiliated with high status by their sexual activeness, and with low status by their prescribed infertility.

Given the pleasure, excitement, and freedom of adolescence, it is not surprising that young people seek to perpetuate it as long as possible. We have seen that Tikopian junior brothers often never marry at all, and Firth reports that in most cases this is voluntary (1963: 373). Even the senior brother sometimes has to be physically coerced into marriage, because in this case he, along with his junior siblings, is allowed to participate in the adolescent dalliances (Firth 1957: 440). In Tahiti one-fifth of the population is estimated to have belonged voluntarily to the *arioi* society (Oliver 1974: 914). Throughout the area unmarried girls abort, kill, or give away babies in adoption on the explicit motive of prolonging the girls' youth and freedom (Firth 1957: 373, 528; Loeb 1926: 84; Suggs 1966: 44; Oliver 1974: 943). Throughout the area too, both boys and girls express directly their commitment to and enjoyment of adolescence, and their unwillingness to end it with marriage. Their views are echoed by older married people, who look back on their own adolescent freedom with great sentimentality (Firth 1957: 465; Marshall 1971: 142; Handy and Pukui 1958: 167).

Ultimately, however, most people marry *of their own accord*. Because for the most part only the highest elite marriages are arranged (to insure the reproduction of the senior line, as well as its proper breeding) all other marriages are undertaken voluntarily. Why people marry, and what happens when they do, is the subject of the next and final section of the analysis.

SPOUSES AND PARENTS

Husbands and wives. Marriage in Polynesia may be said to be only weakly structurally motivated. Almost all of the important social relations are kin relations, and specifically sibling relations and their derivatives—uncles, aunts, and cousins. Affinal relations are of very little social consequence, and throughout the literature one can scarcely find references to them, no less extended discussions.

Part of the "weak" motivation for marriage, and the lack of cultural interest in affinity, derives from the fact that marriage normally takes place within the descent group, between people who are already related to one another by kinship. Not only is this the normal state of affairs, it is pre-ferred. The Maori view is typical: "Marriage within the *whanau* ["tribe"] met with much approval, in that problems in the marriage would not have political repercussions as opposed to intertribal marriage" (Best I 1924: 447; see also Hecht 1977: 193; Firth 1963: 316; Buck 1932: 35; Suggs 1966: 127; Beaglehole and Beaglehole 1941: 77; Oliver 1974: 638). Mar-riage is thus secondary to or encompassed by kinship as a social organiza-tional principle. It neither expresses nor forges important social or political alliances between groups, nor does it generate any important new personal relationships for the bride and/or groom. It does not tie either husband or wife into extensive affinal obligations with the other's kin, nor alternatively does it bring either husband or wife any special help in cooperation from the affines.[26]

Economically, too, marriage is only weakly motivated. Because both men and women inherit property, neither needs a spouse in order to have the means of self-support. (See note 10 for exceptions.) As for labor, hus-bands and wives provide each other with little that they cannot legitimately get from kinspersons, or at least from someone other than a spouse. Al-though there is (relatively balanced) division of labor by sex throughout the area, there is virtually no productive or domestic work, including child care, that must be performed by a spouse, or even that ought preferentially to be performed by a spouse.[27] Indeed in the Marquesas, there are certain intimate services that can only be performed for a man by a kinswoman, which is one of the cultural reasons given for preferentially marrying one's cross-cousin rather than an unrelated woman (Suggs 1966: 127).

One might at least expect that a wife provides a man with one thing a mother or sister cannot: sex. It is true a man cannot get this from his (close) kinswomen, but a wife is by no means his only legitimate source. Sex is available with widows, divorced women, and with most unmarried girls. In addition there is always the possibility of sex with other men's wives, and al-though this is culturally unacceptable, it is certainly frequent enough: High rates of adultery are reported throughout the area (Loeb 1926: 48, 79; Mead 1949: 68; 1930: 84; Suggs 1966: 131; Best I 1924: 474–75; Gold-man 1970: 566; Malo 1903: 82, 91, 284; Henry 1928: 284; Oliver 1974: 354, 358).[28]

The situation with respect to sexual dependence is somewhat different for women, at least at the formal level. Because unmarried girls are relatively less sexually free than boys, and because, as will be explored shortly, married women are theoretically out of bounds for men other than their husbands, a woman is apparently dependent on having a husband for having legitimate sexual relations. In practice however, we have seen that most unmarried girls are tacitly permitted much more sexual freedom than cultural ideology allows, and married women appear to engage in extramarital sexual relations nearly as often as their husbands. It seems, moreover, that divorced women may have almost complete and legitimate sexual freedom, even in those societies in which premarital female chastity and marital fidelity are strongly emphasized. In Tonga, for example, "when once divorced, [women] may remain single if they please, and enjoy all the liberty that the most libertine heart can desire" (Mariner II 1827: 145–46). Mariner also points out that some Tongan women choose never to marry, and have similar freedom (1827: 145–46).

The relative lack of material mutual dependence between husband and wife, as well as the relative paucity of larger social implications of their marriage, may well account for the widely reported "amiability" of husband-wife relations in Polynesia (Firth 1963: 122; Loeb 1926: 76; Huntsman and Hooper 1975: 422; Mariner II 1827: 148, 226, passim; Buck 1932: 119).[29] Because there is little practical or social necessity for staying together, one may assume that when couples stay married (or for as long as they do stay married) the parties simply like each other.

But the arguments that account for the amiable quality of relations between Polynesian spouses also account for the high rates of adultery and divorce.[30] There is little holding the relationship together either from the outside (structures of affinal obligations) or the inside (mutual dependence), and the relationship is largely sustained (or not, as the case may be) on personal sentiment. Personal sentiment is, of course, a rather shifting business in any society. But it is perhaps particularly so in Polynesia where, as noted earlier, the habit of not getting deeply emotionally involved with other individuals is often inculcated in childhood, and is strongly reinforced during the adolescent period of moving quickly from one lover to the next; such habits probably die hard, if ever. If we then add in the fact that a woman can always return to her kin group, where she has land, and where she and her children are always welcome additions, we see most of the reasons for what Mead called the "brittle" quality of Polynesian marriage (1949: 69). The high rates of adultery throughout Polynesia have already been noted; the rates of divorce are equally high (Buck 1938: 143; Hecht 1977: 192; Mead 1949: 69; Handy 1923: 100; Suggs 1966: 133; Buck 1932: 54; Mariner II 1827: 141; Gifford 1929: 16; Loeb 1926: 78).

At this point, however, it is worth distinguishing between getting married and staying married. Much of the discussion thus far pertains to the weak motivation for staying married; clearly the motivation for getting married is stronger, and remains to be explored. On this issue it is important to distinguish further between male and female "interests." We begin with the men, and specifically with the junior males for whom whether to marry or not is a question.

Young men, as we have seen, are at least ambivalent about getting married. Ultimately however they have a real "interest" in doing so: Only by getting married can they reproduce offspring that are legitimately theirs, and only by producing such offspring can they acquire any independent standing in the status system (as the head of a recognized social unit, no matter how junior and how small), as well as any possibility of mobility within it. This "interest" is culturally codified (or equally, is a precipitate of a prior cultural value) in formal markings of the higher status of the married state as such. In Samoa, for example, only married men may get the aristocratic titles that allow them to sit on the *fono*, the governing council. Men who are divorced or widowed must lay aside their titles and resign from the *fono* in order to go courting again. Unmarried men are grouped with untitled men in a separate and subordinate organization, the duties of which consist of carrying out *fono*-decreed work projects, and serving food and drink to the members of the *fono* when they are meeting (Mead 1930: 14). In Tikopia, too, married men are classed with "elders" and have community authority, whereas bachelors have more freedom but remain social subordinates (Firth 1957: 509; 1963: 335; see also Buck 1932: 51 for Tongareva).

Even where married men do not have higher public status, it is nearly universal throughout Polynesia that a husband/father has absolutely high domestic status. The role of husband/father is generally defined as one of absolute superiority and authority vis-à-vis wife and children, no matter how junior the man may be in the public hierarchy (see Best I 1924: 477; Oliver 1974: 813; Mead 1949: 69). In some cases the relationship is formulated through the metaphor of the husband as "chief" and the wife as "commoner" found in a number of Western Polynesian societies (Loeb 1926: 63; Gifford 1929: 17, Kaeppler 1971: 177; Firth 1963: 80). In Mangareva, an

Eastern Polynesian island, wives feed their husbands by hand, as servants feed chiefs (Buck 1938: 224). The metaphor of husband as chief expresses both the actual and potential status benefits of marrying and producing children—the higher status of heading one's own social unit as opposed to being a dependent in another unit, as well as the potential for status mobility inherent in fathering (legitimate) children and thus founding an incipient descent line.

The "chiefly" status of the husband gives him (among other things) the culturally defined right to expect fidelity from his wife, explicitly parallel to the right any chief has to fidelity from his subjects. Thus in Tonga "there was no word for chastity except one which means 'remaining fixed and faithful,' applied only to a married woman, and also to a warrior vis-à-vis his chief" (Mariner II 1827: 130). In both Tonga and Tikopia married women are labeled "sacred" and/or tabu, and should not under any circumstances be trifled with (Gifford 1929: 16; Mariner I 1827: 124, II 1827: 141; Firth 1957: 474, 1963: 118–19). In fact, sexual fidelity was demanded of wives at all levels of society throughout the area (see Best I 1924: 450, 474; Oliver 1974: 358), although the more "real" (i.e., the higher ranking) the chief, the more severely was adultery with his wife penalized (Sahlins 1958: chap. 1 passim).

It is in the context of these rules, related to the metaphoric chiefliness of husbands, that the pattern of intense husbandly jealousy, seen throughout Polynesia, becomes intelligible. In the Marquesas, for example, jealous husbands "would beat or even kill their wives," their wives' lovers, or both (Handy 1923: 100; Suggs 1966: 132). "Most of the murders [in this society] were motivated by sexual jealousy" (Handy 1923: 56). Among the Maori, "adultery was very serious. . . . The wife was sometimes killed by her husband, or he may have killed her lover. . . . Occasionally a man would discard an adulterous wife, or expose her on a path spread-eagled, with her limbs pegged down or compose and sing a song reviling her" (Best I 1924: 474). In both the Marquesas and Mangareva, men commit suicide out of sexual jealousy (Suggs 1966: 131; Buck 1938: 472. See also Oliver 1974: 54, 826, and Henry 1928: 230 on Tahiti; and Marshall 1971: 159 on Mangaia).[31]

Such intense jealousy may seem surprising in light of the points made earlier to the effect that a man does not really "need" a wife for goods, services, sex, or significant social relations, and also in light of the patterns of low emotional involvement in personal relations described for at least some

Polynesian societies. We can see now, however, that "husband" is not merely a social role, but a prestige status, as expressed by the metaphor of husband-as-chief. Wifely infidelity is thus not merely a violation of some sort of "contract" between the husband and wife, but an offense against the husband's pride of status. The link between sexual jealousy and other forms of prestige sensitivity is explicit in the Marquesas and Mangareva, where male suicide may be motivated by offenses in either category. At issue in male sexual jealousy, in other words, is not (primarily) either material need or deep emotional involvement, but rather the pride in status culturally associated with husbandhood itself. And given the intensity of status pride throughout the area (see Best I 1924: 389; II 1924: 225; Firth 1957: 440; Suggs 1966: 134–35), the intensity of husbands' jealousy makes sense.

We have taken this little detour through the problem of wifely infidelity as part of establishing the point that marriage provides men with both actual and potential status benefits, such benefits in turn being among the primary motives for Polynesian men to settle down and get married. Little of this applies to women. It is true that in marrying women gain their only legitimate source of sexual relations. In practice however, the heavy penalties on wifely adultery mean less sexual freedom for married women than for adolescent girls, as well as the loss of gratification of being sought after by many men, which girls have been socialized to maximize and enjoy. It is also true that some women gain personal mobility from marriage, because a wife shares her husband's status (but generally not vice-versa), and because most marriages are probably de facto hypergamous (see the earlier discussion that men are more likely to marry down as a result of the social composition of adolescent cohorts). This minor status accretion, however, is surely offset by a woman's demotion to "commoner" vis-à-vis her husband as chief. And wifehood *is* a demotion: Throughout much of Western Polynesia the status of sister is formally higher than that of wife (Hecht 1977: passim; Mead 1930: 184; Gifford 1929: 59, 79; Kaeppler 1971: passim). But even where a sister does not have formal superiority, nowhere is she categorically inferior to a brother (although she may be relatively inferior to some brothers by virtue of birth order). As a wife, on the other hand, her inferiority vis-à-vis her husband is categorical and absolute.[32]

It is difficult then to see the benefits of marriage for a woman, and it is easy to see its costs: a loss of both status and freedom. It may thus be suggested that girls marry more at the instigation of their lovers, than out of any overwhelming motive of their own.[33] It may also be suggested, although the data are not available to prove it, that women are probably the prime instigators of divorce. Given the losses of status and freedom; *and* given the freedom of divorced women; *and* given a woman's higher status as a kinswoman; *and* given the interest of her kin group in attracting her and her offspring—it is highly probable that women are less personally committed to their marriages than are their husbands.[34]

The relations of husbands and wives to marriage are thus structurally different, and probably emotionally different as well. These differences continue into parenthood, to which we now turn.

Fathers and mothers. The social role of parent as we know it—as central supporter, nurturer, and socializer of one's children—is not a highly significant role in Polynesian society. Parenting functions are spread over a wide range of kin of the biological parents (Best I 1924: 361; Firth 1963: 130; Linton 1939: 159; Mead 1949: 22, 32; Handy and Pukui 1958: 90), and children are encouraged to see themselves as belonging to the wider kin group. Tikopians have explicit ideology to the effect that biological parents and children should not be exclusively attached to one another (Firth 1957: 192). Institutionalized adoption and/or fosterage, which are *universal* throughout Polynesia, and at a high rate, implicitly carry the same message (Carroll 1970; Levy 1973: 473–84).

But the general deemphasis on parenthood is differently realized for men and for women. The differences are virtually direct functions of the differential structural relationships of husbands and wives to the marriage. Specifically, a strong paternal role, like a strong husbandly role, is supported by cultural ideology, whereas a strong maternal role is not.

Fathers are granted metaphoric "chiefness" vis-à-vis their children, as husbands are to their wives. Their authority over their children is absolute and unquestionable. They are granted certain privileges symbolic of this status in their households, and are even hedged about with tabus similar to those surrounding a chief (see Firth 1963: 80, 163; Buck 1932: 51; Gifford 1929: 17, 18; see also Handy and Pukui for the reverse metaphor—the chief as father to his people [1958: 198]). All of this provides them with additional personal prestige; it also probably strengthens their "interest" in the paternal role and in the durability of their relationships with their children. The result is that Polynesian fathers do appear to take a strong interest in their paternal roles. Thus, Linton claimed that Marquesan fathers were the sole socializers of their children (1939: 164), and although this was probably an overstatement, it surely reflects some of the tendencies described here. Similarly, a Maori text says, "The salvation of the men of old was the attention they paid to raising children" (Best II 1924: 24). In Tikopia, "In infant nutrition, education, discipline and ritual of adolescence a father is closely associated with his child . . . he is expected to be emotionally concerned in its welfare" (Firth 1963: 118). The metaphoric chiefly status of fathers both fosters this greater investment in the paternal role and expresses its very "paternalism"—its strong authority combined with its caring, nurturing, and protecting qualities.

The pattern of strong fatherhood relates to, among other things, the "political" interest men have in children. Legitimate children, in fact, are the primary raison d'être of marriage. They are not only a source of greater personal status for a man; they are his social and political "base." We have seen that a chief (or a "chief") is only as strong as the social unit he heads, and that heading a flourishing social unit is also the only potential source of status mobility in the system. Thus children must be not only (legitimately) produced, but raised as loyal adherents to their group. And thus fathers have a structurally induced interest not only in having legitimate children, but in overseeing their development as loyal and adhering members.

All of this is less true, if at all, for mothers. Mothers have little "political" interest in their children, a fact that may well contribute to the high rates of abortion and infanticide throughout the area (*Abortion*: Best I 1924: 247; Firth 1957: 373, 527, 528; Loeb 1926: 84; Linton 1939: 164; Oliver 1974: 63; Malo 1903: 103. *Infanticide*: Best I 1924: 413; Firth 1957: 374; Loeb 1926: 84; Oliver 1974: 63; Handy and Pukui 1958: 79; Goldman 1970: 563). Because women are not directly involved in the processes of maintaining or building descent lines, women do not "need" children for social or political purposes. At the same time, women gain virtually no personal status from motherhood. Birth is not ritualized except in the case of high-status women producing the senior child who will carry on the senior line, and even in these cases the birth rituals are generally conceived as being for the child and not for the mother (Goldman 1970: 522ff.; Best II 1924: 2; Buck 1938: 510; Henry 1928: 184; Oliver 1974: 414; Malo 1903: 183).[35] And the mother role is not granted any special cultural prestige: The Marquesan mother is "respected but a figure of indifference" (Linton 1939: 159). In Tonga a mother is as much a "commoner" to her children as a wife is to her husband (Gifford 1929: 17). And in Tikopia, "They recognize no unvarying moral obligation; they do not subscribe to the opinion that a son is bound to remain attached to his mother by any filial sentiment *per se*" (Firth 1963: 162; see also Mead 1949: 111 for Samoa).

The mother–child bond is thus much like the wife–husband bond from the wife's point of view. It receives little cultural support and is largely a matter of (variable) personal sentiment. The bond has, like marriage, an optional quality, depending largely on how well the parties get along. Not surprisingly, then, mothers and children do not (somewhat to the chagrin of Western observers like Linton) appear to be strongly committed to one another. Mothers may easily give children up for adoption or fosterage. Even if they do not do so, they do not necessarily take an intense interest in the care, nurturing, and socialization of their children. In both the Marquesas and Hawaii, wet nursing is apparently common practice (Linton 1939: 164; Malo 1903: 94). Hawaiians even have a notion that some women's laps are inimical to their children's health, and that the child of such a mother has to be raised by someone else in order to survive (Handy and Pukui 1958: 48, 49). More generally, it is reported throughout the area that women turn over the care of younger children to older children as early as possible. Children in turn are free to wander off and affiliate with other "parents" if they choose (see Mead 1949: 33; Handy and Pukui 1958: 71).[36]

The parallels for women between motherhood and wifehood (as for men between fatherhood and husbandhood) are systematic, as might have been predicted by the fact that both are metaphoric "commoner" statuses. Just as wives have no great economic or "political" stake in their marriages, so mothers have little in their children. Just as wives gain no prestige from marriage, and indeed lose some, so mothers gain none and perhaps lose some in motherhood. And thus as the wife–husband bond is "weak" and easily broken, so the mother–child bond is weak and, if not easily "broken," then certainly easily attenuated.

At the same time, just as the husband–wife relationship is generally reported as "amiable," so is the mother–child relationship, and doubtless for the same reasons. I said earlier that the fact that husbands and wives did not "need" each other could account in large part for the reported "amiable" quality of marital relations, when those relationships survived, or for as long as they did. The same point may now be made of mother–child relations, which similarly lack structural motivation or "interest." Observers repeatedly remark that, although the mother is not a very significant figure to the child, nonetheless mother–child relations are generally "easy" and affectionate (see Firth 1957: 172; Linton 1939: 159; Kaeppler 1971: 191; G. Rogers 1977: 159). It may be suggested that such easy affection is possible in part precisely *because* mothers and children do not "need" each other in any structurally significant way. Predictably, on the other hand, father–child (and especially father–son) relations are often reported as "strained" (Firth 1963: 153; G. Rogers 1977: 159; Oliver 1974: 724; Handy and Pukui 1958: 49).

The differential relations of fathers and mothers to their children may be seen to have effects that link back to the very earliest discussions in this essay, and specifically to the general cultural prominence and particular social dynamics of sibling relations. The father's more active role in the care and socialization of his children manifests itself later in the domestic cycle in the particular protection of daughters with which we began this whole excursion. In addition, his "interest" in the unity of his children as a group, and in their loyalty to his (and his successor's, their brother's) line, would manifest itself in the nonnormative but systematically seen pattern of giving special affection and attention to those of his children whose loyalty is not structurally assured—the daughters and the younger sons. Hence the pattern of babying and petting those other children, which probably does foster their loyalty, but which may also incidentally contribute to the reproduction of the pattern of elder-to-younger sibling envy and mistrust. Potential elder–younger sibling cleavage in turn underlay many of the patterns of male adolescence discussed in the section on brothers. And finally, the mother's relative distance from her children also has important implications for the children's sibling relationships. Here, I would particularly stress the point that when mothers turn over child care to others, as they frequently do, the preferred choice appears to be one of their older children (see Mead 1949: 23; Levy 1973: 456). In other words, it is often siblings themselves who are among each other's significant caretakers and protectors in younger years, and this point is surely consequential for the emotional underpinnings of the sibling relationship.

The "status of women." There is one more important link from the patterns of parenthood back to the patterns of siblingship with which we began this essay. The point may be made by raising the question: If women are not primarily wives and mothers, in terms of cultural emphasis, and apparently in terms of personal commitment, then, what, socially, are they? Where are they socially focused, and what are they doing of social significance? The

answer, of course, is that they are continuing to be what they always were—
kinswomen to their kin, sisters to their brothers, and now that they are in
the parental generation, aunts to their brothers' children. As adult kinswomen they may be important as family genealogists, ritual participants,
economic managers, and even, if their brothers are "kings" (paramount
chiefs), as their "queens" (see Hecht 1977: 196; Huntsman and Hooper
1975: 424; Firth 1957: 196; 1975: 105; Gifford 1929: 181, 232; Mariner
II 1827: 10). And, as discussed earlier, as aunts to their brothers' children
they may also be key ritual sponsors, as well as important authority figures
in the children's socialization. If as mothers married women are hardly visible in the ethnographic literature on Polynesia, as adult sisters and aunts
they are everywhere. Indeed, the strong continuing participation of women
in their natal kin relations is clearly a large factor (as both cause and effect)
in their "weak" wifely and motherly roles.

More importantly, it may be argued that women's continuing kinship significance is one of the major sources of their relatively high overall social
status throughout the area, despite their "commoner" status in relation to
their husbands and children. It may surprise the reader to learn that most
observers consider Polynesian women to have quite high social status,
and further that I would agree with them (e.g., Loeb 1926: 82; Linton
1939: 162; Mariner II 1827: 95, 119, 211; Oliver 1974: 1132).[37] This assessment is made despite the strong (but not absolute) sexual control of
daughters and wives; despite the high incidence of rape and other forms of
violence, sexual and otherwise, against women; despite the typical (though
not total) exclusion of women from high religious ritual and high office; despite (a certain amount of) cultural ideology of female weakness and pollution; and despite the formal subordination of wives and the lack of marked
respect for mothers.

The concept of "the status of women" has been notoriously difficult to
pin down. It certainly requires a great deal more theoretical clarification
and specification than I have space for here. For present purposes I will use
the following indexes of relatively "high" or "low" status: formal cultural
ideology concerning women's "nature," quality of male–female relations,
access of women to significant public roles, and degree of male control over
female behavior. My sense of the relatively high status of Polynesian
women, then, derives from at least the following comparative observations: Ideology of female pollution and inferiority is far less elaborated
than, for example, in the New Guinea highlands;[38] the occasional sexual

violence does not, as in New Guinea, manifest itself in antagonistic gender relations in everyday life; women in Polynesia do occasionally succeed to high office, and more frequently than in many other societies; and sexual control of women is less consistently and less effectively applied than, say, among Muslims or among Indian Brahmins. Among these points the most significant in my view is the relatively low elaboration of cultural conceptions (both formal ideology and general folklore) of female inferiority; Polynesians simply do not express, whether in word or deed, many notions of women as inherently less worthy sorts of persons than men.

The problem then is to account for this (provisionally defined) "high status" of Polynesian women. I would argue that the answer lies in two interrelated points: that *kinswomen*—daughters, sisters, aunts—have culturally defined high status, *and* that kinship is analytically the "encompassing" domain of social relations. I said earlier that marriage is subordinate to kinship in organizing critical social relations—most people marry kin; marriage performs few functions and establishes few relations not already performed or established by kinship; and it is kinship (specifically, descent) rather than marriage that generates rank and prestige. Another way of stating this would be to say, in the Dumontian sense, that kinship encompasses marriage in Polynesia—that the symbols and values of kinship are the hegemonic symbols and values in the system. The high culturally assigned status of women as kin thus encompasses their lower status as wives, and produces an overall *cultural* respect, or at least lack of disrespect, for women in general. Sisters are more respected than wives, *and* women in general appear to be seen more *as* sisters than as wives (see also Shore 1981).

Thus if we look again at the list of indexes of *low* status of Polynesian women, we see that most of them pertain to sexual and reproductive functions, and thus essentially to wives, lovers, and mothers. The assignment of formal subordination to wives and mothers is straightforward. Much of the violence, as we have seen, is sexual violence, and/or violence stimulated by sexual faults. Notions of pollution and weakness center primarily around sexual relations and/or birth. The bias against succession of women to high office works categorically only against wives; sisters and other kinswomen occasionally do succeed to public office within their kin groups (Best I 1924: 353, 453; Buck 1938: 156; Gifford 1929: 88; Mariner I 1827: 137).

As for the strong control of sisters'/daughters' sexual behavior, which might appear on the surface to signal low status for women *in kinship roles*, it must be recalled that such control is culturally associated with high, and sometimes very high, status. The Samoan sacred maid formally outranks her male counterpart, the successor to the chiefship, and the Tui Tonga's sister's daughter—one of the very women who as a girl must have been oiled and massaged and had her knees tied together every night—is formally the highest-ranking person *in the whole society* (Gifford 1929: 74, 80).

Thus most of the negative ideology concerning women centers upon their sexual and reproductive activities as lovers, wives, and mothers; kinswomen, who are neither sexual nor reproductive from the point of view of their kinsmen, escape the problematic associations of such activities and functions. It is not, however, a matter of simply balancing off one set of cultural evaluations (low status of wives, etc.) against another (high status of sisters), from an external point of view. The culture must provide the weighting, and in the Polynesian case, as I said, kinship has priority over marital role definitions in the hierarchy of cultural ordering systems.

Conclusion: Prestige, Kinship/Marriage, and Gender

The reader may well be saying by now, "This is all very well and good, but Polynesia is only one isolated, and possibly quite idiosyncratic part of the world." It remains for me then to place Polynesia in a larger comparative context, in relation to a range of other hierarchical societies, to show that this is not the case. The key texts for the discussion will be the extremely useful compendia essays by Goody and Tambiah, in their joint volume, *Bridewealth and Dowry*.

Goody and Tambiah derive many generalizations about the treatment and status of women in "complex," "stratified" societies, from the fact that women in such societies are given substantial wealth from their families in the form of dowry or inheritance. Goody surveys the world in general, but particularly the area from Western Europe to Sri Lanka. He links dowry to "complex forms of stratification," arguing that dowry functions as a way of preserving the status of daughters as well as sons. From female endowment in turn flow many implications reminiscent of what we have seen in Polynesia: control over the premarital sexual activity of daughters; endogamy and other forms of in-marriage, including brother–sister marriage in some scattered cases; significant patterns of adoption (for purposes of creating "fictitious" heirs); significant patterns of filiacentric unions (in-marrying sons-in-law) for the same reasons. Tambiah confines himself to a smaller area (India, Sri Lanka, and mainland Southeast Asia) and fewer variables, but his data show essentially the same familiar patterns. He finds dowry linked with hypergamy, guarding of female virginity, in-marrying sons-in-law, and certain patterns of institutionalized adoption. Tambiah, unlike Goody, systematically distinguishes between dowry and female inheritance, seeing the latter as a "shift" from the former (I will return to his argument on this point shortly). He then finds the "shift" to bilateral inheritance to be associated with a shift to: bilateral kinship; higher rates of uxorilocal residence; kin-group endogamy; easier divorce and higher divorce rates; more adoption; and more equal status of women.

Before discussing the (close) parallels between Polynesia and these other areas, it should be noted that Goody considers the kinship/marriage/sexual/inheritance patterns listed here to be associated not only with "complex forms of stratification," but with "large states," having economies based on "plough and intensive agriculture" (1973: 26). Neither of these latter developments, however, is characteristic of Polynesia. State formation comes quite late (in fact, post-European contact) in its historical development; agriculture nowhere entailed the plough, and in only a few parts of the area did it approximate the intensity of Eurasia (see Sahlins 1958). It would appear, then, in Polynesia at least, that hierarchical social organization historically preceded state formation and economic intensification, and was at least as much a cause as an effect of these other phenomena. Moreover, we have seen that the hierarchical status system alone, without these other aspects, has most of the correlates pertaining to gender discussed by Goody and Tambiah, and is thus clearly the most relevant social structural dimension for the analysis.

We have seen in this essay that Polynesian sex/gender patterns closely parallel those manifested by some or all of the societies covered by Goody and Tambiah. And as noted, both authors consider that the critical factor linking these patterns to hierarchical social organization is female endowment or inheritance, both of which have (analogous) effects on the way the girl is treated before, during, and after marriage, and on the ways in which marriage itself tends to be organized.

But giving daughters substantial wealth is actually itself more of a puzzle than either author notices, and requires some more systematic explanation. Women could easily be construed as social and economic dependents of men, and usually are. There is thus no reason to give them much of anything, certainly not real estate, but not even valuable movables in the form of jewels and money that they may keep for themselves for life and dispose of as they wish. The fact that women in hierarchical societies do systematically get substantial durable wealth from their natal families thus means that some prior factors are already in operation, which need to be brought to light.

I would suggest that both dowry and female inheritance express certain preexisting, general features of the social situation of women in hierarchical societies. It is inherent in the nature of hierarchies that certain nongender-based principles of social organization take precedence over gender itself as a principle of social organization. In these systems social units (castes, ranked lineages, or whatever) that contain both men and women are ranked on the basis of principles such as (in Polynesia) genealogical seniority. The status of the individual in turn is based in the first instance on birth within one or another such unit, and only secondarily (if at all) on any of the following: personal biological characteristics (age, gender); individual talents, skills, or achievements; or functionally defined roles ("hunters," "shamans," "midwives," and so on). Any or all of these other ways of classifying and ordering persons may subsequently enter into further construction of social categories and groups, and the location of individuals within them. But the peculiar feature of hierarchical systems is that the highest level principles of social organization do not divide, but rather unite, women and men in social categories and social units from which both derive their primary statuses, and in which both share common "interests."

There is a sense, then, in which the logic of hierarchical systems inherently tends toward (even if it never reaches) gender equality. At any given level in the system, men's and women's statuses are more similar to one another's than to persons of either sex at other levels.[39] It is in the context of these points then that we can understand why women in such systems inherit or are endowed with property: They are, in varying degrees in various hierarchical societies, full-fledged members of their "classes," and their rights to a share of the wealth of their natal units appear, at one level, as "natural" as the men's.

Having said this, however, one must also hasten to add that there is still an overall male-favoring bias in the system: Within the "strata," men are formally superior to women, have near-exclusive access to positions of social leadership, and dominate decision making on issues of importance to the unit as a whole. It is this point that requires the analyst to continue to take the male point of view, and to look at the ways in which women (as well as junior men) are "used" by senior men in the transactions that reproduce the system as a whole, and the dominance of senior men within it.

Returning to Goody's and Tambiah's arguments, let us agree that hierarchy has "something to do with" certain widespread gender patterns found in hierarchical societies. The real question is, what is the logic of the relationship? Here I diverge from both authors. We have seen in the present essay that the link between rank and gender lies in the organization of the kinship/marriage system. Critical for the Polynesian analysis has been the cognatic-endogamous nature of Polynesian descent groups, and the fact that marriage relations are subordinate to kin relations within such an organization of descent. The cognatic-endogamous type of kinship/marriage organization prevails, with minor variations, from Polynesia, through Southeast Asia and Sri Lanka, to a number of societies of south India (see Tambiah). Most of the "variations" from this pattern are in the direction of matrilineal descent, most famously among the Nayar, but also in many parts of Southeast Asia.

Cognatic kinship organization is not, however, the only type possible in hierarchical systems. In India and China (to take the two most familiar examples) internally stratified kin groups tend to be patrilineal and exogamous. In other words, there appear to be at least two major ways of organizing descent and marriage in hierarchical societies or, to turn the point around, hierarchical systems may be built upon two very different types of kinship systems, a patrilineal exogamous type, and a cognatic-endogamous type with occasionally realized tendencies toward matriliny.

The first lesson to be drawn from this is that the type of kinship system involved is a relatively independently varying factor in the analysis. It is neither a logical precondition nor a logical consequence of hierarchical social organization. Whether a given society is of one or the other type is often largely a function of geographic area, or at any rate, a function of historical factors probably largely beyond our retrieval. I stress this point because I consider it important to see the operation of certain indeterminate cultural factors in the analysis, and not to sustain an illusion of airtight structural determinism. I will return to this point shortly.

The split (whether viewed areally or typologically) between the patrilineal and the cognatic systems in fact lines up neatly with a split between patterns of female property accession through dowry (in the patrilineal systems) and through inheritance (in the cognatic systems). Both Goody and

Tambiah obscure both of these splits, although they do so in different ways. Goody, in a drive to make a fully structurally determined argument, simply merges dowry and female inheritance under the rubric of "diverging devolution," seeing both as correlates of "stratification," and ignoring major area differences as well as the different empirical correlates of the two types. Tambiah, who is more area-conscious, recognizes the break between India on the one hand and Sri Lanka and Southeast Asia on the other, but proceeds to analyze Sri Lanka and Southeast Asia as "weakenings" of the classical Indian system, with Indian patriliny, virilocality, and dowry "weakening" toward cognatic (or "bilateral") kinship reckoning, balanced patterns of virilocal and uxorilocal residence, and equal male and female inheritance. Although Tambiah argues vehemently against some unnamed opponent that the pattern should be viewed in this way, I submit that Sri Lanka and a few south Indian groups are far more straightforwardly seen as typologically (and probably historically) part of the Polynesian/Southeast Asian pattern, rather than as "weakenings" of the classical Indian type.[40]

The concordance between patriliny, exogamy, and dowry on the one hand, and between cognatic descent reckoning, endogamy, and female inheritance on the other, gives radically different significance to marriage in the two systems. In the first, marriage carries an enormous burden in the reproduction of status relations. Daughters will be married into other groups, and unrelated women will be entering one's own group. Seeing that the daughter marries "well," and that incoming women are of suitable statuses, are issues of great importance for both internal "quality" and external "show" of the group, as well as for the quality of intergroup relations. Dowry, which is given at marriage, is generally appropriate to the marriage-emphasis of the system; it also specifically (as most authors have emphasized) aids in procuring desirable mates and marriage connections, and in putting on a good "show" for the group itself. It is further important that dowry almost never involves land. In a patrilineal system, a woman's children will belong to the group of their father. If she obtained land from her kin group, and passed it to her children, it would automatically be alienated from her group. If women are to get wealth in patrilineally organized hierarchical systems, as our earlier logic suggests they should, then they will nearly inevitably get it in the form of dowry, that is, as a set of *movable* goods endowed upon the women *at marriage*.

For reciprocal reasons, female inheritance is equally consistent with cognatic descent and endogamous marriage. As discussed at length in this essay, marriage is not of great significance in such systems, and the absence of any special bestowal of wealth, designated *as a marriage portion*, is consistent with this overall nonemphasis. At the same time, a woman's children in a cognatic system are as much hers as her husband's, their more active affiliation depending primarily on where they live. Thus female inheritance of land and the further devolution of such land to her children does not automatically alienate it from her kin group, and the problems that militate against female land inheritance in patrilineal systems are absent.

The relative deemphasis on marriage in the cognatic-endogamous systems, on the one hand, and the heavy emphasis on marriage in the patrilineal-exogamous systems on the other, in turn may be seen to influence (or at least correlate with) differential patterns of divorce. We have seen in Polynesia that divorce is easy and frequent, and we suggested that this pattern is at least partly explicable in terms of the fact that Polynesian women retain significant roles in relation to their consanguineal kin throughout their lives. In the patrilineal systems, on the other hand, women generally do not retain such roles, or at least not to anywhere near the degree seen in Polynesia. Correspondingly, divorce in these systems tends to be more socially unacceptable (often wholly so), and in practice infrequent.

The descent rules in the two systems feed into these differential patterns. In the patrilineal systems a woman's children belong to her husband's kin unit, and if she leaves she must either leave the children with her husband's kin or bring them back as non-kin into her own group. In cognatic systems on the other hand, the children belong as much to the mother as to the father, and are as much kin to her kin as to his. Thus although personal conflicts over children may arise, such conflicts are not built into the system as *structural* constraints against divorce. And finally, the differential patterns of female property accession in the two systems also support the differential divorce patterns. We have seen that female land inheritance (versus dowries of movable goods) is facilitated by the cognatic-endogamous social organization. Such inheritance, unlike a dowry, can in turn provide women with means of self-support in case of divorce, and thus contributes to the greater ease and feasibility of divorce in these systems.

The upshot of all this is seen not only in the differential actual patterns of divorce, and in the differential cultural attitudes toward it; it is seen in the gender ideology as well. Whereas Polynesian women are not characterized as innately weak, dependent, and needy of protection and support from men, such notions are prevalent in the gender ideologies of the patrilineal systems. The Indian woman, for example, is culturally described as a "naturally" weak and dependent creature, requiring lifetime protection—first from her father, later from her husband, and finally from her sons.

The general hegemony of kinship over affinity in defining personal status in Polynesia, Southeast Asia, and similar societies, and the specific point that women are defined more in terms of kinship than of marital roles in such systems, has even more general implications. In exogamous/dowry systems women are seen more in terms of the marriages they will contract, and the affinal connections they will engender for their groups, than in terms of their ongoing value as members of the group itself. I have argued for Polynesia, on the other hand, that there is a priority of kinship over marital role definitions of women, and that this priority tends to accord women more social respect or, if you will, higher status. Correspondingly, it appears that in the dowry systems, in which marital status, present or future, takes precedence over kinship status in defining the overall role identity of women, women's social respect is generally lower. Assessments of low, as of high, status are difficult to pin down, but certainly the women of India or China hardly appear to be "appreciated" in the same way in their societies as the women of Polynesia or Southeast Asia.

We might pause here to consider for a moment why an emphasis on a marital as against a kinship definition of women would tend to have a "downgrading" effect. It seems to me that here again the answers lie beyond the structural logic of particular systems, and lie rather in dimensions intrinsic to marital relations and kinship relations as such. It would seem that in marriage a woman's distinctively *feminine* (as against generically human) attributes—mainly centering on biological reproduction—are highlighted, whereas in kinship roles they are not. Thus in marriage a woman is more open to being seen as a radically different type of human being, whereas in the context of kinship she is more easily seen as simply occupying different social roles. In all societies, of course, women (like men) are both kinspersons and spouses; what is at issue is the relative dominance of one or the other dimension.

There is one pattern that might have been expected to be differentiated by the dowry/female inheritance divide, but is not, namely the guarding of daughters' virginity. This is a pattern that appears throughout virtually all hierarchical societies, whether patrilineal or cognatic. Most of the analyses of the phenomenon have centered on its relationship to marriage implications—keeping up the girl's "value," thus assuring her of a good marriage

and/or assuring her family of good marital connections (Goody 1973; Ortner 1976 [this volume]; expressing her natal family's high status by giving
the virgin as a precious "gift" in marriage, the same point being made by
sending her off with a valuable dowry (Tambiah 1973); or protecting her
status group (e.g., her caste) from improper status infusions through wrong
marriages (Yalman 1963). One would thus expect that guarding daughters'
chastity would be more associated with the dowry systems, where young
women are seen primarily in terms of their marital futures. In fact however,
we have seen that premarital female chastity is also emphasized in Polynesia, where women are seen more as kinspersons, and less as marriage export items.

It would appear, then, that an emphasis on virginity may have to do with
more general features of hierarchical systems (it is virtually nonexistent in
"simpler" societies) and less with the specific variations of kinship and marriage organization within them. Both Goody (1973) and I (1976) have separately made this claim, although neither of us, I now think, did so for the
right reasons. Based on the discussions of the present essay, I would now
suggest that the concern for the virginity of daughters in hierarchical societies, across the dowry/female inheritance divide, relates more to the argument made earlier concerning the general elevation in status of women in
such systems. That is, stratification by nongender-based principles places
women in each "stratum" on a more equal footing with men, raising them
toward equivalence with men at any given level. In this sense, I argued,
women's status tends to be higher in such societies than in simpler societies
in which gender itself is often a dominant principle of social ranking. It
must further be noted that the cultivation of virginity, whatever we may
think of it coming from our own cultural backgrounds, is in fact associated
in *all* hierarchical systems with high cultural value. In Polynesia we have
seen that this is the case, but in patrilineal India too the virgin is seen as a
"gift," a precious and valuable object (see Tambiah 1973). And of course
virginity has very exalted significance in Christian ideology too. Virginity
thus appears in its *cultural* contexts to be an expression and cultivation of
the overall higher "value" of women in such systems. I would suggest then
that the meaning that gives virginity high value in all hierarchical societies
is the same as that which gives women relatively higher status in such societies—that women are, first of all, co-members of their own status
groups, and only secondarily females. For clearly virginity downplays the
uniquely feminine capacity to be penetrated and to give birth to children.[41]

A virgin is still a generic kinsperson; a non-virgin is downgraded to mere womanhood.

The question then of whether virginity is "really" oriented toward a girl's marital prospects, as the arguments noted earlier would claim, or rather expresses her ongoing importance within her kin group as the Polynesian analysis would have it (see also J. Schneider 1971), is actually a question of secondary interpretations placed by specific cultures on the more generally available symbol. In the dowry systems, with their marital emphasis, the marriage-oriented interpretations correspond with cultural views and are probably appropriate for their cases, whereas in the female inheritance systems the interpretation stressing the symbolic retention of the girl for her kin group is probably more appropriate.

The whole emphasis on dowry and/or female inheritance has tended to focus discussion on women, and I must now also say a few words about the men. Although the Polynesian female patterns are consistent with many of the female patterns common to hierarchical societies in general, and with virtually all of the patterns seen in the Sri Lanka–Southeast Asian area, Polynesian male patterns may appear divergent from all the rest. Nowhere else do we see the extreme emphasis on male sexual activity so characteristic of Polynesia, and here it might be thought that we are in the presence of something culturally idiosyncratic, having little to do with general structural characteristics of hierarchical social organization.

In fact, however, I would argue quite the contrary. The problem of junior male siblings discussed in this essay for Polynesia is in fact endemic to all hierarchical systems. Only one sibling can succeed to the headship, whether that be the position of head of household, or the kingship of the whole realm. The differences of privilege and opportunity between senior and junior siblings in hierarchical societies are thus everywhere potential sources of social cleavage. And everywhere junior siblings must somehow be "taken care of," whether by methods that ensure their dependency and loyalty to the "house," or by methods that effectively remove them from direct interest in kinship and status affairs, or by some combination of the two approaches. The Tibetan system of impartible male inheritance and fraternal polyandry, for example, responds to the first impulse, while Tibetan Buddhist monasteries that took in one-fifth of the male population, ideally always junior siblings, responded to the second (see e.g., Stein 1972).

Focusing purely on "diversionary" or "removal" tactics for dealing with the problem of junior siblings, however, the encouragement of hyperactive (but nonreproductive) sexuality for junior Polynesian males is clearly simply one among several functional equivalents that would serve these purposes. Other possible solutions would include frequent warfare (for which of course there are other motives as well), and/or perpetual warfare training, to which some Polynesian societies were devoted (see also, for example, the Nayar). And as the Tibetan example suggests, another major possibility would be religious monasticism. Monasticism in fact was the great solution of Eurasia, in both Christianity in the West and Buddhism in the East.[42] Polynesia historically escaped the (early) influences of either of these "high" religions, while at the same time not developing an ascetic tradition of its own. It is not too farfetched to suggest, however, that the asceticism of the European and Asian religions and the (nonreproductive) eroticism of Polynesia are simply inverse transformational solutions to the same general problem, the problem of what to do with junior male siblings in hierarchical societies.

In sum, Polynesia is hardly an idiosyncratic case. Polynesian patterns of female "treatment" are well within the range seen in other "hierarchical" societies, and the male patterns appear as functional equivalents of, and simple symbolic transformations upon, male patterns over the same range. It is clearly possible to say that what we have seen in Polynesia is at least as much a set of structural correlates of "hierarchy" in general, as of peculiar Polynesian cultural traits. On the other hand, I have also argued that idiosyncratic, historically evolved, cultural differences play a major role in affecting variations within the general pattern. The marriage-cum-dowry orientation of the patrilineal systems of Europe and Asia, and the kinship-cum-female inheritance emphasis of the cognatic systems of Southeast Asia and Polynesia, are both congruent with hierarchical macro-organization, but are not directly derivable from it. Each in turn has different consequences for the views and treatment of women in their respective areas.

If the prestige system and the kinship system are thus somewhat independent of one another, at least analytically, it may be suggested that we could also look for different kinds of relationships between the two "levels." If, for example, in Polynesia, hierarchy in general raises the status of women, and so (independently) does the fact that kinship encompasses and subordinates the significance of marriage, we can say that the status system and the kinship system are consistent with one another. In India, on the other hand, stratification raises the status of women but the marital orientation of the kinship system has a depressing effect on female status; thus the status system and the kinship system could be said to be a contradictory relationship with respect to women. It would be interesting to pursue, for example, the high degree of elaboration of notions of female pollution in India, compared to the relatively low degree of elaboration of such notions in Polynesia (or Southeast Asia) in light of this contrast. But that is another paper.

The Problem of "Women" as an Analytic Category

The most serious deficiency of a model based on two opposed spheres appears, in short, in its alliance with the dualisms of the past, dichotomies which teach that women must be understood not in terms of relationship—with other women and with men—but of difference and apartness.

Rosaldo, 1980: 409

This paper began as a rethinking of some patterns in my own past feminist work. For one thing, although I have been systematically concerned with the cultural construction of gender categories, I have done very little on women as social actors. For another, I have never attempted to explore issues pertaining to gender (or women) among the Sherpas, the people among whom I have done all my primary ethnographic research. Thus for this paper I decided to tackle the role of Sherpa women in the founding of the first Sherpa nunnery.

As the paper progressed, however, I realized that there was another rethinking going on in the analysis, a kind of illumination of a programmatic paper by Michelle Rosaldo called "The Use and Abuse of Anthropology: Reflections on Feminism and Cross-Cultural Understanding" (1980). Rosaldo argued, *inter alia*, (1) that even though men are universally "dominant" vis-à-vis women, we should stop paying so much attention to this point; (2) that empirical work upon the lives and experiences of women should not be the primary focus of feminist research; (3) that even though the opposition between "domestic" and "public" domains (which Rosaldo herself had established as central to the analysis of gender [1974]) seems to be heuristically useful, it is actually of negative value, since it leads to an emphasis on "difference" between women and men rather than on "relations"; and (4) that ultimately gender cannot be adequately understood except in relation to other structures of social asymmetry.

Laid out schematically like this, Rosaldo's points seem reasonably clear. Yet the paper itself, at least to me, was not at all clear at the time, insofar as it seemed simultaneously to give and take back most of its own points: we must insist on universal male dominance but ignore it analytically; we must study women but not give "women" as such undue analytic emphasis; the domestic/public opposition "is as telling as any explanation yet put forth" (1980: 399) for many gender patterns, but it should be dropped as an analytic tool; and so on. Yet as I worked my way through the Sherpa nunnery analysis that follows here, I found that what I was doing, essentially, was illustrating most of Rosaldo's points. Without forecasting the results any further, then, I will simply perform the analysis, and allow those points to emerge at the end as outcomes rather than as prescriptions.

The Sherpas are an ethnically Tibetan group living at high altitudes in a relatively remote area of northeastern Nepal bordering on Tibet. Their traditional economic base combines agriculture, dairy herding, and long-distance trade. They live in small villages, in nuclear family households, and property in both land and animals is privately owned by families. They practice the Tibetan Buddhist religion. In the past 30 years, they have become internationally famous as guides and porters for Himalayan mountaineering expeditions (von Fürer-Haimendorf 1964, 1975; R. Paul 1970; Ortner 1970, 1978).

Early in the twentieth century, the Sherpas began to build Buddhist monasteries. They had always practiced a "folk" form of Tibetan Buddhism, in which local married priests (*lama*) conducted rituals in village temples and in households for the benefit of the general populace. But the Sherpas had never before had the more "orthodox" monastic institutions, in which celibate individuals live and practice religion on a full-time basis. Monastics are normatively removed from ordinary social life, do not do any productive labor, and devote themselves maximally to their own spiritual improvement (and incidentally, but not primarily, to the general welfare).

The first (male) monastery, Tengboche, was founded in 1916. The initiative for the founding apparently came from high-status individuals—a very high reincarnate Tibetan lama, and three wealthy Sherpa laymen. The high reincarnate lama's motives in stimulating the founding may be interpreted partly in terms of religious empire building—this man had already, at quite a young age, founded his own monastery in Tibet, and was now apparently looking further afield (Aziz 1978).[1] The lay sponsors, for their part, were all successful traders who had recently become quite wealthy. In the late nineteenth century, major transformations had been taking place in the larger north Indian–Himalayan region. In north India, the British were in their most active phase of economic development. In Nepal, the Rana family had taken all effective power from the king, and had begun a process of rationalizing tax collections throughout the country. The three Sherpa traders involved in founding Tengboche monastery had all been rather dramatically enriched, directly or indirectly, by the economic boom created by the British. In addition, two of them had been appointed tax collectors for the Rana regime, and their tax collecting positions generated both additional wealth and some real local power. The third man was the son-in-law of one of the other two. As a result of both their sudden rise to wealth, and their involvement with the alien and suspect Nepalese state, these men would have had difficulties in maintaining social respect and legitimacy of leadership within the Sherpa community. To make a very long story (Ortner 1989) short, it appears that their involvement in monastery building represented, in part, an attempt to shore up such respect and legitimacy.

The story of the founding of the first Sherpa nunnery, Devuche, is quite different. There is no evidence of instigation on the part of high religious leaders or wealthy patrons. Rather it appears that a group of religiously inclined women got together and, in a grass-roots way, sponsored and built the institution. Since the women were not involved in public politics, as the "big men" behind the founding of Tengboche were, the two foundings seem to contrast in "typical" female/male ways: Whereas the founding of Tengboche appears to be understandable in terms of changes in the "public" domain (macro-politics and economics), the founding of Devuche appears to pertain more to the world of women's "private" or "domestic" experience. Yet although this impression is created by the different emphases in the accounts of the two foundings, I shall try to show that the situation was far more complex than that.

Devuche Nunnery

Devuche nunnery was probably begun around 1925, and was completed in 1928. The nunnery complex, consisting of a temple and associated structures, as well as individual houses belonging to the nuns, is situated in a glade in a high valley of Khumbu, the upper Sherpa region. It is located a short distance from Tengboche monastery, a bit further north on the trail leading to some of the highest Sherpa villages, and ultimately to Mt. Everest.

Currently, there are eight fully ordained celibate nuns (*ani*), and five other women attached to the nunnery in the status of "peripheral ones" (*korwa*).[2] The distinction between the fully ordained nuns and the *korwa* pertains to matters of ritual participation rather than levels of religious achievement; there are in fact no such levels in the nunnery, as there are in the male monasteries. The monasteries also have grades of spiritual or moral distinction, the lower being called *rabchung*, and the higher called *gelung*, but all Sherpa nuns are only *rabchung*.[3]

The nunnery, like a monastery, has a number of rotating managerial offices—the *konyer*, who keeps the keys to the temple and is in charge of seeing that the premises are in order, and two *nyermu*, who are essentially the business managers, one keeping accounts, and the other buying food and being in charge of the kitchen when collective meals are prepared. The official head of the nunnery is the (male) head lama of Tengboche monastery, who sits on the "throne" in the nunnery temple during important religious rituals which he comes to lead. Devuche is actually defined as a branch of Tengboche, although it handles most of its own internal affairs.

The financing of the nunnery is no different from that of a monastery, and works as follows. Gifts are usually in cash, but in the past also included some land.[4] The cash may be given outright, either for immediate expenditure or to be used as lending capital, or it may be pledged in the form of annual interest on a designated body of capital retained by the donor. Big donors, both lay and religious, tend to give specifically earmarked gifts— endowments for the annual performance of particular rituals, or lump sums for the purchase of particular temple items (or, in the early days, for the construction of particular structures, including the temple itself). When gifts are given to the nunnery "as a whole," they go toward the maintenance of the temple, the purchase of temple paraphernalia, and the feeding of the nuns *when they are engaged in collective activities*—daily communal tea drinking, and the performance of temple rituals.

For ongoing subsistence, however, each nun must provide for herself. She must buy or see to the construction of her own house, and must provide her own food, except on those ritual occasions when she is supported by the general fund.[5] Normally, a woman's family will provide both the house and the ongoing subsistence for her. They may set aside fields for her support, to be worked by family members or, in a wealthy family, by tenants or wage laborers. Or they may simply obligate themselves to provide her with food from their own holdings. In addition, the nun will be fed, and receive a certain amount of money and grain in donations, whenever she performs rituals for lay people, individually or with other nuns.

We have virtually no information on day-to-day life in the nunnery. We know that there is daily communal tea drinking. Beyond that, when there are no rituals scheduled, it appears that the nuns (like the monks in the monasteries) normally cook and eat in their own individual houses, and privately perform their own devotions.

At least once a month, however, some collective ritual is scheduled. On the tenth day of each month, the nuns perform a *tso* ritual, which entails large offerings of foods to the gods, distributed to all the mortals present afterwards.[6] Once a year the nuns also do a ritual of spiritual purification called *Kusem* (analogous to the monks' *Dorsem*) for seven days. They also do a more intensive version, called *Karwi Chagye*, of the annual laypeople's ritual of atonement and merit-making (*Nyungne*); the nuns' version entails fasting every other day for sixteen days. In summer, there is (ideally) one month of retreat, or *yerne*, during which time all the nuns must remain in the nunnery and participate in daily rituals.[7] In addition to all this, the nuns may be invited at any time to participate collectively in mortuary rituals in private homes, and they may also be invited individually to perform other rituals for households.

The Story of the Founding of Devuche

The account I received of the founding of Devuche came from one of the founding women, Ngawang Samden (her religious name). When I interviewed her in 1979, she was eighty-three years old. Many years before, she had broken her nun's vows and married, in fact several times over.[8] Her last husband was now deceased, and she was living in a small house on the grounds of Tengboche monastery, as a *korwa* of the monastery.

As I was able to piece together from other sources, Ngawang Samden was born into a family of some substance. Her father may have been a *pembu*, a tax collector. One of her brothers had been a *pembu*, and he and another brother were both apparently powerful men in their time.[9] One of these brothers in turn was the father of a man serving as a local government official (*pradhan panch*) at the time of my fieldwork. And one of her sisters married another *pembu*, whose son in turn has become one of the most prominent, respected, and influential men currently active in the area. There is good reason to believe that most of the early Devuche nuns (as well as most of the early Tengboche monks) were from relatively well-to-do, high-status families. Given the fact that a nun or monk must be supported by her or his family, the pattern of drawing monastics from the higher levels of Sherpa society still generally holds today.

When Ngawang Samden was twenty-four, her father betrothed her to a wealthy older man who already had one wife.[10] She did not want to get married, and so ran away from home with the intention of becoming a nun. Lacking money and needing the appropriate attire for taking her vows, she dyed a white blouse red. Another woman, who was to become another of the founding nuns, kindly gave her some food to carry on her journey. She fled to Rumbu monastery, over the border in Tibet, where she took vows from the high reincarnate lama who had been instrumental in the founding of Tengboche monastery.[11]

All the other founding nuns[12] also took their vows at Rumbu, although whether or not they did so at the same time as Ngawang Samden is not clear. All of them eventually migrated back to the Khumbu area, where they pursued their religious studies together, probably under the instruction of one of the Tengboche monks. Ngawang Samden said that she mastered the first two books of reading and writing after only one winter of study.

Eventually, the nuns hatched the idea of founding a nunnery in Khumbu. As Ngawang Samden tells it:

One night, she and the other *ani* were sitting together and drinking tea. They were talking about building a house where they could do religious work together. They did not sleep all night. The next morning they got up and decided to go and put their request to Lama Gulu, the head of Tengboche monastery. He said that it was good that they had come, and he gave them the "order" or the authority to build a temple/nunnery.

Lama Gulu told the nuns to come back on New Year's day. They came back and he gave them some money, but more importantly, he gave them an idol, a prayer book, and a *chorten* [a Buddhist symbol of the cosmos. The three items were symbolic of the three essential spiritual supports of a religious institution and of religious practice]. All the Tengboche monks also gave them money, from their personal resources.

Lama Gulu also told the nuns to go out begging for donations. He gave them a letter of authorization and some religious medicine to take with them to distribute to people.[13] They went to each village and gave the letter and medicines to a prominent man, who then called everybody together and explained the women's mission. They received enormous donations. They went as far away as Phaphlu and Zhung, villages in the lower Sherpa valley, about forty miles south of their area.

The story continues, enumerating additional contributions from religious donors:

> Lama Gulu gave principal from which interest could be used to support the monthly *tso* ritual. The Zatul Rimpoche[14] [the high lama from whom the nuns had all taken their vows] gave principal for the support of three other rituals. The Zatul Rimpoche also sent two large loads of old woolen clothing from Rumbu monastery.[15] Ngawang Samden sold these clothes to make more money for building the nunnery.

As for lay donors, many of these were either the same people involved in the founding of Tengboche monastery, or else closely associated with them. One was Karma Lama of Zhung, one of the original three wealthy and powerful patrons of Tengboche. Ngawang Samden described Karma Lama's support as second only to Lama Gulu's, and one of Karma Lama's daughters became one of the founding group of nuns. Another important lay sponsor was a certain Pule, who was married to a kinswoman of Karma Lama. Pule sponsored the large prayer wheel on the site of the nunnery. Takto Kusang, Karma Lama's son-in-law and another former sponsor of Tengboche, "also gave a lot." In addition, there were smaller donations from virtually every adult in Khumbu. Ngawang Samden's mother gave food, and a turquoise which could be sold. Another man gave a valuable gem, a *zi*. And so on.

Ngawang Samden and Karma Lama's daughter, Ani Tarchin, built their own small houses at the nunnery site even before the temple was begun. Once the building work began,

> Lama Gulu stayed in Devuche from start to finish. He and all the Tengboche monks helped very much with the labor. All the Khumbu village people came to help. There are so many people there weren't enough plates to feed them on.[16] The nuns bought a bolt of cotton cloth and laid it out on the ground, and people sat behind it. The food portions were dumped directly on the cloth [an unheard of mode of serving food]! Each of the nuns also gave the workers one day's food, out of her own resources.

All the structural work on the main temple and the large prayer wheel associated with it, as well as the painting of the frescoes, was finished by the time of the consecration, the *ramne*, in 1928. (Ngawang Samden and others recalled that many wealthy and powerful people came to the *ramne*.) But the temple still required more internal furnishings, and once again Ngawang Samden went into action:

> After the *ramne*, she and two other nuns [including Karma Lama's daughter] went to Lhasa, where they contacted Gembu Tsepal [the third of the three big Tengboche sponsors and a former head tax collector—*gembu*—who had fled to Lhasa after being involved in a murder case] and also her two younger brothers. These three men helped the *ani*, calling people together, buying them all beer, and raising a lot of donations. With the money the *ani* bought carpets and dragon-hangings in Lhasa for furnishing the interior of the temple. You can still see all these things inside the temple today. On the way back from Lhasa to Khumbu the nuns stopped in Shigatse, where another Sherpa [?] man gave them more carpets. Thus they furnished the temple.

In this account of the founding of Devuche, then, what is emphasized are the initiatives of the young women involved, both in launching the process, and in carrying it through to completion. Although the roles played by high religious leaders and wealthy lay sponsors (including, indeed, most of the same people involved in the founding of Tengboche) are fully noted, these people are not presented as the prime movers in the process, as they are in the case of Tengboche monastery. This difference in the accounts of the two foundings may of course be an artifact of the interviewing. Had I interviewed male informants about the founding of Devuche, perhaps they would have described the initiatives as coming from the high lamas and wealthy sponsors rather than from the nuns.[17] Alternatively, had I been able to interview some of the original Tengboche monks (none of them were alive at the time of the research), perhaps they would have described the founding of Tengboche more as a product of their own grass-roots efforts (as Ngawang Samden describes the founding of Devuche) than as having been generated by the higher-ups. Unfortunately, we lack the space and/or the data to deal with questions of variations in narrators' perspectives here, although we shall return to the possibility of a more ground-level angle on the founding of Tengboche below.

All of this aside, however, we have here an account of the founding of Devuche nunnery that portrays it as the fruit of initiatives on the part of a group of women. It seems reasonable, then, to attempt to understand this event at least partly with reference to certain patterns of Sherpa women's lives. I should declare at the outset, however, that I do not believe one can get very far in the analysis by focusing on women actors alone. That is, even though Devuche is an institution created by and for women, I shall argue that we cannot understand the forces behind its founding without exploring the parallels (as well as the differences) between women's and men's lives, and without contextualizing the experiences of *both* sexes within certain larger structures of social relations.

The Situation of Women among the Sherpas

The position of women (and more generally, the pattern of gender relations) among the Sherpas deserves a paper in its own right, and only the barest sketch can be given here. The following is based on my own field observations and conversations, as well as on March (1979), the only extended treatment of the subject currently available.

At the level of formal ideology, both Sherpa men and Sherpa women say that women are "lower" than men. Femaleness is a lower form of rebirth.[18] A human born as a woman is being punished for past sins. Women in turn have more propensity than men to accumulate even more sins since, among other things, mothers acquire the sins of their young children, as well as the demerit of their own bad deeds. If a woman nonetheless manages to accumulate much merit, the best she can hope for is rebirth as a man.

One aspect of women's "lowness" is that they are *gamchu*, or that they generate *gamchu*, a kind of negative force which causes persons or things with any special powers to be drained of these powers. Thus, for example, a woman should never touch the head or shoulders of a man, and especially of a lama, or he might lose his greater spiritual potency. Potency thus lost can never be restored.

Women are also mythically blamed for a number of mishaps that have harmed the Sherpa community as a whole. For example, one lama's wife, in a folktale, intruded herself into a situation in which a god was visiting her husband. The lama had been lamenting to the god that there was no salt in the Sherpa area, and the god had been on the verge of agreeing to rectify the situation. But when the wife arrived, the god (who couldn't stand women because they are *gamchu*) withdrew, and never visited humans again. Thus the Sherpas still have to make arduous trading expeditions to obtain salt. In another tale, the ancestor Mempali and the ancestress Ikpali owned many cattle. Mempali warned Ikpali not to say "phew" when she got tired of doing her cattle chores. But after rounding up one hundred cows, she was tired and involuntarily said "phew," whereupon all the cows ran away. Now, the tale concludes, nobody, not even the richest people, can keep more than one hundred head of cattle. And a third little story: In the time of the Guru Rimpoche, the founder of Tibetan Buddhism, people used to live for one thousand years. One day the Guru Rimpoche invited all the lamas to take *ong*, a ritual of long life. But one lama's wife would not let him go, and so now people are doomed to short lives.

In modern Sherpa social life, women are seen as being more driven than men by greed, materialism, and envy. As a result, it is believed that they may become poisoners (poisoning unsuspecting guests is thought to be a magical way to gain wealth) or witches (who make people ill out of envy of their possessions). At the same time, men are not seen as perfect either. They are given to competitiveness and violence. Yet women's assumed propensity to poison and bewitch others is felt to be more insidiously threatening than men's tendencies to compete and fight with one another, probably because poisonings and witchcraft attacks are invisible and unpredictable.

At the social level, women have two major disadvantages compared with men: a norm of virilocal residence, which means that they must move to their husbands' homes at marriage, and the rules of inheritance which give all productive property to men. A brief look at the Sherpa domestic cycle will illustrate the impact of these rules on female experience.

The Sherpas live for the most part in nuclear families which (ideally, and generally in practice) own all of their own productive resources—land and herds of dairy animals—and which support themselves largely by the labor of their own members.[19] All the members of the household become active contributors to the support of the family from very early ages. Daughters as well as sons work hard in both agriculture and animal care, and are valuable members of the household economy. Daughters, further, do much more domestic work than sons. Indeed, some women said that they would rather have daughters than sons, since daughters help their mothers with domestic chores as well as doing productive labor, while sons just sit around the house "like kings." These sorts of comments aside, however, the family is a relatively tight and efficient social unit, with a high degree of internal solidarity, until the children begin approaching marriageable ages.

Marriages are finalized relatively late, when the children are in their mid to late twenties. The lateness of marriage (and the frictions that develop around it) is partly related to the children's importance in their parents' domestic economy. But it is also connected with problems created by the inheritance system: The transmission of property takes place at this stage of the children's lives, rather than at the death(s) of the parent(s). Thus when each child marries, he or she gets his or her final share of the family estate. Sons inherit the land and the herds, while daughters inherit only movable goods—jewelry and household effects.[20] Thus men are the owners of the means of production, while women are technically propertyless.[21]

Marriages are generally arranged by the parents. Sons have little more say than daughters in arranged marriages, and a son may be just as unhappy, in a given case, with the chosen wife, as a daughter is with a chosen husband.[22] The rate of divorce, primarily in the early stages of marriage, is about 30 percent (Oppitz 1968: 124).

But it is the woman who must move to her husband's house after marriage, and virtually every young Sherpa woman I knew expressed some apprehension about this move. The norm of virilocal residence works somewhat differently in Khumbu, the northern Sherpa area, and Solu, the southern one. In Solu, the villages are mostly single-clan communities. Since a woman must marry a man of a different clan, she *must* move out of her natal village. She must thus go and establish herself among relative strangers, with little of the family support she had at home.[23] Further, since men are very geographically mobile (for trade, and for wage labor), the woman may be left alone in this relatively strange place for long periods of time. Indeed, in cases of arranged marriages where the man is unhappy with his parents' choice of wife (or, in many cases, where he simply feels that he is not ready to be married), he will tend to stay away as much as possible. Given nuclear family household organization, the young wife—and I knew of quite a few such cases—feels quite isolated and unhappy. (See also the biographical sketch of Ani Chodon [Aziz 1976: 45]).[24]

In Khumbu the situation appears to be different. Khumbu villages are generally multi-clan communities, and the rates of local endogamy (inmarriage) are quite high—63 percent (von Fürer-Haimendorf 1964: 45–46) or 77 percent (Lang and Lang 1971: 3). Yet these figures require some interpretation. In one instance, for example, von Fürer-Haimendorf took two adjacent villages as a single marriage unit and calculated only one rate of endogamy for the two together. Lang and Lang, with their even higher rate, may have done the same thing for other parts of Khumbu as well. Such calculations seem quite reasonable, since Sherpas are in general quite casual about long distances and very difficult terrain. Yet in the context of the issue of residence change at marriage, the picture for women appears rather different. I heard several Khumbu women who married into villages adjacent to their natal ones express the sense that they were moving "far away." The subjective experience of distance is thus transformed in this context. Further, even though many young Khumbu women *will* remain in their natal villages, or relatively close, none can be sure before marriage that *they* will not be among the 23 percent (or 37 percent) who will in fact have to move further away.

Although the statistics are not available on which girls are more likely to move longer distances, in most instances for which I have specific information, it is girls from higher-status families. A higher-status girl is also more likely to be shipped off earlier to her husband's village, because her family does not need her labor, and does not need a long time to put together her dowry. These points are of particular relevance for the present analysis, since most of the women involved in the founding of Devuche (and indeed most women who become nuns) were/are from higher-status families.

Next come the problems of bearing and raising children. It may be assumed that, in this remote area with no medical facilities before the 1960s, there was considerable risk to women in bearing children. Nonetheless, I never heard a Sherpa woman express fear of dying in childbirth. What women do worry about, however, is *children* dying, and such worries are quite realistic. There is a 15.8 percent rate of deaths of infants in the first year of life, and an overall 28.8 percent rate of mortality before adolescence (Lang and Lang 1971: 4).

Finally, both women and men always express a great deal of concern about the ability to support the children adequately, except in the wealthiest of families (see also von Fürer-Haimendorf 1976: 148). Young parents with a number of small children must work extremely hard. There are more mouths to feed than workers to produce, and the requirements of child care cut into the wife's productivity as well. Again, the problems are intensified by nuclear family residence (and the ideal of nuclear family autonomy): the couple cannot expect much help from others, with either child care or productive labor.

Yet despite the ideology of women's lowness and associated bad characteristics, and despite the rather heavy social constraints just sketched, Sherpa women hardly strike one as oppressed creatures. If one had no access to all the above information, and if one based one's assessment of Sherpa women's status solely on behavioral or interactional observations, one would probably say that Sherpa women are the virtual equals of Sherpa men. In ordinary behavior and interaction, Sherpa women are assertive, outgoing, self-assured, and enormously independent. There is little sex-segregation in the society: there are no men's clubs or coffee shops or plazas where men alone congregate. Almost all social life takes place in private homes, where the wife is as active in hosting a social event as her husband is, if not more so. When husbands go off on trading expeditions, or to do wage work, wives manage home and land on their own for long periods of time, making financial decisions, organizing and performing the labor involved, and generally taking care of themselves and their families. They are not seen as incompetent, vulnerable to rape or seduction, stupid in worldly affairs, or in any other way requiring special protection and sheltering. (See, along these same lines, von Fürer-Haimendorf 1964: 81.)

Summing up the total situation of Sherpa women, then, it is clear that the components are somewhat internally contradictory. Women are encouraged to be competent, self-assured, independent actors, but they are also hemmed in by distinctive structural constraints, and burdened by negative ideology. It would be important to try to understand the roots of this contradiction—both in its individual components and its totality—but such an undertaking would carry us far beyond the confines of the present paper. For the moment we may only suggest one point of immediate relevance, namely, that high-status women might experience the internal contradictions of the total female situation more deeply than other women. That is, they would tend to have particularly positive self images (indeed many of them have probably been quite spoiled as children), and might thus feel much more unjustly abused than other women by the social restrictions and negative ideology constraining women generally.

The Decision to Become a Nun

The central vow of monasticism is that of celibacy. The woman swears not to engage in sexual relations nor to marry. More generally, she is not supposed to engage in most of the ordinary practices and relations of secular social life. Even if she returns to reside in a secular household after taking the vows (a possible, and not infrequently chosen, option for nuns), she is not subject to the normal obligations of kinship, neighborly reciprocity, social hospitality, and the like, and is not supposed to become involved in such activities. A nun must also not engage in productive labor, as agricultural work entails killing the tiny insects and worms that live in the soil, and in any event it (like most other normal activities) takes time and energy away from the full-time pursuit of religion. Finally, while there is no actual vow of poverty, in general a nun is supposed to lead a simple material life. Sex, marriage, family, work, social exchange, material goods—all of these are both generally distracting from concentration on religious work, and (in various ways) specifically inimical to the long-term goal of such work— the reduction of egotism and of the cognitive and emotional attachment to self.

In taking the vows of a nun, a woman breaks out of most of the disabilities of the female state. From the nun's point of view, this "breaking out" is envisioned in terms of setting herself on a lifelong course of religious action that can ultimately lead to rebirth as a man. One nun (at Bigu nunnery, in Solu) expressed the hope

> to be reincarnated as a god, or at least as a human, preferably a man. "As a woman one is always inferior," she argued, "however much one learns one is never given as much respect as a lama. Even corrupt lamas are still treated with some respect; a man can lead a sinful life, and yet later become a lama and be considered superior to any woman." (von Fürer-Haimendorf 1976: 148)

The nun thus aims for a better rebirth, through renunciation of sin and pursuit of merit. In leading a simple material life, she can avoid the sins of greed and envy. In not doing agricultural work, she avoids the sins of killing worms and insects. In not having children, she avoids accruing their sins as well as her own. In not marrying and not entering into family and social life, she avoids distractions and is able to pursue her devotions and other meritorious religious work.

From a more analytic perspective, however, we can see that a nun gains a great deal not only toward improving her next life, but also in raising the quality of her present one. In relation to negative cultural views of women, a nun is less likely—in theory—to be endowed with the unpleasant characteristics normally attributed to women. By renouncing an interest in worldly goods, a nun can separate herself not only from the sins of greed and envy, but also from the *attributions* of greediness and materialism placed upon women in the culture. And by renouncing normal social relations, she can escape the various cultural charges of female social troublemaking: poisoning, witchcraft, and general meddling.[25]

In relation to social and economic disadvantages, next, monasticism is again a rather neat way out For one thing, the nun—in sharp departure from the property rules—gets her own real property from her family: a house. In addition, either some land is allocated for her support (which— the best of all worlds—she does not have to work herself) or in any event a pledge is made of material support from her family's lands and herds.[26]

It may be noted that nuns do not stress the acquisition of property as an advantage of taking vows, either because this is not part of conscious moti- vation, or because it would be unseemly to emphasize the acquisition of property in the context of the anti-materialistic ideology. What they *do* stress in terms of social motivation is something that is perfectly consistent with religious ideology—the desire to avoid marriage. Indeed, from the point of view of the women with whom I spoke, this was the most salient motive for becoming a nun. We have seen that Ngawang Samden ran away from home and took vows because her parents had arranged an unattrac- tive marriage for her. Other women, who either expressed a desire to be- come a nun, or had already taken vows, also cited many of the problems surrounding marriage discussed above—the possibility of having a "bad" husband, the possibility of children dying, the possibility of having to move away from their natal homes, sometimes great distances away. Becoming a nun avoids at least the problems of husbands and children, even if it does en- tail moving away from home.

But moving away from home to join a nunnery would appear to be quite a different story from moving away from home in marriage. A woman gets to join a community of individuals who share many of her goals and aspira- tions. There may be an expectation that such a community will provide a context of personal warmth and supportiveness. There is some suggestion in Ngawang Samden's text, for example, that she sought and found "sister- hood" in this sense with some of the other nuns. Unfortunately, the data are not available to indicate whether such expectations are widespread among women contemplating becoming nuns, and/or whether, in practice, such "sisterly" supportiveness actually crystallizes. It may be noted, however, that both the ideology and the social organization of the celibate institu- tions (nunneries and monasteries alike) do not encourage the formation of close personal ties among the members: ideologically, each individual is there to pursue his or her own salvation; socially, each individual lives, eats, and sleeps alone, and performs religious devotions in her or his private house, except when engaged in collective rituals. Further, we noted in pass- ing earlier that it is acceptable for nuns (but not for monks) to return to live with a kinsperson back in the village, and quite a few in fact do this. The sum of these points, then, suggests that the idea of joining a close and supportive community when one takes the vows is either not envisioned or not realized by women who become nuns.

Indeed I suspect that what the nun seeks and gets, in a positive sense, from taking the vows, is rather the chance to be more fully autonomous (see also Aziz 1976: 45). We have already seen that Sherpa women are encouraged to be quite independent, even while they are constrained by both the ordinary bonds of social life and the special constraints of womanhood. In "escaping" these various bonds and constraints, which constitute one-half of the (contradictory) situation of Sherpa womanhood, the other half—the autonomy and independence—is in effect liberated. Although there are many rules in a nunnery, there is almost no supervision, and every nun (like every monk in a monastery) is responsible for her own moral behavior.

Finally, it is important to translate all of the above points into religious terms. Becoming a nun (or a monk) offers the opportunity of a major transformation of one's present self, and one's future existences. Once past the desire for "escape" and independence that probably dominates the initial decision to take the vows, the nun can focus without distraction on building merit, reducing ego, and other major Buddhist objectives which hold out the promise of transcendence not only of woman's lot, but of the painful human condition as a whole. In the process, one gains social respect, security, and autonomy, but in theory such gains are quite incidental to the spiritual benefits.

An example of such a shift in perspective can be seen in the case of Ngawang Samden, whose text on the founding of Devuche was given above. Her initial motivation for becoming a nun was framed in terms of escaping an unappealing marriage—or marriage in general. Yet when I asked her what the nun's vocation is, she answered in entirely spiritual terms: "Nun's work is to practice religion—what else? One is afraid of dying [and having a bad rebirth] and so one must do religion all the time."[27] The quality of her religious faith and devotion may be seen in her remark that, at one point in her life she was losing her sight, but she did numerous *mani* (repetitions of the central mantra of Tibetan Buddhism) and her sight was restored. She neglected to mention what to her was incidental to her religious efforts—a doctor performed a successful cataract operation on her eyes.

In becoming a nun, then, a woman can resolve many of the problems of women's lives in Sherpa culture—she can escape certain cultural stigmas, get around certain social and economic restrictions, and feel herself to have reduced certain moral disabilities with respect to present well-being and future rebirth.

Women and Some Men: Relative Structural Position

At this point, we have approached the limits of analysis pursued from the point of view of female actors. In asking why Sherpa women might become nuns, we have been forced to concentrate on the *differences* between men and women in Sherpa society. These differences are real enough. Nonetheless, they are perhaps less dramatic than they have appeared, particularly if we compare the women to certain *categories* of men, rather than to "men" as a whole. My general point here, to which I will return in the conclusions, is that analysis focused through a polarized male/female distinction may produce distortions at least as problematic as those which ignore women and gender in the first place.

On the surface, the situation of Sherpa men is more attractive than that of Sherpa women. Men are formally considered "higher." They do not have to cope with the supposed moral disadvantages of the female state, nor with the assault on self-esteem posed by the negative ideology surrounding women. Nor do they face the possibility of being sent to a distant village, far from home, at marriage, where they will have to make their way into the social system from scratch.[28] They will, however, be subject to arranged marriages just as women are, with the same prospects of being placed in an unhappy relationship. They will, moreover, be faced with the same heavy responsibility of supporting children. In addition, as the property owners, and despite the fact that their wives will do at least an equal amount of productive labor, the men (unlike the women) view themselves as having the responsibility of supporting their spouses. Not surprisingly, then, men's motives for becoming monks stress the avoidance of marriage much as women's do, although their emphasis tends to fall more on avoiding the burden of responsibility for support of family, than on some of the other unpleasantnesses of marriage stressed by women.

But the analogies between men's and women's motives go even further than this. We pointed out earlier that one of the most salient differences between men's and women's social positions is the fact that men are the owners of all the productive resources—land and herds. In point of fact, however, there are certain men who are almost as disadvantaged as women with respect to property—middle sons. Although all sons are supposed to get equal shares of the parents' productive estate, in practice things do not always work out so neatly. As each son gets married, the father is supposed to build or otherwise provide him with a house, and give him his share of the land and animals. Generally, the first son gets his full share, including the house, although he may have to wait a relatively long time to get it, since his marriage comes at a relatively early stage in his father's economic career. With later sons, on the other hand, providing houses may become increasingly economically difficult, and it is middle sons, more than any others, who may find themselves out in the cold. They may in theory have land and herds to work, but no place to set up a household. Only a youngest son (or an only son) has a relatively unproblematic property situation, since he will inherit the parental house and the remaining portion of the productive resources.

Nor surprisingly, according to Sherpa ideology, it is middle sons who should normally become monks. Only slightly more surprisingly, social practice conforms quite closely to ideology. The available statistics on birth order among monks run in the appropriate direction. At Tengboche in 1957, out of ten monks reported on, seven were middle sons, one was an eldest, one a youngest, and one an only son (von Fürer-Haimendorf 1964: 140). At three other monasteries (Thami, Takshindo, and Chiwong) surveyed in 1967–68, of twenty-two monks for whom data were available, eleven were middle sons, five were eldest, four were youngest, and two were only sons (R. Paul field notes).[29]

What is being suggested here is that, at least in some contexts, gender in pure form may be a less useful (and more misleading) analytic construct than something like "relative structural position." Women's sense of the difficulties of marriage, though different in some specifics from men's, is not without strongly felt male analogues. More importantly, Sherpa women's formally prescribed exclusion from property ownership has its non-normative, but systematically reproduced, parallels among certain categories of men. These men's structural disadvantages are hidden—by the culture, and by us—by the use of a global category of "male," associated with general social superiority vis-à-vis women. In other words, in attempting to rectify male bias in anthropological analysis, we slip into a different sort of distortion, which might be labeled (for lack of a better term) "big man bias." We take the privileges of certain men—leaders, or elites, or last-born sons, or whatever—and assume them to apply to male actors in general. We thus obscure (and thereby unwittingly collude with cultural

ideologies) what many men have in common with women in general, or
with specific sectors of women. Again, I will return to the broader implications of these points in the conclusions. For the moment, however, let us
consider how a more structurally based, rather than gender-based, catego-
rization of actors and their motives might inform our understanding of the
founding of Devuche nunnery.

Interpreting the Founding of Devuche . . . and Another Look at Tengboche

We began the paper by noting that, in accounts of the founding of Tengboche monastery, prominence is given to the initiatives of religious leaders
and wealthy lay sponsors. In accounts of the founding of Devuche nunnery,
on the other hand, the prime movers appear to be the young nuns themselves. The emphasis on the leaders in the Tengboche stories, in turn, tends
to give the founding of the monastery a distinctly "political" or "public"
cast. The founding of Tengboche appears as the outcome of large-scale
political-economic changes—the Rana coup in Kathmandu, the activities
of the British in India, the consequent enrichment and rise in power of local
Sherpa elites who in turn sought social legitimation through building monasteries.[30] The founding of Devuche, on the other hand, appears as the
product of more "personally" or "privately" motivated efforts on the part
of a group of women seeking to avoid certain specifically female constraints. To be sure, the large-scale political-economic changes could be
added into the story, but primarily in *facilitating* roles: contributing to an
overall rise in surplus in the Sherpa economy, and to the enrichment of the
founding women's families, thereby providing the resources to found the
nunnery and support the nuns. But the changing political-economic conditions do not appear to play a *motivating* role in the building of Devuche
nunnery, as they do in the account of the founding of Tengboche.

But let us look at the data again. In the first place, it is quite possible to
view the founding of Tengboche in much the same terms as the founding of
Devuche. There is suggestive evidence to the effect that the monastery was
as much a product of "grass-roots" pressure on the part of certain young
monks, as Devuche was on the part of the young nuns. There was in fact a
group of four young monks involved in the Tengboche story, who acted in
some respects much as the nuns who founded Devuche did. These men had
taken vows in Tibet, but then had returned to the Sherpa area, where they
formed their own little community under the tutelage of a higher-ranking

lama. Eventually, they became the first group of Tengboche monks. The anology between the proto-monastery formation among these monks before the founding of Tengboche, and the proto-nunnery formation among the nuns (who, it will be recalled, lived and practiced religion together before the nunnery was founded) is most suggestive. And in the case of a later-founded monastery (Thami), for which we have much more information, it is quite clear that grass-roots efforts on the part of certain monks played a major role in the process. The point of all this is that the founding of Tengboche may have been less of a "big man" initiated event than appears from the accounts we are given.

Yet if the founding of Tengboche was less fully a product of the initiative of the big leaders, motivated by macro-political considerations, than would appear from the accounts, I would also argue that the founding of Devuche, for its part, was more a matter of "public" politics than would appear from the accounts. I have already suggested, in considering why Sherpa individuals might take monastic vows, that a gender-based analysis might be less useful than an analysis grounded in analogous structural disadvantages. The same point may now be applied, *mutatis mutandis*, to the interpretation of the foundings of the nunnery and the monastery. The young nuns and monks involved in these events, if similarly *dis*advantaged (by gender in one case and birth order in the other), were also similarly *ad*vantaged. As has been noted, most of them were from relatively high-status families. They were thus, in effect, the collective children of the class of men whose political legitimation needs loom so important in the founding of Tengboche. But insofar as the young people's fathers' positions were changing, *so too were theirs*, a point that would have become particularly apparent, to both parents and children, as the children approached the stage of marriage and property devolution. Although such arrangements are always somewhat problematic, they may have been particularly so at this historical moment, with the fathers' positions and estates only newly established.

It is possible, then, that the young monks and nuns *shared* some of their fathers' interests in founding the religious institutions—contributing to the consolidation of the prestige of their families, and providing respected positions for themselves and future daughters and middle sons of this class who might otherwise lose status and/or suffer economic decline at the point of marriage and the division of property. It is equally possible, however, that the young nuns and monks saw themselves as *rebelling* against the pressures coming down on them as the second generation of the new elite—that they saw themselves as rejecting these new (or newly intensified) games of status and power. Ngawang Samden's history, for example, shows her to have played both sides of the fence: On the one hand she ran away from home and took nun's vows to avoid an undesirable marriage arrangement. It is likely that this betrothal was politically motivated, since the prospective husband—described as "wealthy"—already had a wife, and polygyny (which is very rare in any case) only occurs among "big men." On the other hand, when it came time to raise funds for the furnishing of the nunnery temple, Ngawang Samden turned to her two powerful brothers for help, and drew upon their influence and their contacts.

One way or the other (or both), however, the point is this: the dynamics eventuating in the foundings of Devuche and Tengboche were probably pretty much the same. The two cases do not contrast, with the founding of Tengboche as more "politically" motivated, and the founding of Devuche as motivated more by women's "domestic" concerns. Rather, they shared the same motivating structure, which may be summarized as the *domestic* fallout (on the second generation of a certain socioeconomic sector) of major changes in the *public* domain. That the actors in the drama perceived the commonalities of their positions is perhaps visible in all the personal contributions—of money and labor—made by the Tengboche monks to the founding of Devuche nunnery.

Conclusions

To the extent that women are excluded from positions of leadership and public initiative, we tend to think of them as excluded from the public domain. We sometimes forget, however, that most men are excluded from leadership and public initiative as well, and so we succumb to what might be called, not the male bias, but the "big man bias" in social science analysis. This bias prevents us from seeing the degree to which many men are as disadvantaged as women with respect as property, marriage, and the like. At the same time, it also prevents us from seeing that women, however much their day-to-day lives appear immersed in domestic concerns, systematically participate in the larger social rankings of their natal and marital families, and so participate in important ways in macro-political and economic processes. This, I think, is part of what Rosaldo was getting at in attacking the domestic/public opposition as a device for analyzing gender problems, and in attacking more generally the emphasis on gender "difference" in much of current feminist scholarship.

If these points are accepted, then we must seriously consider whether we create as many problems as we solve by insisting on "women" and "men" as bounded analytic categories in and of themselves. Do we not in fact aggravate the very problem we seek to counter—the hegemony of gender distinction as a basis for organizing social life and thought? Sexism, of course, is real enough. It is still the case, in the material just discussed, that women are disadvantaged in various ways simply by virtue of being women, while the same is not true of men. If it is *this* that we wish to understand, then of course we must look for "difference." Yet an over-emphasis on difference, regardless of context, can create serious mystifications in our analyses, blinding us to the disadvantages women share with many (if not indeed most) men, and allowing us to sweep under the rug the many real advantages that *some* women share with *some* men.

There is, of course, both heuristic and practical value in utilizing polarized male/female categories. Heuristically, we gain the capacity to see the (ideal-typical) genders as cultural constructs, and we begin to ask questions about how and why such constructs are organized the way they are in different cultures and historical periods (e.g., Ortner and Whitehead 1981). On the practical level, further, there is perhaps no other way to organize against sexism than to try to get women together *as women*, regardless of other social differences. (That such an effort has not succeeded, and that the women's movement is essentially bounded by class and race, is not, however, irrelevant to the point I am making here).

Granting certain contexts of usefulness for operating with pure female/male analytic oppositions, and with pure women/men political oppositions, we must at the same time be aware that there are real dangers in such a position. Specifically, an emphasis on "women" as an analytic category, when pushed too hard, tends to move in the direction of a very problematic naturalism—another of Michelle Rosaldo's points. That is, there is a tendency to slip from an "as if" posture, in which we isolate gender categories for heuristic (or political) reasons, to an assumption that "women" in some global and sociologically unqualified sense really exist out there in the world, as a natural class of objects with their own distinctive attributes. This tendency, I think, is part of what is behind certain problematic directions in current feminist theory, which concentrate heavily on female physiology, sexuality, and reproductivity. Personally, I thought the whole point of feminism was to bring about a situation in which women were *not* seen as a natural class of being, defined primarily by their bodies.

Then again, a more structurally based perspective on gender relations, such as the one taken in this paper, has its own problems. Most seriously, it threatens to lose gender and women as significant analytic categories in their own right, and to merge them with, or dissolve them into, other structures of social inequality. Thus, for example, while showing the parallels of structural advantage and disadvantage between Sherpa women and some Sherpa men, I was put in the position of playing down both the ideology of male privilege, and the actual male control of all significant leadership positions. Ultimately, then, we will have to learn to tread that fine line between reifying (and thereby "naturalizing") the genders on the one hand, and, on the other, allowing the male/female distinction to disappear back into the fog of gender-insensitive "variables" from which it has only recently been rescued.

Gender Hegemonies

Back in the early seventies, in the fresh years of the feminist movement, anthropologists were often asked about matriarchies. Was it not the case, people wanted to know, that there were societies in which women had the kind of power and authority men have in our own society? With a reasonable degree of unanimity, anthropologists said no.[1] Well then, continued the questioners, weren't there matriarchies in the past? Here there was somewhat less unanimity among the anthropologists, but by and large no professional scholar in the field was willing to make a strong claim for any past matriarchies either.

And how about egalitarian societies? Here the anthropological consensus fell apart completely. The first round of responses to the egalitarianism question, or at least the first round to receive widespread attention, consisted of several articles published in the 1974 Rosaldo and Lamphere collection, *Woman, Culture, and Society*. In our respective essays, Michelle Rosaldo, Nancy Chodorow, and I (this volume, pp. 21–42) all rather firmly said no, that men were in some way or other "the first sex" in all known societies, that there were no truly sex egalitarian societies in the world. Later, in 1981, Harriet Whitehead and I coedited a collection of articles on the cultural construction of gender and sexuality (*Sexual Meanings*), and, seeing no reason at that time to revise the universalist position, we reaffirmed it.

But quite a few anthropologists disagreed, and one or another of their reactions to the universalist claim has continued to appear in print since the publication of *Sexual Meanings*. At first I was not inclined to respond. I believed that interested and/or skeptical readers could evaluate the evidence themselves and that they would arrive at conclusions matching those set forth in *Sexual Meanings*. Yet the critiques kept mounting, and eventually it seemed that I had to either defend or revise my position.

The Debate

Let us begin by sorting out some terminology. There seem to be at least three separable dimensions of the phenomenon of relative gender status. These three dimensions may covary closely in a given empirical case, but they will not necessarily do so, and to confuse them is to create a hopeless conceptual muddle. Part of the disagreement between the universalists and the nonuniversalists derives from confusion over the level of discussion.

There is first of all, then, the dimension of relative prestige,[2] as in a claim that men are "the first sex" and women are "the second," or that men are preeminent, or have "higher status," or are accorded greater cultural value of charisma, or have greater authority. In all of these statements, what is at issue is a culturally affirmed, relative evaluation or ranking of the sexes, something that is perhaps most commonly called "status." Nothing is said here about the quality of male-female relations, or about male and female behaviors.

Quite distinct from this issue is the question of male dominance and female subordination. These are terms describing a particular kind of relationship, in which men exert control over women's behavior (with varying kinds and degrees of legitimacy/authority for doing so) and women find themselves compelled to conform to men's demands. An emphasis on female "autonomy" pertains to this level of discussion, since autonomy is indeed (one) obverse of domination.[3] Again, factors of dominance and factors of prestige may vary independently of one another, and this has been a major source of confusion in the debate over the universality of "male dominance."

Finally, there is the question of female power, which again seems to be largely distinct. Here there is a presumption that neither greater male prestige nor actual male dominance, nor both, however extreme, could wholly negate women's capacity (again, with varying kinds and degrees of legitimacy/authority) to control some spheres of their own and others' existences and to determine some aspects of their own and others' behavior. "Female power" refers to these capacities and may be considered to some extent as separate from the other two levels.

The first thing to note about the universalism debate, then, is that the authors who took the position that gender asymmetry is universal were talking essentially about prestige and not about either male dominance (which was taken to be variable rather than universal) or female power (which was granted to be present in varying degrees in all cases). None of the authors ever claimed that men directly "dominate" women in any normal sense of the term in all known cultures, nor did any of them ever claim that universal male prestige negates all female power. A reasonable reading of the 1974 essays by Rosaldo, Chodorow, and Ortner, or of the introduction to *Sexual Meanings*, shows that the language was not primarily that of domination or power but rather of prestige, charisma, and status.

The universalists' claim, then, was that it was in some sense culturally accepted in every known society that men have greater prestige and/or status, whether or not they exert dominance over women and whether or not women have a great deal of official or unofficial power. Broadly speaking, there have been two quite different reactions to this position. In one, it is agreed that explicit or tacit cultural assumptions of male superiority are universal, but it is argued that these cultural assumptions are undercut in practice by various forms of on-the-ground female power. In the other reaction, it is denied that men have culturally defined greater prestige than women in all societies. I will examine each of these positions briefly.

The first view emphasizes the importance of "balancing off" or weighing cultural attributions of male prestige and status, on the one hand, and, on the other, the realities of practical life in which women have a great deal of power and influence. In this view, even societies that may appear at first glance to be quite asymmetrical may be shown analytically to have a certain type of sex equality. Thus, Susan Carol Rogers (1975) argues, using French peasants as her example, that men have less power than they appear to have and women have more, so that there is actually a balance; this balance is maintained by what she calls "the myth of male dominance," in which both sexes sustain the formal notion that men are superior to women and have greater prestige and status (1975: 746). Later she says more directly that there is a "power/prestige balance" between men's and women's spheres (1975: 747). Similarly, Peggy Sanday, in her widely read and widely assigned *Female Power and Male Dominance* (1981), argues for establishing a category of societies with "sexual equality." Confining herself to "the

level of secular politics" (that is, power), Sanday says that "male suprema-
cism or sexual asymmetry is not as widespread as some anthropologists
have argued" (1981: 8). She then picks up Rogers's notion of "mythical
male dominance," in which men are given a token sort of prestige but
women make many of the important decisions, as "a form of balanced sexual opposition" (1981: 168).

My objections to this position in the past have been twofold: first, prestige and power cannot be "balanced" against one another. Weighing on-
the-ground female power against male status and prestige is like trying to
add the proverbial apples and oranges: without cultural prestige, female
power is not fully legitimate and can only be exercised in hidden and/or dis-
torted ("manipulative") ways. And second, as these points imply, I have
continued to consider the cultural assertion/acceptance of male superiority
to be definitive. If men in a given society have culturally stated higher status,
then by definition this is a "male dominant" or gender asymmetrical society, regardless of how much de facto power women may exert.

It should be noted that both Rogers and Sanday agree with the universal
male dominance position at a certain level: they agree that *cultural assertions* of greater male prestige are universal. As Rogers asks (in some de-
spair) at the end of her vehemently argued paper, "Why is it that men always
seem to play a dominant role, if not actually, then at least mythically?"
(1975: 753).

It is precisely on this point, however, that proponents of the second anti-
universalist position would disagree. In this view, associated most prominently with the work of Eleanor Leacock (1981), it is asserted that there are
culturally defined egalitarian societies in the world—mostly hunting/gath-
ering societies—in which greater male prestige and status are not asserted
or assumed in the first place. Universalists like myself, Whitehead, etc., ignore or misread those cases, not because they fail to give due weight to female power but because they fail to see that these societies are put together
on quite different ("egalitarian") principles. Like the other theorists, Leacock prominently uses the phrase "the myth of male dominance," but she
means by that not some cultural ideology the natives endorse. Rather it is a
"myth" created by analysts who take the universalist position. (See also
Poewe, who called it "an ethnological illusion" [1980: 111].)

Leacock's arguments seem problematic in a number of ways. For one
thing, her expectations of equality in simple societies seem largely derived
from her theoretical framework—a slightly updated version of Engels's no-

tions of "primitive communalism," as set forth in *The Origin of the Family, Private Property, and the State*—rather than from any actual ethnographic case(s). For another, she seems to set up her examinations of cases in a sort of heads-I-win-tails-you-lose way, such that any instance of *in*equality in simple societies could not be indigenous; it has to be a product of capitalist penetration, observer bias, or both. In point of fact, modern informants in the group she uses as her prime example of gender egalitarianism did say that men were superior, but she discounts these assertions as effects of long-term capitalist penetration (Leacock 1980).

At this point we have all reached an impasse. There is no point in trying to look for more or better cases, since what is at issue is precisely the interpretation of cases. But fresh interpretations require fresh theoretical perspectives, and these must be considered next.

On the Mutual Illumination of Feminist Theory and Theories of Social Value ("Prestige")

Whitehead's and my interest in *Sexual Meanings* was to arrive at the most powerful ways of interpreting gender ideologies, of discovering the different logics that different cultures use in constructing their notions of male and female, sexuality and reproduction. In addition, we sought to locate those aspects of cultural thought and social practice that seemed to exert the strongest force in shaping those cultural logics. Our conclusion was that it was cultural notions and practices related to "prestige" that seemed to provide the most powerful interpretive keys for understanding the social and cultural ordering of gender, sexuality, and reproduction cross-culturally. We argued further that there is a simple reason for this fact: it is because gender is itself centrally a prestige system—a system of discourses and practices that constructs male and female not only in terms of differential roles and meanings but also in terms of differential *value*, differential "prestige."

I would still argue that prestige is central to understanding the logic of gender discourse and practices. I also think, however, that there are limitations to the concept that need to be faced and overcome. Thus it will be useful to look more closely at some past uses of "prestige" in social science discourse. It is Max Weber who, more than any other theorist, draws out the implications of the distinction between prestige categories and political/economic ones (Weber 1958, 1978). In the realm of class relations, he distinguishes between classes and status groups; in the realm of politics, he distinguishes between power and authority. In both cases there is a category defined largely in terms of "hard" social realities of some sort (economic position, political domination) and a category defined largely in terms of cultural values of what is socially worthy and morally good.

Weber's ultimate interests were processual: he was concerned to observe how these elements interact with one another over time. Thus he was interested (for example) in the decline of aristocracies that had high social status but little economic power, and in the ways in which a rising political group sought and gained cultural legitimacy. But with the waning of a historical perspective in the social sciences, what remains of Weber's processual model is simply a set of dualistically opposed categories—status and class, prestige and power—which in turn become lined up with other dualisms— the soft and the hard, Weber vs. Marx, Idealism vs. Materialism.

The oppositional construction of the relationship between prestige and power in contemporary social science is perhaps best seen in Louis Dumont's important book about the caste hierarchy in India, *Homo Hierarchicus*. Dumont argues that there is, within Indian culture itself, a radical split between prestige and power. The Brahmins have no political power and, in many regions, very little economic power as well, yet Brahmins have preeminence in terms of prestige, and as a result their values are the hegemonic values of Indian society. Prestige and power are opposed and seemingly have little influence on each other. The power of the Kshatriya caste, from which are drawn the warriors and the rulers of political society, appears marginal and almost unreal in Dumont's book.

The oppositional construction of the relationship between prestige and power has in turn established a set of perennial and by now somewhat fruitless debates over which term is the controlling term of the opposition. Does prestige in effect "neutralize" power, as in Dumont's arguments about Brahmins and Kshatriyas? Or, on the other hand, is power the reality and prestige simply the myth, power the base and prestige the (dispensable) superstructure? Or—to return to the male dominance debate—can there be such a thing as a "power/prestige balance" in which men have prestige but little power, while women have power but little prestige?

In *Sexual Meanings*, Whitehead and I tended toward a Dumontian perspective, emphasizing the cultural level of prestige and giving little systematic attention to the practices of power. This no longer seems an adequate position—the "cultural level of prestige" and "the practices of power" cannot be divorced from one another, as Weber himself recognized, and as anyone concerned with social practice would recognize today.[4] This paper thus represents, in part, an attempt to return to the historical dynamism of Weber's argument, in which one distinguishes between power and prestige not to eliminate one or the other or to try to add them together, but in order to see how they interact.

But there are other dimensions to rethinking the prestige problematic as well, in terms of reconceptualizing the way in which "prestige" is socially present. In *Sexual Meanings* Whitehead and I spoke of "prestige structures" and "prestige systems," with the terms "structure" and "system" intended to stress the point that there is a kind of logic and order to cultural frameworks of social evaluation, a logic that is pervasively embedded in language, ideology, institutions, and the practices of social life. These points are still important and are not being rescinded here. But the terms "structure" and "system" carry several problematic implications. For one thing, there is an implication of singularity and of totalization: a "society" or a "culture" appears as a single "system" or as ordered by a single "structure," which embraces (or pervades) virtually every aspect of that social and cultural universe. For another, there is an implication of ahistoricity: systems or structures presumably must change, but the basic mode of systems analysis or structural analysis has been to look for the synchronic integration of the elements rather than for their transformations over time. And third, there is an implication of functionality: systems or structures are either explicitly (in the case of Parsonian systems theory) or implicitly (in the case of Lévi-Straussian structuralism) beneficial to the people who live within them, socially functional and/or "good to think," and there is virtually no examination of the ways in which they might articulate and indeed embody politically biased arrangements.

If for all these reasons, then, one would greatly restrict the terminologies of system and structure, one finds oneself with a real problem of language. It would not be unreasonable to speak of cultural prestige orders as "discourses"—which indeed they are—except that "discourse" has a largely linguistic connotation, whereas prestige categories and evaluations are embedded not only in language and symbolic representation but also in practices and in institutions. Raymond Williams's concept of "hegemony," adapted from Gramsci, is explicitly articulated against the traps of singularity, ahistoricity, and functionality associated with earlier frameworks. A cross between the anthropological concept of culture and the Marxist concept of ideology, it embodies the pervasiveness of culture and the biased nature of ideology. It also captures the combination of explicit discursive expression and practical and institutional embeddedness being sought here:

> "Hegemony" goes beyond "culture," as previously defined, in its insistence on relating the "whole social process" to specific distributions of power and influence. To say that "men" define and shape their whole lives is true only in abstraction. In any actual society there are specific inequalities in means and therefore in capacity to realize this process. . . . It is in [the] recognition of the *wholeness* of the process that the concept of "hegemony" goes beyond "ideology." What is decisive is not only the conscious system of ideas and beliefs, but the whole lived social process as practically organized by specific and dominant meanings and values. (Williams 1977: 108–9)

While the term "hegemony" is not perfect either, and other theoretical languages will probably slip in from time to time, it does carry most of the theoretical benefits we need.

My central argument will be as follows: no society or culture is totally consistent. Every society/culture has some axes of male prestige and some of female, some of gender equality, and some (sometimes many) axes of prestige that have nothing to do with gender at all. The problem in the past has been that all of us engaged in this debate were trying to pigeonhole each case (is it male dominant or not?) either through data purification (explaining away the inconvenient bits of information) or through trying to add up the bits and arrive at a score (add a point for balanced division of labor, subtract a point for prevalent wife beating, etc.). I will argue here, however, that the most interesting thing about any given case is precisely the multiplicity of logics operating, of discourses being spoken, of practices of prestige and power in play. Some of these are dominant—"hegemonic." Some are explicitly counterhegemonic—subversive, challenging. Others are simply "there," "other," "different," present because they are products of imagination that did not seem to threaten any particular set of arrangements. The analytic question will be precisely that of the relationship between the elements, both at a given moment and—ideally—across time.

Looked at in this way, the view of the ethnographic record on the question of universal male dominance does indeed appear quite different. There are clearly societies with what must be described as egalitarian hegemonies. Are there some elements of exclusive male authority in those societies? Of course there are. Does that make those societies "male dominant"? It would be absurd to claim that they do, although the question of the relationship between those elements and the prevailing hegemony, both within and across time, must be looked at very carefully and not explained away. From this point of view we are also prepared to recognize some female-centered hegemonies, to which the same caveats would apply.[5] And finally, we would argue that the same sort of approach should be taken with respect to male dominant hegemonies: are there counterhegemonies and "loose ends" (of egalitarianism, and of female authority) in these systems? Of course there are. Thus their relations to the hegemonic order past, present, and future must be analyzed.[6]

I have found that viewing prestige orders as hegemonies—that is, as culturally dominant and relatively deeply embedded but nonetheless historically emergent, politically constructed, and nontotalistic—is analytically quite liberating. It means that all the pieces of a given ethnographic instance do not have either to fit together through heroic analytic efforts or to be explained away. The loose ends, the contradictory bits, the disconnected sections can be examined for their short- and long-term interactions with and implications for one another.[7] This does not mean that everything has equal analytic weight and plays the same sort of role in the overall dynamic. There *is* an ordering—a "hegemony" in the sense of a relative dominance of some meanings and practices over others. It is both this ordering and *its potential dis-ordering* in which I am interested.

Egalitarian Societies? The Andaman Islands Case

It will be recalled that Eleanor Leacock, among others, argued that there are what might be called "culturally egalitarian" societies in which there is no indigenous ideology of asymmetrical gender prestige, of greater male social value and status. I said that this claim represents a more serious challenge to the universalist claim than the attempts to argue for a prestige/power "balance," since it works from the same premises as the universalist arguments: the insistence on the encompassing status of prestige valuations—in this case, egalitarian valuations. In the past I was not convinced by the cases put forth as examples of such culturally egalitarian societies. They all seemed to have one or another flaw that allowed one to dismiss them as, in effect, tainted with male dominance. Thus, for example, in reviewing the case of the Crow Indians in an earlier paper, I point out that women seemed to have a wide range of rights of participation, even to high offices in "the public domain" (Ortner 1972; this volume, p. 24). Yet I fasten on some evidence of menstrual pollution and use this to reclassify the case as "male dominant." How would such cases now appear, in light of the theoretical discussions just presented?

The case I have chosen for reconsideration of this question is that of the Andaman Islanders, who were brought to my attention as a relevant example by Mary Klages in an outstanding Dartmouth College undergraduate thesis (1980). The Andaman Islanders have the additional virtue of not having already been chewed over in the universal male dominance debate, and so it seems possible to look at them with a relatively fresh eye.[8]

A few words first about the nature of the sources. By far the best study of the Andaman Islanders was published in 1883 by a British administrator called—rather charmingly for the present context—E. H. Man. Man spent eleven years in the Andamans and describes himself as having acquired "a fair knowledge of the South Andaman dialect" (Man 1883: 69). A. R. Radcliffe-Brown later worked in several different parts of the area over a two-year period (1906–1908) and is candid about his difficulties with the language and his use of interpreters (Radcliffe-Brown 1922: viii). These two works provide the bulk of the source material for this discussion, with some supplementation from other sources.

There are many problems in using these sources. Man had certain very obvious Christian biases[9] and also probably a variety of "administrative" biases that are less immediately visible. As for Radcliffe-Brown, it has been argued with reference to another context that he actively discriminated against female colleagues; this might imply significant male bias in his ethnographic work as well (Rohrlich-Leavitt et al. 1975). In my readings of their texts, I have tried to work against the grain of these biases as much as possible. The major limitation on doing so, I have found, is the fact that neither author presents virtually any account of the people's own views of what things meant. In general, my strategy is to try to establish meaning contextually, putting bits of information together with other bits to suggest particular lines of cultural "thinking" or cultural valuation.

After a very careful and self-critical reading of the source material, then, I have concluded that it is reasonable to argue that the Andaman Islanders (and probably many other "simple" societies) did indeed have an egalitarian hegemony, which is to say that there was a very strong cultural tendency to render male and female roles and statuses equal and complementary.[10] This egalitarianism was largely embedded in language and in practices, rather than in formal ideology. The first part of the discussion, then, will be to sketch the various dimensions of this practical hegemony. I will then examine certain patterns of male power and/or prestige and consider their relationships to the egalitarian order.

It is important to note that the hegemony of egalitarianism is not meant to be seen as an "ideology," contrasted with some "reality" of domination and inequality lurking beneath the surface. This is not a base-and-superstructure model. To say that the egalitarianism is hegemonic is to say that it pervades a variety of domains and/or "levels" that, in a different framework, might have been parceled out between the "base" and the "superstructure." The relevant distinction concerns those modes of social and cultural life that are ordered by the hegemonic (here, egalitarian) assumptions and those that are not encompassed/pervaded by them and are organized on different principles.

PATTERNS OF EQUIVALENCE AND EQUALITY

Before starting the discussion, I must warn the reader that in what follows I present only a relatively sketchy and compressed account of the relevant ethnographic information. Anthropologists may well find the discussions too sketchy (while lay readers may find them too detailed!). In general I have tried not to put in any unnecessary detail but believe at the same time that no relevant information has been omitted.[11]

The Andaman Islanders' division of labor, first, appears to have been relatively balanced—men hunted or fished, women gathered; everyone seems to have done a lot of child tending. It also appears relatively flexible, such that women might go on collective hunts, men might do a lot of gathering in certain seasons, and both men and women might jointly gather honey (which is highly valued). Both men and women worked on hut building, men cutting and erecting posts, women collecting leaves and weaving the mats for the roofs. Men and women made their own respective tools and artifacts.

As noted above, the exegesis is not available that would tell us how the people themselves assigned value to these various tasks. We read these items as pieces of an egalitarian picture partly because they fit with theoretical expectations derived from other cases (e.g., relatively *in*flexible divisions of labor—as in Mediterranean societies—seem to go with "hard" gender distinctions and strong "male dominance" [see Sweet 1967]), and partly because they fit with further details of the Andaman case itself to be presented here. I ask the reader's patience as I try to build the case.

One may also speak of a division of labor in social spheres. Men made intergroup feuds, but women were the active parties in making peace, and this was a very prominent social and ritual role for them. Men composed and sang songs, and this was a source of male prestige (women formed the chorus); but women alone did body scarification and body decoration, and this was a source of female prestige. Women also made certain kinds of highly prized necklaces from the bones of the dead, and these were always in great demand for medicinal purposes, being both used and exchanged. Men divided and shared hunted meat according to prescribed patterns.

In terms of ritual treatment, young men and women were given very similar initiations. Both were subjected to similar food taboos. Both were said to be in a state of "hotness" or apparent pollution (largely to themselves) during their respective phases of seclusion. Socially, both were accorded similar freedoms as adolescents, moving out of their parents' huts and into adolescent residences.[12] Sexual intercourse was said to have been "promiscuous" before marriage, marriages often being brought about by the boy and girl forming their own attachment. Some marriages were arranged, but the arrangements were made by all parents. There seems to have been no question of men exchanging women. If there could be said to have been any exchange of persons at all, it was an "exchange" of children in widespread patterns of adoption and fosterage (often operating as child betrothals). Postmarital residence was optional for the couple, who might choose to reside near either the wife's or the husband's parents, or even elsewhere if they so chose.

At the wedding, both bride and groom were lectured on fidelity. After marriage, there was an explicit single standard, and both husband and wife were expected to be faithful to one another. An adulterous man was said to lose prestige in the community.[13] Concerning the birth of children, in late stages of pregnancy both husband and wife had to observe similar or identical food taboos, lest the child, or the husband and wife themselves, become ill. With the birth of the first child, the couple moved into full adult status. The egalitarianism and level of affection of the husband-wife relationship was worthy of special comment by Man:

> [O]ne of the most striking features of their social relations is the marked equality and affection which subsists between husband and wife; careful observations extending over many years prove that not only is the husband's authority more or less nominal, but that it is not at all an uncommon occurrence for Andamanese Benedicts to be con-

siderably at the beck and call of their better halves; in short, the consideration and respect with which women are treated might with advantage be emulated by certain classes in our own land. (Man 1883: 327)

Concerning community influence or "leadership," the question of equivalence gets a bit trickier, and—depending on one's reading—men may seem to have had a slight edge. Thus Man describes a system of "chiefs" and specifically says that "females (like minors) . . . cannot be chiefs" (1883: 109). He goes on to say, however, that "females . . . have a similar position relatively among the women, to that held by their husbands among the men of the tribe" (ibid.), and that "chiefs . . . and their wives are at liberty to enjoy immunity from the drudgery incidental to their mode of life, all such acts being voluntarily performed for them by the young unmarried persons living under their headship" (ibid.). Similarly, Radcliffe-Brown says that "the affairs of the community are regulated entirely by the older men and women" (1922: 44) and that "[w]omen may occupy a position of influence similar to that of the men" (1922: 46). It would seem that the relevant social unit for purposes of leadership is actually the senior couple, rather than the classic male "chief." I will return to this point later.

Finally, one may look at the realm of the spirits and the supernatural. The information here is particularly vague, contradictory, and confusing. Radcliffe-Brown himself complains about it, although he is unsure as to whether the apparently poor quality was the result of his own linguistic deficiencies or whether the confusions and contradictions are objectively present in the culture. Skipping all the details, we may say that the supernatural level, like the level of human social relations, appears to have been relatively balanced. Supernatural beings of both sexes played significant, generally complementary, and sometimes reversible roles. The most prominent divinity was a figure of variable (but usually female) gender who had as much power and authority as any male supernatural figure, if not more.

Again, I have been able to present only a sketchy account of the Andaman Islanders' gender patterns, in turn derived from less than ideal sources. Nonetheless, I consider the picture that emerges to be reasonably describable as an egalitarian hegemony in the sense that, although the Andaman Islanders did not seem to elaborate an ideology around it, there was a pervasive structuring of relations and practices in an egalitarian direction. The main dimensions of this picture are as follows: there seems to have been both quantitative and qualitative balance in assigned sex roles and flexibil-

ity in the enactment of sex roles. Men and women seem to have been ex-
pected/entitled to participate equally in all forms of social relations (child
care, production, exchange, leadership, intergroup relations, etc.) and appear to have been treated equally—or comparably—in ritual. Both sexes
had sources of personal creativity and prestige that were admired by the
group as a whole. Most of the features that correlate with strong male dominance cross-culturally were absent. There were no hard-edged male and female "spheres," no inflexible policing of gender boundaries, no radical
asymmetries in the division of labor. Further, there was no obvious "male
dominance": men did not control production, did not control the marriage
system, did not have exclusive access to leadership, and did not have secret
and/or male-only rituals. Men and women appeared to have respected one
another.

CORRELATES OF EQUALITY

The Andaman Island society had several features that have been remarked
on in earlier theoretical discussions as correlates (even, if one were given to
such language, "predictors") of egalitarian gender relations. The first is that
gender does not appear to have been the dominant axis or order of prestige.
In another context, I have argued that gender tends to be constructed in a
more egalitarian way when prestige or social honor is allocated primarily
on nongender grounds—on the basis of age or hereditary rank, for example
(Ortner 1981; this volume, p. 107).

    In fact, as we have seen, both Man and Radcliffe-Brown provide indica-
tions of an alternative, basically gender-undifferentiated, prestige hegemony for the Andaman Islanders: a pattern of age-defined statuses and obligations. Juniors of both sexes owed respect, obedience, gifts, and services
to seniors, while seniors owed love, care, consideration, and protection to
juniors. We saw the point earlier, when Man says that senior men and
women were exempt from most work, which was done for them by juniors.[14] Radcliffe-Brown describes the pattern in similar ways: "There is no
organized government in an Andamanese village. The affairs of the community are regulated entirely by the older men and women. The younger
members of the community are brought up to pay respect to their elders and
to submit to them in many ways. . . . The respect for seniors is shown in the
existence of special terms of address which men and women use when
speaking to their elders" (Radcliffe-Brown 1922: 46). The widespread patterns of "child exchange," or adoption and fosterage, fit in with these points

as well. The fact that parents exchanged children (both in general forms of adoption and in child betrothals), while men did not "exchange" women (as is the common construction of many marriage systems cross-culturally), indicates again that age and generation were more significant axes of authority than was gender.[15]

The second feature of Andaman society that was consistent with the egalitarian gender hegemony and that was forecast by earlier theorizing on the subject was the virtual absence of "genderization" of domestic and public domains. We need to take a moment here to say a few words about the domestic/public opposition. It will be recalled that Michelle Rosaldo (1974) speculates that sexual asymmetry is grounded in the tendency for men to occupy the "public" sphere of social life, while women tend to operate largely within the "domestic" sphere. The reason for this differing preponderance of the sexes in the two spheres has to do with the mother role: mothering activities tend to restrict those who do them—mostly women—to the domestic realm, whereas men, who are not so restricted, are free to monopolize the realm of public affairs. The Rosaldo framework has been subjected to several critiques, including one of her own (1980). The issues are complex, and space prohibits addressing them in any detailed way here. Rosaldo's own critique, picking up on points raised by Sylvia Yanagisako (1979), is that binary oppositions like domestic/public necessarily carry cultural baggage about the supposedly inherent differences between women and men; rather than opening up the question of the politics of these terms—of how those supposedly inherent differences got assigned to the genders in the first place—the continuing analytic deployment of the oppositions simply carries along the old baggage.[16]

My view is that Rosaldo is somewhat hasty in dropping a distinction that, as she says elsewhere in her article, is "as telling as any explanation yet put forth" for universal male dominance, at least as the question was posed at that time (1980: 399). I agree that the domestic/public distinction as such may tend to presuppose certain gender differences that should not be presupposed, but it also embodies some very useful distinctions that should not, I think, be thrown out. In particular, I would pick up on a point set out somewhat in passing in the Introduction to *Sexual Meanings*. There Whitehead and I proposed that all the oppositions so frequently used to characterize the implicit logic behind the male/female split—domestic/public, nature/culture, self-interest/social good, particularistic/universalistic—could be resolved by observing that "the sphere of social activity predominantly associated with males encompasses the sphere predominantly associated with females and is, for that reason, culturally accorded higher value" (Ortner and Whitehead 1981: 8). The more general distinction thus is that of encompassing/encompassed (which carries no particular gender implication in itself), and the central characteristics of this distinction have to do with such things as universal/particular, collective welfare/individual interest, and so forth. In any given culture, these abstract distinctions, which are approximations of general social orientations rather than places or things, will nonetheless be concretely embodied in places and/or roles and/or practices of the mundane world, including quite commonly, though not universally, the places and/or practices that we shorthand as the domestic and the public.[17]

In retaining a distinction like that between sites of social life that are "encompassing"—that make claims (often untrue) of operating in the interests of the whole—and sites that are "encompassed"—that operate with respect to more local and particular interests—I do not propose ramming it uncritically through every ethnographic and historical case. But, since it has been shown *empirically* that such distinctions often link up in complex and problematic ways with the gender distinction, I retain it as a potentially powerful point of leverage in looking at specific cases and inquiring about their dynamics. The point is always to ask how encompassing and encompassed sites and projects of social life are distinguished, organized, and interrelated in a given society, to inquire into the underlying politics of these distinctions and interrelations, to ask whether a given culture does or does not fuse a gender opposition to these more abstract dimensions of social value, and finally, and very importantly, to examine the ways in which such fusions are used, contested, and sometimes effectively shifted over time. Returning then finally to the Andaman Islanders and to the question of the ways in which the apparent egalitarianism of the gender order might line up with prior theoretical expectations, I said a moment ago that there is a virtual *absence* of cultural genderization of domestic and public domains. Using here a commonsense image of domestic and public, with domestic as the household and public as associated with both public spaces and trans-household activities, we have seen that men and women participated equally, equivalently, and complementarily in all the affairs related to the household (provisioning and child care) and to the public domain (singing in the plaza, being initiated, settling disputes, making war/peace). This absence of gender exclusivity in both domains (or, as some might say, the absence of a domain split, period) is precisely the situation in which, according to Rosaldo's original model, one would expect to find relative sex equality (Rosaldo 1974: 40–41).

The egalitarian hegemony of Andaman society is thus both empirically visible in the ethnographies and consistent with theoretical expectations. But, as noted earlier, there were a few elements that stood outside this hegemony. There were in fact two ritual roles that were implicitly (in one case) and explicitly (in the other) reserved for men. The first was the role of shaman, involved primarily with controlling the weather and other spirit-caused misfortunes. The second was the role of the ritual performers who released the initiates from their eating taboos at the end of the initiation rites. I will examine each of them briefly, in terms of their relationship to the egalitarian hegemony.

ELEMENTS OF INEQUALITY

Concerning the role of shaman, Man says that they were "invariably of the male sex."[18] Shamans were thought to be able to communicate with the spirits involved in causing storms and illness. Man portrays the shamans quite negatively, as extorting gifts and favors from people because people were afraid of the shamans' supernatural powers: "It is thought that they can bring trouble, sickness, and death upon those who fail to evince their belief in them in some substantial form; they thus generally manage to obtain the best of everything, for it is considered foolhardy to deny them, and they do not scruple to ask for any article to which they may take a fancy" (1883: 96). Man portrays them as in a sense abusing the kinds of authority that normally gave elders the right to ask for and accept gifts without return: "Sometimes, owing to the multiplicity of these gifts, it is inconvenient to the [shaman] to take charge of them; he then enters into an arrangement with the donors that such articles as he does not at present need shall be available for his use or appropriation whenever he may require them" (1883: 53).

If there is truth to this portrayal, then the shamans, though performing necessary functions of weather and illness control, violated the hegemony in several respects: in their exclusive maleness, in their special powers for harming others, and in their exploitation of the senior/junior gifting relationship. The shamans thus tended toward a kind of dominance that was not countenanced elsewhere in the culture.

It is difficult to evaluate the status of the shaman within Andaman Island society. Even assuming Man's descriptions to be accurate (and, because of his religious biases, this assumption may not be justified), we have no idea whether these individuals were respected or simply feared. We do know that many cultures have roles involving the inversion of the culture's central values. The classical interpretation is that such roles confirm the hegemony through its inversion, by providing a glimpse of the undesirability of alternatives. This interpretation may be applicable here: if indeed, as Man implies, shamans were not respected but simply feared, then their relationship to the egalitarian hegemony may have had this "perverse" quality, providing the negative image of the unequal (male dominant, power dominant) life.

One might also look at a seemingly contradictory institution/practice like this as a possible node of historical transformation. This point will be more central to the discussion of the Hawaiian case, where much better historical evidence is available, but the question may be raised in a small way here: were the exploitative shamans the wave of the future for Andaman society? Interestingly enough, it does not appear that this was the case, at least not in any direct sense of their dominance becoming more institutionalized over time. On the contrary, between Man's and Radcliffe-Brown's times, the shamans dwindled in numbers and evidently lost some of their social standing: "Most of the old [shamans] are now dead. Amongst the younger men there are a few who pretend to the position, but the recent intercourse with foreigners has produced a degree of skepticism in such matters" (Radcliffe-Brown 1922: 176).

There was one other arena of systematic gender imbalance: the administration of initiation rites. It was the senior men who decided when the young initiates of either sex were to be released from the various food taboos that they were observing, and it was the senior men who then hand-fed the first bits of these de-tabooed foods to the initiates. It is specifically noted several times that only the senior men, and not women, officiated, even in the case of a girl's initiation (Man 1883: 129–35 passim; Radcliffe-Brown 1922: 92–106 passim). Moreover, Radcliffe-Brown calls these the most important rituals in the society, and this makes sense on analytic grounds as well, given the centrality of the senior/junior axis of social differentiation discussed earlier: the rituals played a major role in turning "juniors" into "seniors." The significance of feeding the initiates is not explained, but cross-cultural patterns of this sort suggest an interpretation: that the initiates were being reborn as adults, and that it was the senior men who were symbolically claiming to deliver them into adulthood, as women delivered them into the world as infants in the first place.

In the past, this is the sort of thing that would have led universalists to switch the Andaman Islanders from the "possibly egalitarian" box to the "male-dominant" box. But this is precisely the kind of move that no longer seems justified. How shall we think about the situation now?

The egalitarianism of Andaman Island society was, as I said, hegemonic in the sense that it was structurally pervasive—reappearing in many contexts and in many patterns of relations. The male ritual role, while quite important, was a more or less isolated element, *not* woven into some larger pattern. Such isolation or fragmentation is precisely part of *not* being in a hegemonic position: we have seen again and again that men qua men had no special privileges or sources of authority vis-à-vis women in virtually any sphere of ordinary life in the society. Moreover, it is conceivable that the role of ritual rebirther was itself redefined in an egalitarian direction, given the prevailing hegemony. Although the cultural exegesis necessary to establish this point with any certainty is not available, we are told that the initiation itself was not enough to render a boy or girl a full adult, the transition to such status requiring, in addition, marriage and the birth of the first child. In other words, the cultural position may have been that women and men had equivalent and complementary roles in the social production of adults: women (as wives) bore the children that made both themselves and their husbands parents and, hence, adults, while men did the rituals that accomplished the same thing; neither alone was sufficient to produce a full adult person.[19] Thus, male ritual authority may have been not only isolated, vis-à-vis the prevailing hegemony, it may actually have been reinterpreted so as to fit the hegemony itself.

Yet even if this interpretation was held in the culture, the exclusive role of senior men in initiation rites could also have been a point of cultural transformation. While in theory anything can be reinterpreted and can form the basis for significant cultural change, something like this had powerful transformational potential precisely because it was outside of, and in some sense challenging to, the hegemonic order: it appears to have accorded special authority to one group (senior men) over all others, on grounds (gender plus seniority) other than the dominant grounds (seniority alone) of social valuation. It had powerful transformational potential for another reason as well: because it was culturally defined as "encompassing," performing acts seen as beneficial to the wider social welfare, or in other words because it, like the role of the shaman, was situated in the "public domain." Thus one may ask, Did the authority initially granted to senior men in this limited (though important) role become more general? Looking again at the fifty-year period between Man's and Radcliffe-Brown's observations, the answer appears to be no; if anything, Radcliffe-Brown's account would seem to suggest a slight increase in egalitarianism (compare the quotes about chiefs and their wives presented earlier). But here one reaches the limits of the available information; the Andaman Islanders continued to decline demographically after Radcliffe-Brown's study,[20] and in any event the area was never studied again in anything like the detail of the two accounts utilized here. In order to see how a potential "node of transformation" might become a real one, we must look at a case for which high-quality historical information is available. I turn now to eighteenth-century Hawaii for an inverse example: a case of a "male dominant" hegemony showing significant instances of female power and prestige. Once again, I can only sketch the case, but I hope to provide enough detail to establish the argument.

Historical Transformations: Ancient Hawaii

Traditional Hawaiian Islands society, as observed in the late eighteenth and early nineteenth centuries, appears to have been a male dominant hegemony. [1996 note: The Hawaiian Islands only partly conform to the general model of "Polynesia" set forth in "Rank and Gender." Every Polynesian society varies in some degree from that ideal type, depending on location (Eastern vs. Western Polynesia), degree of stratification (the Hawaiian Islands being at the most stratified, class-like end of the spectrum), and many other factors.] Male dominance was pervasive in both formal ideology and in the structuring of many institutions. In terms of ideology, men were defined as sacred (*kapu*) and women as profane or unsacred (*noa*). There were taboos against men and women eating together, lest women offend the gods with whom men were in communion. There were thus separate men's and women's eating houses. Young boys ate with the women, but at the age of nine they were ritually transferred to the men's eating house and never ate with the women again. There were also a large number of "male" foods, which were part of the sacrificial offerings that men shared with the gods and which women were not allowed to eat. Women were also not allowed in the temples, where male priests made sacrifices to the gods on whom the welfare of the society as a whole was said to depend. Menstruation was deemed polluting and offensive to men and gods, and women had to retire to menstrual huts during their periods each month.

Next, at the level of economic and political institutions, property was generally inherited by the oldest son. While daughters and younger sons had certain usufruct rights, they were formally noninheriting. In terms of political leadership, most chiefs were men; at the same time, all men were metaphoric "chiefs" vis-à-vis their households, performing the domestic sacrifices that maintained the well-being of the household. In sum, male dominance in Hawaiian society must be considered hegemonic, in the sense that it was formally articulated as a cultural statement of greater prestige, and in the sense that it was pervasive throughout a wide range of relations and practices—public and domestic rituals, public and domestic authority.

But there were also significant arenas of "equality" or "equivalence" in traditional Hawaiian society. The most notable of these concerned the tendency to allow the first-born child, regardless of gender, to succeed to the chiefship at the very highest and most sacred levels of the aristocracy. Thus there were a significant number of ruling female chiefs in the Hawaiian royal genealogies.

There was a similar (though unformalized) tendency toward equivalence with respect to property, inheritance, household headship, and related matters, in a variety of ways. While in general the first-born son was the favored heir, "land transmission to and through women was always a possibility" (Linnekin 1985: 103), and women could and did act legitimately as heads of household: "The home was centered in the parent and provider. The 'head of family' (*makua*) could be any relative, any age, sex, or even adoptive—he or she is physically and spiritually the king-post of the house" (Handy and Pukui 1958: 174). Evidently daughters were also allocated land to live and work on as part of a general strategy to keep daughters with the family and to bring in in-marrying sons-in-law (normally nonsenior sons who did not inherit land in their own families) (Linnekin 1985: 105; Handy and Pukui 1958: 44; Goldman 1970: 237–38; Ortner 1981, this volume, pp. 68–71).

If the inheritance system tended to create a certain equivalence between sons and daughters in the sense of giving daughters property more often than one might expect, it also created a certain equivalence between sons and daughters in a negative sense as well: many noninheriting sons and daughters tended not to marry, living at home with their natal families (as dependents of the inheriting sibling) but living lives of great sexual freedom. (Sexual activeness, skill, etc., were strongly valued culturally.) This applied to both men and women, and the Hawaiians were famous among Europeans, especially missionaries, for (as the missionaries saw it) not having an institution of marriage at all (Linnekin 1985: 61). While it is not the case that the Hawaiians had "no marriage," marriage was more likely to be associated with aristocratic status, property-inheriting status, or both. The effect of this was to give many women, like many men, great behavioral freedom. Should an unmarried woman in such a situation have a child, her freedom was not necessarily hampered, because having a child out of wedlock was not seriously frowned upon: giving a child away in adoption was considered normal, and the woman's parents were often happy to adopt the child.

The Hawaiian system thus displayed a dramatic conjunction between a male dominant hegemony and a series of areas in which there was significant equivalence between men and women—in "prestige," in chiefly succession, and in "autonomy." As in the case of the Andaman Islanders, one may ask what other features of Hawaiian culture and society might be expected to be found in conjunction with these patterns on the basis of prior theoretical discussions. These can be located in relation to features of both the patterns of male dominance and the patterns of equality.

Concerning male dominance, we see once again the relevance of the encompassing/encompassed opposition: men occupied all the positions that were defined as integrating and sustaining the social order—they were the preferred holders of the chiefship, the exclusive practitioners of the state rituals, and the exclusive practitioners of the domestic rituals.[21] The distinction was made not so much between domestic and public (for although women were largely excluded from public affairs, men were very actively involved in domestic affairs) as between sacred and profane, between arenas in which connections with the supernatural supports of society were made and those in which they were not. Sacred/profane in turn was precisely the cultural idiom within which the male/female opposition was cast: Hawaiian men were *kapu*, Hawaiian women were *noa*.[22]

A second correlate of the male dominant hegemony that could be theoretically anticipated is the greater elaboration of asymmetrical relations in general. Unlike that of the Andaman Islanders, Hawaiian society was decidedly not an egalitarian social order, and its rankings pertained not only to men and women but to the elaboration of hierarchical distinctions between older and younger siblings, descendants of older and younger siblings, aristocrats and commoners, chiefs and everyone else. While it is not necessarily the case that all forms of inequality automatically amplify one another (the relationship between different forms of inequality in particular times and places is always an empirical question), nonetheless it is clear that in the Hawaiian case (and probably a large number of societies that are similarly ordered), gender inequality and other forms of inequality were directly linked *culturally*: as Marshall Sahlins (1981) in particular has emphasized, men were to women *as* chiefs were to commoners. The effect of this linkage, in turn, was to accomplish precisely what was not accomplished in Andaman Islands culture: to turn a context-specific (which is not to say unimportant) role (like Andaman male leadership in the context of one specific stage of initiation rituals) into a general social principle.

Turning next to the arenas of equivalence in Hawaiian gender practices, here too there are several theoretically predictable correlates. The first is one that was encountered with respect to the Andaman Islanders, although here in a restricted rather than a general and hegemonic form. For certain purposes (succession to the high chiefship), an alternate principle of prestige ranking (here, birth order) overrode gender as a status principle. This is not simply a structural point but apparently a historical progression: Goldman argues on the basis of chiefly genealogies that the Hawaiians seem to have shifted from the more "traditional" pattern of male-only succession to a more purely seniority-based pattern in about the fifteenth century.[23]

One might add to this point one other area in which seniority seems to have been a more important ordering principle than gender and which might have provided a cultural basis for the political shift. The Hawaiians had (and still have) what has come to be called (even in other cultures) Hawaiian kinship terminology, in which the kinship positions are divided primarily by generation and in which gender is only a secondary modification. Thus—and this is the most extreme form of this—even the Hawaiian terms for mother and father were not initially distinguished by gender. There was a single term to indicate "parent" that could be modified by a gender marker if necessary.[24]

I began this discussion by describing Hawaii in the late eighteenth century as having a male dominant hegemony in which there were nonetheless significant arenas of gender equivalence/equality. Male dominance or, more precisely, male preeminence, was linked largely to men's "sacredness" and their consequent control of the ritual system that generated the principles of order, value, and authority for the society as a whole. As Valeri put it, "the relationship with [the] divine [was] obtained by two different means: the sacrificial means, in which men dominate[d], and the genealogical means, which [was] equally accessible to men and women" (1985: 113). And in the traditional Hawaiian order, at least at the point of early description, "sacrifice [was] superior to genealogy" (1985: 114).[25]

Yet it may be suggested that by the time of European contact the relative hegemony of ritual succession vs. genealogical succession (or more precisely, a combination of genealogy plus ritual, vs. genealogy alone) is precisely what was at issue.[26] High chiefs succeeded to office through a combination of genealogical and ritual proceedings—born to the right families (but so were their brothers, half-brothers, and cousins), their rights to rule had nonetheless to be confirmed by the priests through appropriate ritual practices. But the growing tendency seen in the genealogies, to let seniority override gender and to let women succeed, suggests that the pure seniority (or "genealogy") principle was approaching near equal status with the genealogy/ritual combination, if only for certain (restricted but highly significant) purposes.

The situation created major contradictions. Women could succeed to the chiefship on the basis of genealogical and birth order criteria but then did not have the necessary sacredness to enact all parts of the rituals that went with the office. Thus a certain female chief, "having the supreme rank on the island of Hawaii, had the right to enter state temples—normally taboo to women—to consecrate human sacrifices to the gods. But . . . it was still forbidden for her to eat a portion of the offerings" (Valeri 1985: 113). These contradictions suggest that we are looking at a situation in which the hegemony had been virtually breached. The only thing (though not a small thing, by any means) standing between the existing situation and the full political equivalence of men and women was the ritual system, the system that conferred chiefship on some individuals and not all their genealogically similar (even superior) kin, the system that conferred *kapu* status on men and *noa* status on women. Gender equality at this point was more than an isolated element in the system: it was a virtual counterhegemony. It is in this context that we may understand the famous overthrow of the ritual system in Hawaii.

THE OVERTHROW OF THE *KAPU* SYSTEM IN HAWAII

Captain James Cook landed in the Hawaiian Islands in 1778, initiating Western contact with the area that continued and intensified, largely in the form of commerce, throughout and beyond the time period to be discussed. Subsequently, there was also significant Christian missionary activity in the larger region. The Hawaiians were aware of this in some way, but there were no actual mission stations in the Hawaiian Islands until after the indigenously initiated overthrow of the *kapus*.[27]

The events of the overthrow, in sketchy form, were as follows: in 1819, Kamehameha I, the chief/king who had for the first time succeeded in unifying most of the Hawaiian Islands under a single rule, died. It was normally the case that when a high chief died there was a ten-day period during which all the taboos were suspended: women and men ate together, women entered the temples, various forms of sexual license (e.g., sexual relations between high-born women and low-born men) prevailed. At the same time, the heir to the chiefship was supposed to leave the island and separate himself both from the pollutions of the chiefly death and the license of the people, returning at the end of the ten-day period when he (or she) would be installed in the chiefship and would, as his or her first chiefly act, reinstate the taboos. The period following Kamehameha's death was no exception in all these points. The heir, Liholiho, Kamehameha's son by his senior wife, was the designated successor, and he left the island for the prescribed period.

Probably because Liholiho, according to many sources, was by temperament a rather inappropriate successor, Kamehameha had designated his favorite wife, Kaahumanu, to be regent for some period of time. (Earlier, Kaahumanu had adopted Liholiho. She was thus the adoptive mother of the successor as well as the designated regent.) But Kaahumanu, it turns out, had rather more ambitious things in mind than a temporary regentship. During Liholiho's absence she worked out a quite intentional scheme to undermine the *kapu* system by enlisting some high-ranking men to eat publicly with the high-ranking women at the feast celebrating the return and installation of the heir. Also involved in the scheme was Kamehameha's senior wife, Liholiho's birth mother, a chiefly woman of the very highest possible birth rank. The two women succeeded in enlisting Liholiho's younger brother to eat with them, and Kaahumanu sent a message to Liholiho asking him to join as well. On this occasion he did not do so, although he did nothing to stop the younger brother. Kaahumanu made an extraordinary speech:

> Kaahumanu . . . presided over the installation of Liholiho as Kameha-meha II some days later, taking the occasion to pronounce before the assembled Hawaiian notables the purported will of the deceased King that she rule jointly with his heir. Kaahumanu also seized the opportunity to proclaim that those who wished to follow the old tabus might do so, "but as for me and my people, we intend to be free from the tabus. We intend that the husband's food and the wife's food shall be cooked in the same oven, and that they shall eat out of the same calabash. We intend to eat pork and bananas and coconuts [sacrificial foods formerly prohibited to women], and to live as the white people do." (Sahlins 1981: 63)

On this occasion, however, the breach did not fully "take," perhaps because not enough high-ranking men participated. Thus Kaahumanu continued to work on bringing about a more general and thoroughgoing transformation of the status quo. Liholiho left the island again, for about five months. There was to be a memorial feast for Kamehameha on Liholiho's return. Again Kaahamanu sent him a message to join and eat with the women at the feast. In this case he agreed, although evidently at some cost to his peace of mind: he and his friends went on a two-day drinking binge at sea, and Kaahumanu had to send out canoes to tow them in to shore. There was another feast, and this time Liholiho, as well as a high priest and several other high-ranking aristocratic men, joined the women and ate with them.[28]

Needless to say, these changes did not go unopposed. The brother's son of Kamehameha I, who was the designated heir of the deceased king's god, violently opposed the permanent breaching of the taboos. Some time after these events, he rallied an army, and there was a battle. Both he and his wife, who went into battle with him, were killed, this fact seeming ironically to signify that the gods were on the side of those who wished to overthrow the *kapu* system.

The result of these events was the profound and pervasive transformation of Hawaiian culture, affecting all aspects of Hawaiian life. With regard to the issue of gender, there were long-term political and religious/ideological changes. On the political front, Kaahumanu saw to the institutionalization of her new position in the government, called *kuhina*—"regent" or "prime minister." Kaahumanu evidently defined it as a "female" position, and it was thus subsequently filled by her female relatives (her sister's daughter, and her half-sister) for the next several decades, that is, for as long as the chiefly system continued in the form it had at the time. The creation of this position in turn involved a more general reorganization within the government; the high priests, who as performers of the rituals had been extraordinarily powerful under the old arrangements, were made organizationally subordinate to the *kuhina*.

The subordination of the high priests, in turn, represented a complete shift in the status and value structure of traditional Hawaiian religion. The eating taboos, which both represented and constituted the superiority of men over women, were in turn tightly linked up with parallel taboos representing and constituting the superiority of chiefs to commoners and gods to all Hawaiians. The unraveling of the first level was the unraveling of the whole system. Thus in the weeks and months following the events recounted above, the high priest who had been involved in the breach of the eating taboos at the feast, as well as other priests throughout the islands, went on to desecrate the temples and either to burn the statues of the gods or throw them into the sea. In what amounted to an act of autoethnocide (which of course is why it has attracted so much anthropological attention), gods, chiefs, and men were desacralized, and men and women (as well as chiefs and commoners) were defined as equal within the framework of a disenchanted world.

INTERPRETING THE OVERTHROW OF THE *KAPUS*

Why were some Hawaiian women able to mount this sort of challenge to their own gender ideology? And why were they able to succeed? There have been many attempts to answer these questions, and I can only summarize them briefly here. Broadly speaking, the answers fall into two general camps: placing the causality in the Hawaiians' contact with the West vs. placing the causality in structures and processes internal to Hawaiian society. Proponents of the second, "internal" camp in turn fall into two groups, those who tend to emphasize general political/economic/religious features of Hawaiian society/culture and those who tend to emphasize the factor of gender (without necessarily ignoring the other dimensions).

Robert Redfield most firmly takes the position that the overthrow of the *kapu* system in Hawaii must be blamed largely on the impact of external forces: "when we ask if the reform would have been attempted had the civilization of the white man not come into the South Seas, we ask a question that is unanswerable but that raises doubts that the reform would have then been attempted in the absence of influences from civilization" (Redfield 1953: 128). Redfield's position is not so much opposed as ignored. It was not until Marshall Sahlins's recent study that a serious second look was taken at the impact of Western commerce and religion on the events under consideration here (1981: 63). Unlike Redfield, Sahlins does not overstate (and in some subtle way glorify) Western impact but considers, rather, the complex interplay between Western and Hawaiian cultural dynamics. In the period between Redfield's and Sahlins's discussions, the majority of anthropologists emphasized the significance of internal factors, largely political/economic factors related to the processes of state making.[29] In some but not all cases the authors specifically oppose a gender interpretation of the events. M. C. Webb, for example, begins his discussion with a reference to the interpretations of the historian R. S. Kuykendall (who in turn utilized firsthand accounts of the events provided by Europeans resident in Hawaii at the time):

> R. S. Kuykendall ... suggests that the abolition of the taboos was largely at the instigation of the two royal women, who would have found the system especially irksome and humiliating and who would have been successful because unpunished breaking of the taboos by foreigners had weakened faith in the system. ... [Kuykendall's] solution follows the traditional history of David Kalakaua. Yet one is loath to see so great a change as being caused essentially by the whim of a pair of even very powerful women. (Webb 1965: 25)

This rather patronizing quote aside (not only with respect to women but to a native Hawaiian historian), Webb goes on to present a quite interesting argument to the effect that Hawaii was in the process of indigenous state formation, with Kamehameha unifying the islands under his chiefship, and that the sort of religious housecleaning seen in the abolition of the *kapus* may go along with the process of state formation. This is the case, he argued, because some aspects of religion and of other "traditional" forms of regulating succession and renewing legitimacy involve relatively constraining ways of constructing power. Once states have enough military power to hold themselves together by less problematic means, they tend to deemphasize many religiously based modes of legitimation. Thus Webb points out that in the course of the formation of the Zulu state, Shaku Zulu "broke the power of the traditional witch hunters [and] expelled all of the rainmakers except for his own appointees" (1965: 81). Arguments by William Davenport (1969), Stephanie Seto Levin (1968), and J. L. Fischer (1970) similarly emphasize other problematic dimensions of the relationship between religion and politics in a state-making process. I find most of these arguments to have a great deal of prima facie plausibility. Nonetheless, given what is known about the contradictions in the Hawaiian gender system, about the interlock between the gender system and the chiefly system, and about the leading role of Kaahumanu and her co-wife in the events of 1819, I am inclined to think that gender should play a rather larger part in the interpretation of the events than it does in the arguments just cited.

The gender line has in fact been pursued by a number of other scholars. I noted earlier that Robert Redfield emphasizes the impact of Western contact on the Hawaiian situation. Redfield goes on to say, however, that certain features of the Hawaiian situation itself would have rendered it vulnerable to the challenge posed by Western values and practices. Among these he prominently includes "the inconsistencies between the high position of certain women in the system of political power and the low position of these women as women, as expressed in the taboos" (Redfield 1953: 129). Irving Goldman also discusses these inconsistencies but emphasizes as well the genealogical evidence showing a shift earlier in Hawaiian history from male-only succession to first-born succession regardless of gender (Goldman 1970: 237–38). More than any other writer, Goldman is prepared to see the overthrow of the *kapu* system as a virtual feminist revolution (related in turn to larger evolutionary possibilities inherent in Polynesian chiefdoms):

> Early Hawaiian genealogies favored the male line, and even after the tide had begun to turn . . . men were still preferred as high chiefs, a condition that favored patrilineal succession. Nevertheless, bilateralism and with it the social and ritual equality of women had become overwhelmingly powerful forces. We have reason to assume that when Liholiho finally broke the *kapus* that had separated men and women in some ritual respects, his action was no mere response to Christian or to general political influences, but was indeed the culmination of an irresistible movement toward sexual equality. (Goldman 1970: 214–15)

Most recently, Sahlins has made several arguments concerning the significance of these events. On the one hand, he tends to deemphasize the role of Kaahumanu and her co-wife qua *women* in the overall process. He stresses instead the way in which Kaahumanu was a representative of her kin group who, as affinal (in-law) relatives of the king and thus not potential rivals for succession, would traditionally tend to be entrusted by the king with important regions to rule and important administrative functions. This group had thus been given by the late Kamehameha the choicest properties in the kingdom and had also been entrusted by him to serve as his liaison to the Europeans. By a complex logic that cannot be reviewed here, this group stood to gain in both wealth and status by the abolition of the taboos. In the context of Sahlins's argument, Kaahumanu's gender is not particularly relevant; she is simply the spokesperson for her kin group within the councils of the king. At the same time, Sahlins introduces for the first time significant information on the role of commoner women in these events, showing that they began breaking the eating *kapus* (and doing a lot of other things) with English sailors from virtually the moment Captain Cook arrived. In this context, Sahlins is quite explicit in seeing the women's behavior developing into—even if it did not begin as—a form of resistance to their disabilities as both women and commoners (Sahlins 1981: 63 and passim).

It is now time to synthesize the various elements of this discussion. I am looking at the Hawaiian case because it is an example of a not uncommon form of gender system—a male dominant hegemony with significant areas of female power. Although it is clear that these areas of female power cannot be balanced against hegemonic male prestige so as to classify Hawaiian society as "egalitarian," I am saying that arenas of nonhegemonic power may be the bases of historical moves in a more egalitarian direction. The case of Hawaii is perhaps the most dramatic example of such a historical transformation in the ethnographic record. The question is, What were the forces that led the key actors to act on their contradictions rather than simply living them, and what were the forces that brought about the success of that effort?

Once again, I think it is critical that one arena of female power was in "the public domain," that is, in positions from which statements and practices of social encompassment, of universalistic concern, were enacted. The legitimate presence of female chiefs in the Hawaiian political arena, even though not fully sacred in Hawaiian cultural terms, placed women in positions from which they attended to the affairs of "society as a whole" (however ideological such claims about the universalistic concerns of chiefs and priests might be). After all, the female chiefs were allowed to enter the temples and to perform the highest sacrifices for the general welfare, even if they themselves were restricted from gaining the fullest benefits from them.

But I would go beyond this point, both for the Hawaiian case and for its broader implications. Entry into "the public domain," insofar as that domain (or certain restricted areas of it) is culturally defined as "male," may have quite the reverse effect on female actors. Rather than encouraging them to push for more generalized gender equality, it may encourage them to act—as the modern charge often has it—"like men." What is interesting about the Hawaiian case is the degree to which the elite women involved in the overthrow of the taboos seemed to have sustained both a universalistic *and* a particularistic perspective, to have identified themselves *both* with the encompassing outlook of the male/chief and with the encompassed outlook of the female/commoner. It was their ability to bridge these levels that seems to have been one of the keys to their success.

While it is difficult to establish this point with great certainty from the scanty evidence available, I will use the one little text at hand to try to sketch its outlines: the speech made by Kaahumanu at the feast installing Liholiho in the chiefship. If one asks first whether Kaahumanu was acting primarily as a representative of her kinship/political group or "as a woman," clearly the answer is both. Thus she begins by saying, "as for me and my people, we intend to be free from the tabus," and here the "we" means herself and her relatives regardless of gender. Later, however, she says, "We intend to eat pork and bananas and coconuts," and here the "we" can only mean herself and other women, since only women were debarred from eating those foods previously.

A similar point can be made for the question of whether Kaahumanu and the other chiefly women involved were simply representing an elite perspective or whether they were representing people in general, regardless of rank. Again—although the text is somewhat less clear here—the answer seems to be both. That is, although there is a specification of "me and my people" in the early part of the speech, the general thrust of the text seems directed at a more inclusive audience, without regard to rank. She makes a variety of nonexclusive generalizations: that "those who wish to follow the old tabus might do so"; that "the husband's food and the wife's food shall be cooked in the same oven, and that they shall eat out of the same calabash"; and that women—clearly women of all ranks—will eat the formerly tabooed foods.

The way in which the taboo breaking at the feast was orchestrated displays one more aspect of the impulse toward bridging on the part of Kaahumanu and her coconspirators. The women's plan involved the successor to the high chiefship and other high-ranking men getting up from their places and going to eat with the women, rather than the women joining the men. Several things seem embedded in this construction of the event. First, women had already "invaded" a variety of "male" domains, both legitimately (in the succession of female chiefs) and illegitimately (in all the inter-dining with British sailors and the eating of tabooed foods that had already gone on). Having the men move in the other direction would have both balanced and equalized the roles of the two parties. Perhaps more important, the men's coming to eat with the women publicly signified their *consent*, their voluntary joining not just in an act but in an idea. Insofar as Kaahumanu and the other planners were interested not simply in trading places with men but in negating the oppositions and equalizing the relations that had been inherently unequal before then, the agreement of both men and women to the changes sought was essential.

Many things "caused" the overthrow of the *kapu* system in Hawaii. It is not my intention to substitute a gender-revolution interpretation for all the others, but arguably something like that took place *in conjunction with* the myriad other changes that Hawaiians were undergoing. Pursuing this interpretation, I asked about the conditions that might have favored the gender-revolution dimension of the changes. One important factor, I think, was the presence of women in high office, in "the public domain." This heightened the contradictions in the gender system, gave some women both the opportunity and (some of) the authority to create the all-important public event, and gave them the clout to ride out the consequences afterwards. The fact that commoner women were also involved in breaking the taboos was extremely important as well, but it is not clear how much effect this would have had on the formal *kapu* system without the intentional public actions of the elite women.

Yet, supposing that these events took place partly because of the "public" positioning of certain elite women, I went on to argue that the women's efforts were not directed toward trading places with men in a hierarchical system, but toward destroying the bases of hierarchy—the *kapu* system—and equalizing gender relations. Thus I tried to show that Kaahumanu's words and deeds moved back and forth between encompassing and encompassed positions—between gender-neutral kinship interests and women's interests, between rank-neutral women's interests and elite women's interests, and between an order in which men's positions were encompassing and an egalitarian order in which encompassing and encompassed positions were not defined as gender-specific.

We may go on to ask what happened later. Sahlins points out that Kaahumanu subsequently converted to Calvinist Protestantism and came under
the influence of the notoriously strict Reverend Hiram Bingham, whom
she called (using the term formerly used for the high priests of the Hawaiian religion) "my *kahuna nui.*" She founded a large number of Protestant
churches, and Sahlins characterizes her as "restoring the tabus. Only this
time the tabus at issue were the uncompromising restrictions of a fanatical
Calvinism" (Sahlins 1981: 65).

Yet it would be quite distorting to stop the narrative here. In the mid-
1970s Jocelyn Linnekin studied kinship, landownership, and status in a
community on Maui. She found that 50 percent of the land was owned by
women and that the Protestant churches were virtually empty of congre-
gants. Clearly the moves toward equality that were made in 1819 were
never totally reversed by Kaahumanu's conversion to Protestantism. Indeed, Protestantism itself may have been undermined over time by the more
egalitarian hegemony that was at least partly established in the period discussed here.

Conclusions

I began this paper by sorting out the claims and counterclaims of the debate
over universal male dominance. In earlier work my position had been that
male dominance was universal at the level of cultural ideologies or cultural
patterning, that all cultures posited, either in ideological assertions or in the
patterning of practices and institutions, the belief that men were superior to
women—that men have greater prestige, or charisma, or social value. Some
authors countered that this was false simply at the level of cultural assertions and that there were in fact culturally "egalitarian" societies in the
world. Other authors argued that the claim was false in a different way:
that although all cultures may say/imply that men are superior, in many cultures women have a great deal of power which actually counterbalances
these claims of male prestige, thus producing another kind of "equality."

Both opposing positions, I now think, have a certain kind of truth value,
though not exactly in the forms as stated. Critical to the reformulation is
the necessity of accepting the idea that, although a given ideology and/or a
given pattern of practices may be hegemonic, it is never total. Thus, with respect to the question of cultural egalitarianism, I would now agree that
there are societies, like the Andaman Islanders (and a significant number of
others like them), that are hegemonically egalitarian; but this does not

mean that there are no dimensions of "male dominance" to be found in such societies or that the elements of male dominance must be effects of exogenous forces. Instead, I tried to describe the sense in which such nonhegemonic elements can be important yet, as it were, contained, such that most areas of ordinary life apparently remained organized along other—egalitarian—lines. As for the question of "mythical male dominance," although I find the phrase problematic (it suggests that cultural myths or ideologies are relatively trivial), I would nonetheless agree that one must always look at *both* the cultural ideology of "prestige" and the on-the-ground practices of "power." At the same time, I have argued that one must look at the relationship between these "levels" not so much for purposes of classification—indeed this will never yield satisfactory results—as for purposes of examining the historical dynamics of given cases over time.[30] The analysis of the Hawaiian case is meant to illustrate these points. The case can be taken as a reasonable example of "mythical male dominance," in the sense that the core of male superiority was lodged in the cultural "myth" that men were *kapu*/sacred and women were *noa*/profane. Yet the myth did not exist at some purely cultural or ideological level as opposed to some on-the-ground reality. Rather it was hegemonic, in the sense that a whole range of on-the-ground practices were predicated on its premises—it was part of, in Raymond Williams's terms, a "whole lived social process" (1977: 108–9). At the same time, as with instances of male dominance in the Andaman case, there were other areas of practice in which the hegemony did not prevail, in which women had significant amounts of power, authority, autonomy, and prestige. Moreover, I was able to show, as I was unable to do with the Andaman material, the ways in which these arenas of nonhegemonic practice became the bases of a significant challenge to the hegemony, in this case not only to "male dominance" but to the entire chiefly system.

I am inclined to think (or at least to hope) that this approach goes a long way toward resolving the by now rather sterile debates over the universality of male dominance. It allows us to be hard-headed about the realities of power and status at a given ethnographic moment yet at the same time to be analytically flexible about its long-term possibilities. Hegemonies are powerful, and our first job is to understand how they work. But hegemonies are not eternal. There will always be (for both better and worse) arenas of power and authority that lie outside the hegemony and that may serve as both images of and points of leverage for alternative arrangements.

So, *Is* Female to Male
as Nature Is to Culture?

T he paper "Is Female to Male as Nature Is to Culture?" was my first
piece of feminist writing, and my second professional publication.[1] It was written for the Rosaldo and Lamphere (1974) collection, *Woman, Culture and Society.* The first three papers of the
volume—Michelle Rosaldo's, Nancy Chodorow's, and mine—received a
lot of attention, in good part because they all took the position that "male
dominance" was universal, and then tried to offer some kind of (universal)
explanation for that "fact." The idea that male dominance was universal
was (meant to be) somewhat shocking to many non-anthropologists, who
seemed to think that although our own Western society is patriarchal, "the
anthropologists" would have some little stock of more reassuring cases
of matriarchy and egalitarianism to bring forth. The universal male
dominance position also went up against the intellectual assumptions of a
certain "Marxist" wing within anthropology, and thus played into some
preexisting—and already quite heated—intellectual politics within the
discipline.

"Is Female to Male . . ." has continued to have a life of its own, well into
the present. On the one hand many people seemed to have found it persuasive. On the other hand it attracted—and still seems to attract—a great deal
of very intense criticism. I do not know whether I would write the same paper today, but I assume not, both because the questions have changed (universals are of less compelling interest), and because what would seem satis-

173

factory as answers to those questions has changed (exposing an underlying logic seems less satisfying than exposing the politics of representation in play). Yet the paper's role as theoretical lightning rod over time remains interesting. To borrow a phrase from Lévi-Strauss, the paper has been good to think (Lévi-Strauss 1963b). A brief tour through some of the criticism of this paper will allow me then to reflect on some aspects of both feminism and anthropology as these have (and have not) evolved over the past twenty or so years.

Is Male Dominance Universal?

This seemingly simple question can be constructed in a variety of ways. It may take the form of an empirical question: let us look around the world and see if all cases have this quality. This, I think, is how Rosaldo, Chodorow, and I treated it initially. We looked around and the answer seemed to be yes.

But the first round of reactions, as noted above, came from people committed to a certain Marxist evolutionary paradigm, especially Eleanor Leacock (1981) working from Engels's *The Origin of the Family, Private Property and the State*.[2] Within this paradigm, early human societies were presumed to have been egalitarian, and factors of inequality were introduced in conjunction with the emergence of private property. Thus if examples of egalitarian cases in the contemporary world could not be found, it is not because, in their pristine state, they did not exist. It is because all societies have already been touched in one way or another by capitalism, and/or because anthropology has been theoretically blinded by capitalist culture.

Even granting Leacock's points about both capitalist penetration and bourgeois blinders, there were simply too many cases that could not be worked into Leacock's picture. Nonetheless at another level what she and others were saying is that recognizing egalitarianism is not as easy as it appears, that it is a matter of interpretation. I came to agree with this position, and in a recent paper ("Gender Hegemonies," this volume) I argued that if one looks at certain cases from a certain theoretical angle, they look more egalitarian than not. It is not that these societies lack traces of "male dominance," but the elements of "male dominance" are fragmentary—they are not woven into a hegemonic order, are not central to some larger and more coherent discourse of male superiority, and are not central to some larger network of male-only or male-superior practices.

My point, in other words, was to look again at some cultures at the relatively egalitarian end of the spectrum. I wanted to try to rethink the significance of culturally unmarked elements of "male dominance" in such cases, to try to get a better feel for their relative weight within a culture's gender patterns. I felt that my mistake earlier had been to play up such items too much, to seize upon any indicator of male superiority, female "pollution," etc., and label a whole culture "male dominant." Behind my rethinking are larger shifts in the conceptualization of "culture" in the field of anthropology as a whole, in the direction of seeing "cultures" as more disjunctive, contradictory, and inconsistent than I had been trained to think.[3]

The case I focused on was the Andaman Islanders, and I concluded that it was fair to view them as "egalitarian," despite the presence of certain items of special male privilege and authority. I argued that, since these items were not woven into a hegemonic order, they could not be treated as pervasively redefining the dominant egalitarianism. Interestingly enough, Jane Atkinson and Anna Tsing published papers at virtually the same time as "Gender Hegemonies," taking up similar kinds of materials in similar kinds of ways. Atkinson examined gender relations among the Wana of Central Sulawesi, and Tsing considered material from the Meratus of Kalimantan, both within Indonesia. Their cases are both very similar to the Andaman example I had discussed. In all three cases there is a lack of formal ideology about male superiority; in all three cases there are extensive patterns of gender equivalence and equality; in all three cases there is a tendency not to use gender as a conceptual or social organizational principle at all.[4] Very few things are limited to men simply because they are men, or to women simply because they are women. But in both cases some people nonetheless come to occupy, and/or to create for themselves, positions of influence and authority, and those people tend predominantly to be men.

We three authors wind up in slightly different places with respect to the egalitarianism question, although this seems largely a function of the way each author posed the problem in the first place. My agenda had been to try to learn to "see egalitarianism"—to see how some kinds of de facto male dominance might remain isolated and, at a given moment in time at least, not basically challenge a prevailing egalitarianism in a culture. Atkinson and Tsing, on the other hand, were interested in seeing how male dominance gets produced and reproduced, largely in an unmarked way, in societies that represent themselves as basically egalitarian. Together, however, the papers convey a suggestion that you can call such societies "gender-egalitarian" if you want, and you would not exactly be wrong, but the egalitarianism is complex, inconsistent, and—to some extent—fragile.

Picturing the Emergence of Male Dominance

These papers also raise another point about the male dominance issue, one that was not much debated at the time of the publication of the Rosaldo and Lamphere volume, but that nonetheless seems to me important: how shall we imagine the process of the emergence of male dominance in human societies? Should we think of it as the product of male intentionality, some sort of "will to power" emerging from a "natural" aggressiveness? Or should we think of it—as I did in "Is Female to Male . . ."—as a kind of side effect, an unintended consequence of social arrangements designed for other purposes?

The cases just discussed show how tricky this question is. On the one hand they can be read as supporting my original contention. Whether we call them "egalitarian" or not, these cases show that certain kinds of male privilege emerge in a de facto way from certain relatively functionally defined arrangements. Men emerge as "leaders" and as figures of authority, vis-à-vis both women and other men, as a function of engaging in a variety of practices, only some of which are predicated on power, including trade, exchange, kinship networking, ritual participation, dispute resolution, and so forth. That is, male dominance does not in fact seem to arise from some aggressive "will to power," but from the fact that—as Simone de Beauvoir first suggested in 1949—men as it were lucked out: their domestic responsibilities can be constructed as more episodic than women's, and they are more free to travel, congregate, hang out, etc., and thus to do the work of "culture."

In a subsequent paper, Collier and Rosaldo criticized the functionality of this argument (1981; see also Rosaldo 1980). Although they did not argue that men "naturally" sought to dominate women, they nonetheless emphasized that male power relations, often grounded in violence and threats of violence, had to be at the heart of understanding gender inequality. In general I shifted over to a more political perspective in my own work as well. Yet I retained a certain commitment to the "functionalist" argument in the context of the nature/culture paper, that is, in the context of the origin-of-male-dominance story that is embedded in that paper. We seemed to have two choices: either to imagine that male dominance came about as, in Engels's famous phrase, "the world historical defeat of women" by men (1972), or alternatively that it came about as the unintended consequence of certain functional arrangements and other paths of least resistance.

I preferred the latter interpretation, in part because the will to power position presumed, even if it did not clearly declare, some kind of essentialized male aggression, and I thought essentialized characteristics were exactly what feminists (at least some of us) were trying to get away from. Yet it is clear from cross-cultural data (Sanday 1981, 1990) that issues of greater male physical size and strength, and perhaps greater male "aggressiveness" in some form, do matter in many cases, although in a wide variety of not entirely predictable ways. The issue haunts contemporary feminist politics as well, where one finds a fairly deep split between what I think of as the "body feminists," who focus on rape and other forms of violence against women (e.g., Brownmiller 1975; MacKinnon 1987), as against the more socially and culturally oriented thinkers and activists. I would more fully acknowledge today, then, the challenge to capture bodily issues in our understandings of gender asymmetry, but without essentializing either women or men.

Is Nature/Culture Universal?

The second bundle of arguments against "Is Female to Male as Nature Is to Culture?" concerned its use of the nature/culture opposition to explain (universal) male dominance. Again there were several sets of issues here: Is the nature/culture opposition truly universal? Does it have more or less the same meanings cross-culturally? Does an alignment between gender on the one hand and nature/culture on the other in fact explain universal male dominance? And even if it does not, is there still some significant sense in which female is to male as nature is to culture?

Beneath these various questions, there seems to me to be one large question that is of continuing relevance today: in this era of poststructuralism, does it still make sense to talk about "structures," and if so what do we mean by them? In order to get to this question, I will first yield and set aside those parts of the argument in "Is Female to Male . . ." that now seem to me probably wrong, or at the least, not very useful. And then I will defend what still seems to me right, partly in the spirit of defending myself, but largely— I hope—in the spirit of learning something from all this.

The biggest substantive "error" in the paper may be the main point, that is, the point that a linkage between female and nature, male and culture "explains" male dominance, whether universal or not. Rather, an explanation of universal or near-universal male dominance seems to me largely explicable in ways just discussed: as a result of some complex interaction of functional arrangements, power dynamics, and bodily effects.

The other big problem surrounding the use of the nature/culture opposition concerns the seeming attribution of universality to certain meanings of "nature" and "culture." Here I think it was more a matter of too casual an exposition in the paper than gross "error," but the point is well taken. Thus, for example, even if the nature/culture relationship is a universal structure across cultures, it is not always constructed—as the paper may seem to imply—as a relationship of cultural "dominance" or even "superiority" over nature. Moreover, "nature" can be a category of peace and beauty, or of violence and destruction, or of inertia and unresponsiveness, and so on and so forth, and of course "culture" will have concomitant variations. Such variation at the level of explicit cultural meanings—unemphasized in the paper—is indeed crucial to variation in the construction of gender and sexuality cross-culturally; the argument from the universality of the nature/ culture opposition was in no way meant to suggest a similar universality at the level of "sexual meanings."[5]

As these points suggest, however, there is still some sense in which I would argue, first, that the nature/culture opposition is a widespread (if not universal) "structure," and second, that it is generally (if not universally) the case that female is indeed related to male as nature is to culture. This needs to be elaborated here.

Probably the most consistently articulated charge against "Is Female to Male . . ." is that an opposition between nature and culture is simply not a universal opposition, that it therefore could not be assumed to underlie either "universal male dominance" or—a priori—any given ethnographic case. As with the first takes on the universal male dominance question, the question of the universality of some sort of nature/culture opposition was at first taken to be an empirical issue: does the opposition appear in all cultures? to which the contributors to *Nature, Culture and Gender*, looking at both non-Western examples and pre-nineteenth-century Western cultural history, answered, pretty much, no (MacCormack and Strathern 1980).

The problem here, as a number of observers quickly pointed out, was that many of the contributors to the *Nature, Culture and Gender* volume fundamentally sidestepped the notion of "structure," which I had used in a Lévi-Straussian (e.g., 1963a) sense, and which has only a complex relationship to empirical cultural terminologies and ideologies. That is, nature/culture as used in my essay (or throughout Lévi-Strauss's work) is not an empirical object that can be found through ethnographic scrutiny; it is an assumption of a relationship that underlies a variety of ethnographic "surfaces." An early review by Beverley Brown (1983) took the volume to task for this confusion, as did more recent essays by Valeri (1990), Hoskins (1990), and Peletz (1996). Simply finding an absence of terminological categories in a particular cultural case does not mean that the structure is not there; the structure is a patterning of relations that may exist without cultural labeling.[6]

But what shall we mean by structure? There have been many definitions of the term, and this is not the place to review the state of structural theory in general. Part of the problem, I think, was Lévi-Strauss's tendency to picture structures as binary oppositions,[7] and also in fact—despite disclaimers—to picture them as sets of terms, words. My own way of thinking about structures, however, is to think of them as existential *questions*, even riddles, which humanity everywhere must face. Of these, one of the most central is how to think about the confrontation between humanity and nature, that is, between humanity and "what happens without the agency, or without the voluntary and intentional agency, of man" (Mill 1874, quoted in Valeri 1990: 266), or between humanity and, in Marilyn Strathern's terms, those processes that proceed autonomously in the world, and "that limit the possible" of human action (quoted in Valeri 1990: 266).

Nature/culture in one or another specifically Western sense—as a "struggle" in which "man" tries to "dominate" nature, as a confrontation with a system that obeys "natural laws," and so forth—is certainly not universal. Even the idea that "nature" and "culture" are two relatively distinct kinds of objects is probably not universal. But the *problem of the relationship* between what humanity can do, and that which sets limits upon those possibilities, must be a universal problem—to which of course the solutions will vary enormously, both cross-culturally and historically.

Now add gender into the equation. Gender difference, along with nature/culture, is a powerful question. And the gender relationship is always at least in part situated on one nature/culture border—the body. What I think tends to happen in most if not all cultures is that the two oppositions easily move into a relationship of mutual metaphorization: gender becomes a powerful language for talking about the great existential questions of nature and culture, while a language of nature and culture, when and if it is articulated, can become a powerful language for talking about gender, sexuality, and reproduction, not to mention power and helplessness, activity and passivity, and so forth. The particular articulations of the relationship will vary greatly across cultures, with surprising and unexpected shifts and alignments. But the chances that the two sets of issues will be interconnected in specific cultural and historical contexts still seem to me fairly high.

The chances seem to me high, further, although less so perhaps than the chance of sheer interconnection, that the relationship between the terms will be asymmetrical, and that both women and nature will be in some sense the more problematic categories. The logic that de Beauvoir first put her finger on—that men get to be in the business of trying to transcend species-being, while women, seen as mired in species-being, tend to drag men down—still seems to me enormously widespread, and hardly an invention of "Western culture." From a range of tribal societies with male-only rituals and practices that would be spoiled by women's gaze, to so-called high religions, both Western and non-Western, that exclude women from their higher practices, the basic logic shows up. And it is a logic grounded in a particular construction of the relationship between nature and culture, the idea that culture must at least in part be about the transcendence of nature.

I think the final question for this paper is probably, "so what?" While I do think there are such things as structures in the sense just discussed, large existential questions that all human beings everywhere must cope with, I also think that the *linkage* between such structures and any set of social categories—like female/male—is a culturally and politically constructed phenomenon. From early on after the publication of "Is Female to Male . . . ," my interests lay much more in understanding the politics of the construction of such linkages, than in the static parallelism of the categories.[8]

In conclusion, then, I must say first that it is very odd to have written what has evidently become a "classic"; I certainly did not set out to write one in advance. I and all the other authors in the two founding volumes of feminist anthropology—*Woman, Culture and Society* (Rosaldo and Lamphere 1974) and *Toward an Anthropology of Women* (Reiter 1975)—benefited enormously from the fact that the feminist movement as a political movement had created a virtually ready-made audience for the books. And the argument in "Is Female to Male . . . . ," written from the position of a young, white, middle-class female academic, trying to figure out how to live a life as an embodied woman while launching a career as a disembodied mind, evidently touched something in many others similarly positioned in that era.

Borderland Politics
and Erotics

Gender and Sexuality in
Himalayan Mountaineering

Introduction

The image of the "borderland" is a powerful presence in contemporary theory. Borderland thinking initially took shape within the theorizing of ethnic and minority studies, and emphasized the construction of complex, hybridized identities for those who must live within, yet are excluded from, the dominant cultural order (Anzaldua 1987; Behar 1993). In anthropology the idea of the borderland has been used particularly to rethink the object of anthropological study—to get away from the study of supposedly bounded and timeless "cultures," and to attend instead to sites of social friction and cultural encounter where culture is no longer an inert object but something constantly under challenge and construction (R. Rosaldo 1989; Gupta and Ferguson 1992; Davis 1994; Foley 1995).

Borderland work emphasizes the movements of, and the encounters between, people, images, and so forth across cultural and political spaces (e.g., Appadurai 1991; Chambers 1990; Clifford 1992; Hannerz 1992; Pratt 1992). While always potentially transnational, or even global, in scope, it is—ideally—at the same time local and ethnographic (e.g., Rouse 1991; Kearney 1991; Gupta and Ferguson 1992), looking at real places and asking what kinds of things happen on the ground when people who started from very different places (literally or metaphorically or both) wind up occupying the same space.[1]

In a borderlands perspective the terrain of cultural encounters, of border crossings, is never neutral and never level. It is never neutral because borderlands are spaces that some people call "home" and define those entering it as Other, alien. "Home" may or may not be an advantage: the Others who are entering may come as poor and terrified refugees or as powerful conquerors, but in any event the space from the outset has different relationships to the different parties involved. Similarly, the space of border crossings is never "level," that is, it is almost always a space of unequal power. The people who occupy or enter this space have their own histories, which produce these inequalities, and which set the cultural and political terms within which the encounters will unfold.

In addition, feminist theorizing invites us to see encounters and transactions in the borderlands as always gendered and eroticized, both in practice and in the imagination. Here the work of Ann Stoler (e.g., 1992) on the erotics of the colonial encounter is pathbreaking in opening up the terrain. Stoler shows us that Western categories of the Other, especially racial categories, emerge not only from an economy and a politics of culture, but from an erotics of culture, in which the parties in the borderlands (in this case imperial colonies) meet as gendered beings with gendered fantasies, anxieties, and desires (see also Bloom 1993; Nandy 1983; Rafael n.d.).

Finally, whatever else borderlands politics are about—gender, race, class; material resources and political power—they are always also about "culture." The term "culture" is currently under extraordinary attack. People are writing "against culture" (Abu-Lughod 1992), "beyond 'culture'" (Gupta and Ferguson 1992), and considering whether we should "forget culture" (Brightman 1995). An extraordinary textual struggle has been taking place between Marshall Sahlins and Gananath Obeyesekere over Sahlins's use of the idea of "culture" in the context of interpreting Hawaiian history (Sahlins 1981, 1995; Obeyesekere 1992). Yet for all the problems with the use of the culture concept—the tendency to use it in such a way as to efface internal politics/differences, and to make others radically Other—it does more violence to deny its presence and force in the social process than to keep it in the picture. For "culture" in the borderlands is both the grounds of negotiation and its object: it sets the terms of the encounters, but it is also what is at stake.

What is needed, then, is a sense of culture without Otherness. The idea that people have their own historically sedimented frames of reference, and come at events with their own ways of thinking and feeling, means that people across cultures are different, but not necessarily radically Other. A perception, a construction, of radical Otherness is a possible outcome of intercultural encounters, but it is not intrinsic to the idea that other people are different—come from different histories and practices and ways of being in the world. The attributions and claims of difference (how much, what kind, how significant) is one of the things up for grabs in the borderlands, but difference and identity (or identities) are not the only cultural things under negotiation. Rather, whole issues of meaning and style, forms of practice and forms of relationship, are in play and in question.

In the present paper, which is part of a larger project (Ortner n.d. b), we enter one strange borderland—the space of high altitude mountaineering in the Himalayas, the highest mountains of the world. Since about the turn of the twentieth century, Western mountaineers (and later mountaineers from all parts of the globe) have come to try to climb these mountains. Here they have encountered the Sherpas, an ethnic group of Tibetan origin whose home area is a region of Nepal close to Mount Everest and some of the other highest Himalayan peaks. The Sherpas have done portering and other forms of climbing support for these expeditions for nearly a century now. Their role began as a very subordinate one, in which they were viewed as little more than load-bearing "coolies," and in turn called the mountaineers "sahib" (boss, master). But the work often involves a very close association over several months' time, sharing food, tents, successes, failures, danger and death with the mountaineers, and this has led to personal closeness among some sahibs[2] and Sherpas, a tendency toward equalization of the sahib/Sherpa relationship—and a good deal of representation of and projection onto Sherpas by sahibs that at the same time reveals a lot about the sahibs themselves.[3]

In the larger project I am concerned with a variety of dimensions of expedition politics and culture—authority, resistance, money, death. But in one other paper—"Discourses of Masculinity," which looks at the changing definitions of manhood among both the Westerners and the Sherpas (Ortner n.d. a)—and this one, which looks at the entry of women, and of feminist ideology, into the mountaineering arena since the 1970s—I focus on the gendered and erotic dimensions of relations in this borderland. I attempt to lay bare what I will call, borrowing a phrase from an earlier feminist manifesto (Firestone 1970), a "dialectic of sex."

Central to this discussion is the idea that people come to encounters like this not only with their own prior and ongoing cultures and histories, but with their own prior and ongoing politics (Ortner 1995a). Encounters between Western women and Sherpa men are shaped not only by Western and Sherpa gender *categories* (although those are very important), but by Western and Sherpa gender *politics*, that is, politics between Western women and men, and between Sherpa women and men. It is these distinct politics as well as distinct "cultures" that come into play in the interactions between Westerners and Sherpas, and that give the whole process an extraordinary dynamism and complexity. It is this "politics of politics" with respect to gender and sexual relations that I am calling a dialectic of sex.

Gender Radicalism in Himalayan Mountaineering before the 1970s

Himalayan mountaineering until the 1970s was an overwhelmingly male sport. It was engaged in almost (but not quite) exclusively by men, both Sherpa and "first world"; it built on male styles of interaction derived from other all-male institutions, especially the army; and while it was about many things—nature and nation, materiality and spirituality, the moral quality of the inner self and the meaning of life—it was always in part about masculinity and manhood.

Given this, any woman who engaged in (Himalayan) mountaineering was by definition in some sense what I will call a "gender radical." To say that someone is a gender radical is to say that they are questioning or breaking gender rules, although there are many ways of doing this, and many ideological frameworks within which it may be done. The feminist movement that took shape primarily in Europe and the United States in the 1970s is only one specific historical example of gender radicialism, and it itself encompasses a variety of styles and positions. At the same time it does not—as many minority and Third World feminists have argued (see Collins 1990; Mohanty 1991a, b)—in fact encompass all forms of gender radicalism even in the West, no less in other parts of the globe.

Himalayan mountaineering can be broken into periods—for present purposes, pre–World War II, the post-war period between the 1950s and emergence of the feminist movement in the 1970s, and the period from the 1970s to the present. In the pre-war period, there are scattered examples of individual women, both "memsahib" and Sherpa, climbing in the Himalayas. Most of the Western women active in this period were explorers like Fanny Bullock Workman and, in a more spiritual mode, Alexandra David-

Neel (Blum 1980: chap. 1). But in 1934 a climber named Hettie Dyhren-
furth reached the top of Queen Mary Peak (24,370') in the Karakoram Hi-
malaya as part of an expedition exploring and mapping the Baltoro Glacier
region (Blum 1980: 6).[4] It is more difficult to find traces in the pre-war period of Sherpa women climbing (beyond "local portering," i.e., carrying
loads to the base of the mountain). But we note, for example, a figure called
"Eskimo Nell" who evidently climbed at least part way up Everest:

> And there was Eskimo Nell. I had heard tremendous stories of her ef-
> forts as a porter to Everest in 1933, when she had been the driving
> force among the Sherpas and her caustic tongue had spurred the others
> on to carry to even greater heights. (Bourdillon 1956: 203)[5]

The period between the 1950s and the 1970s saw an intensification of
Himalayan mountaineering in general, and a slightly more visible presence
of women. Among the memsahibs we see, for example, "the first expedition
composed entirely of women ever to explore and climb in the high Hima-
laya" in 1955 (Jackson and Stark 1956), the Women's International Expedition to Cho Oyu led by the French climber Claude Kogan in 1959 (Birkett
and Peascod 1989; see also Lambert and Kogan 1956), and the group of
women led by Josephine Scarr who climbed in the Kulu area in 1961 (Scarr
1966). Again it is harder to find traces of Sherpa women climbing, but we
note, for example, two daughters and a niece of Tenzing Norgay (who had
reached the summit of Everest in 1953), climbing with Claude Kogan on
Cho Oyu in 1959 (Birkett and Peascod 1989: 211).[6]

With such small numbers and generally scant information it is difficult to
generalize about the social positioning of these women. In general, the
memsahibs who climbed in the Himalayas up to the 1970s were western
European and American,[7] all—as far as one can see in the published record—white, and mostly—as far as one can see—broadly middle class.
Most seem to have had at least some higher education; most—but not all—
expressed some form of awareness or consciousness about breaking barri-
ers for women in this quintessentially man's world. Some were married
and/or in long-term relationships with men; some of these had children;
and some were unmarried.[8] As a generalization it is probably safe to say
that these women were part of the more liberal (sometimes verging on bohemian[9] or counter-cultural) edge of the middle classes, a characterization
that would hold true for the most part for the men as well.

As for Sherpa women, there is even less information available. They too probably came from the middling levels of Sherpa society—daughters of "big people" who were gender radicals would have been, at least in the pre-1970s era, more likely to enter a nunnery than to join a mountaineering expedition, while daughters of "small people" would have been unlikely to have the necessary contacts or confidence to achieve any position higher than local porter.[10] Concerning marital status, we know nothing about "Eskimo Nell," but the presence of the daughter and nieces of Tenzing Norgay on the 1959 Cho Oyu expedition signals a pattern that has held true until very recently: Sherpa women have of necessity climbed under the sponsorship of, or in partnership with, a related male, whether kinsman or husband. Sardars—the Sherpa foremen of expeditions—were, and still are, generally unwilling to take an unrelated woman on a climb, and for women who wanted to climb, a relative or husband who was a sardar was generally the only way in. More on this as we enter more deeply into the culture and politics of Sherpa gender relations. We begin with the men.

Sex and Sexism

On a scale of gender inequality across world cultures, the Sherpas are pretty good. "Pretty good" is not exactly a scientific category, but then it is notoriously difficult to assign a score of degree of gender equality or inequality in a particular society. The Sherpas are not "egalitarian," and the culture is in many ways biased in favor of male privilege of various kinds (Ortner 1983, this volume). Yet I would not describe Sherpa male consciousness as organized in terms of "macho" or "sexist" principles. Although I develop these points more fully elsewhere (Ortner n.d. a), let me sketch the argument briefly here.

At one level Sherpa sexual culture is quite bawdy. Unmarried men and women who are potential sex/marriage partners interact with one another in explicitly funny/joky/sexual ways. Groups of young men and women who meet on the trails may shout quite obscene things to one another, and they may exchange verses of made-up obscene songs.[11] At weddings and funerals when large numbers of eligible young men and women get together, there is always a lot of sexual joking, teasing, chasing, laughing, tickling, etc., often culminating in sexual trysts later that night.

On the other hand, sex is heavily devalued by Buddhist ideology. While the Sherpas were always Buddhists, the more ascetic style of Buddhism was only established among them starting in the early twentieth century with the foundings of the first Buddhist monasteries in their midst (Ortner

1989). With the continuing expansion of monasticism over the whole of the twentieth century, Sherpa society was subjected to heavy and continuing doses of the more ascetic, anti-materialist, anti-sexual Buddhist ideology. A good deal of the post-monastic reforms focused on cleaning up the bawdier aspects of Sherpa popular religion and everyday life (Ortner n.d. b).

By the time Robert Paul and I did fieldwork among the Sherpas in the mid 1960s, the more ascetic/monastic Buddhist values had clearly taken hold at least to some degree. The bawdy side did not by any means disappear. But as Paul discusses in his dissertation, while sex was certainly considered pleasurable, it also existed under a pall of negative Buddhist ideas about sin, pollution, and the worldly drudgery it produces in the form of children who must be supported by hard work (1970: 110–17; note also comments by the monk Dorje in Ortner 1977).

Possibly because of these Buddhist constraints, as well as because of fundamentally not-unrespectful views about women (Ortner 1983, this volume). Sherpa male sexuality did not traditionally take a predatory, conquest-style form vis-à-vis women. Men did not traditionally boast—as far as I know—about sexual conquests, and did not seek to rack up high sexual scores. Occasionally one came across a Don Juan figure in the villages who had been married six or seven times, but this was always remarked upon negatively. As Paul commented, "There is not, as in so many other . . . cultures, a sub-culture of *machismo*, a scale by which . . . men compete or strive to achieve in the field of seduction . . ." (1970: 111).

In addition it was my impression as a female researcher that Sherpa male sexuality was always limited by questions of status and power. That is, I felt completely sexually safe while I was in the field, in large part because of the general absence of predatoriness just sketched, but also—no doubt—because I was a "memsahib," a high-status Western woman, and in a broad sense—given my research permits and so forth—under the protection of the Nepal state as well.[12]

Over the course of the twentieth century, that is, over basically the same period as the establishment and spread of high Buddhist monasticism, Sherpa men's experience on mountaineering expeditions was similarly contradictory. In some respects, expeditions imposed a great deal of bodily discipline on the Sherpas—no drinking, no fighting, no sex. (One of my informants described expeditions as being "like monasteries.") On the other hand, from early on in expedition history, and particularly after World War II, sahibs and Sherpas developed a pattern of bawdy joking on expeditions

(Ortner n.d. a). As far as I can tell, the pattern actually originated with the Sherpas, who seemed to have used it to generate greater equality with the sahibs.

It is my impression, then, that for young Sherpa men involved in expedition work a certain western-style machismo—more predatory, more disrespectful of women—began to become a more possible form of masculinity. While much of the evidence is ambiguous and hard to read, it seems that "bawdy" relations between Sherpa men and women, which were previously fairly mutual, may have begun to tip in a more disrespectful direction on the part of at least some Sherpa men. Thus for example the British mountaineer Chris Bonington, who is generally astute in his observations of Sherpas on expeditions, described a situation in which the Sherpas were contributing money to a post-expedition party fund, based on the numbers of (Sherpa) women they had slept with (or boasted of sleeping with) along the way (Bonington 1976: 85). I was also told that the journalist Tom Laird has written (unpublished) about a recent gang rape of a Sherpa woman by some Sherpa men.[13] This, if true, is quite shocking, since rape in Sherpa society has been virtually unknown.

These fragments concerning shifts in Sherpa male attitudes toward Sherpa women are, as I said, quite ambiguous. On the other hand, the evidence is rather stronger for a shift in the direction of a more Western-style machismo with respect to "memsahibs." The general absence of disrespect, as well as the boundaries of status, were apparently somewhat weakened. In part this was the result of the kinds of male-male bawdy incitement practiced between sahibs and Sherpas. But in part it was the result of another dimension of "bodily politics" that must be discussed here.

Sex with Memsahibs

Among other things the 1960s counterculture in the United States and Europe produced the sexual liberation movement. The sexual liberation movement in turn went in several different directions, but one of them was simply a general loosening of rules and inhibitions about sex: sex outside of marriage became morally acceptable, basically good for you, and meant to be fun for all concerned. To a great extent, the double standard in which it was acceptable for men to both seek and enjoy sex, while women should not be observed to be doing much of either, was finally destroyed, or at the very least demoted from dominant ideological status.

Sexual liberation intersected with, but was not isomorphic with, the women's liberation movement. Feminists in general were sexual liberationists, but sexual liberationists were not necessarily feminists, and for some women inviting and enjoying sex was simply part of a more traditional gender positioning—gaining the attention of men and proving one's physical attractiveness.

Nepal was actually one of the earliest sites of the counterculture in the mid-1960s, in part because of the countercultural fascination with "the East" and in part because marijuana and hashish were legal there until recently.[14] And apparently dating from that period, western women coming to Nepal on treks as well as climbs—probably more the former—were inviting and engaging in sex with Sherpa men. It is not known for a fact, of course, who was soliciting whom, but the general view among both western observers and Sherpas is that it was primarily the memsahibs—at least in the earlier years—who initiated the encounters. While one may be suspicious of this view as another form of blaming women, in fact it makes sense on several grounds: because of the Sherpas' relatively unaggressive and unpredatory attitude toward sex; because of the fact that memsahibs have generally not been thought by them to be particularly attractive; because of the fact that memsahibs were definitionally (at least in the early years) high status and the Sherpas were quite careful about transgressions of status and power; and so forth.

In any event, while for obvious reasons it is hard to get data on these sorts of phenomena, the fact of sex between Sherpas and memsahibs on many treks and on some climbing expeditions is widely known in the streets of Kathmandu (see also Adams 1996: 56ff). James Fisher, drawing in part on von Fürer-Haimendorf (1984), reports "forty or so cases of marriage between Westerners and Sherpas, almost all relatively uneducated villagers from Solu or Khumbu[15] . . . and . . . many more informal liaisons, primarily between trekking sardars and their Western female clientele" (1990: 127).

In addition, both Sherpas and Western observers often discuss the sexual goings-on from specific expeditions. What follows must of course be classified as gossip; I report these things not as true stories (though they may indeed be true) but as examples of what observers believe is going on. With respect to a certain Women's Expedition, for example, it was said that one of the women wanted one of the Sherpas to go home with her, but he didn't go. In addition it was said that the Sherpa leader of the expedition had a son by one of the women, now living in America. The Westerner relaying these stories to me was of the opinion that it was the women who made the advances, the Sherpas being "too shy."

Next, one of the Sherpa women climbers I interviewed told me the story of another Women's Expedition, from a different country:

> There was a problem when [M's] son got together (had sex) with the leader. After the expedition succeeded, there was a big party and the Sherpas got drunk. The father [got very angry and] broke all the tent poles. He said he would put it in the papers that [climbers of this nationality] should never come to Nepal again.

The father's reaction illustrates that the issue of young Sherpa men's sexual connections with memsahibs is not unproblematic for other Sherpas. Sherpas in fact exhibit a range of attitudes about this. For the most part there is a relatively mild and benign jokiness about the whole thing. For example, some Sherpas were quoted as joking with a writer about the Annapurna Women's Expedition of 1978:

> There is one other way to go to foreign countries. There was one American Women's Expedition this year and some Sherpas they marry [actually, one married and one had a sexual relationship] with some of those women. Now Sherpas say, "For Women's Expedition you not have to pay, I work for free." We both laughed. (Laird 1981: 124)

But at the less benign end of the spectrum we hear a kind of contempt for memsahibs, coupled with a relatively calculating attitude about Sherpamemsahib relationships, that I am particularly calling attention to here. It is worth stressing that these attitudes are not by any means characteristic of all Sherpa men. Nonetheless they represent an emerging tendency that is clearly disturbing to many observers, Sherpa as well as Western.

The first example is from one of my field trips, in this case with a Granada television crew to make a film about the Sherpas in 1976 (Ortner 1977). While filming up in one of the villages, I met a young mountaineering Sherpa who had gotten involved with a Swiss woman on a trek. He was supposed to follow her back to Switzerland where they would get married. Even at this early stage, however, he seemed a good deal less interested in her than she in him. Later, I was visiting Sherpa friends in Kathmandu when this same young man, R, came into the house:

> R came in with his Swiss girlfriend—very surly [toward her]—he seems to be sick of her. She's leaving day after tomorrow and I said to

him, you must be sad. [Of course I was fishing to see what he would say.] He said, well I've got plenty of friends here. [The woman I was visiting, RJ] said to him, but you can't sleep with your friends. And he said—fast, hoping I wouldn't understand—well, there's plenty of women here [to sleep with].

More directly, here is a rather dreadful "joke" that was making the rounds in Kathmandu in 1990, attributed to "a Sherpa":

Did you hear the one about the Sherpa who said trekking work is very easy? You only need one word of English: "yes." Sherpa climb high? "yes." Carry load? "yes." Cook dinner? "yes." Memsahib wants to fuck? "yes."

If this really is a joke that originates with "a Sherpa," it illustrates several things: first, the perception that memsahibs will initiate sex; second, that the Sherpa is not in a position to refuse; and third, that a Sherpa in this position may become callous toward and openly disrespectful of women, or at least of memsahibs. This "macho drift" in Sherpa male gender attitudes would put (some) Sherpa men on a collision course with feminist, and decidedly anti-macho, expeditions in the 1970s.

1970s Feminism

In this borderland of Himalayan mountaineering, it should be clear that gender boundaries were in some sense under challenge (and in other senses not) both within and across cultural borders, even before the onset of feminism as a political and cultural movement in the 1970s. But the rise of the feminist movement had some dramatic effects on Himalayan mountaineering.

It is worth pausing here to note that, from the perspective of Himalayan mountaineering, the 1970s feminist movement had a completely transnational quality. Women from virtually every "first-world" country, including by this time virtually every country in Asia, came into Himalayan climbing within that decade. We thus see a great deal more ethnic/national diversity, although not necessarily class diversity—my general sense is that the women, whatever their nationality, remain largely middle class.

In any event, feminism produced first of all a large influx of women into Himalayan mountaineering. Not only did the women come, they conquered. In 1975 Mt. Everest was climbed twice by women, first via the traditional southern route by Junko Tabei, who was co-leader of a Japanese all-women's expedition (Birkett and Peascod 1989), and second via the north face by Phantog, a Tibetan woman who was part of a mixed-gender Chinese expedition (actually composed mostly of ethnic Tibetans) (*Another Ascent . . . 1975*).[16] But the feminist movement was about a lot more than making gains of this sort for women. Particularly for Euro-American women, for whom I have the most data and whose point of view I will continue to explore here, it was also about problematizing presumptions of male superiority and boundaries of gender difference. At the very least it took the form of a heightened consciousness of, and sensitivity to, "sexism." Sexism itself took a variety of forms in mountaineering, some more and some less familiar. Generalized disrespect and dismissal by fellow male climbers was probably the most common (see Ridgeway 1979: 119ff, about Arlene Blum's problems on the mixed American Bicentennial expedition; see also Bremer-Kamp 1987; Gillette and Reynolds 1985). Beyond that there was more active sexual harassment:

> . . . this morning Jeff [one of the French men] called me into the mess tent where a little group of them were sitting. They had obviously just been smoking 'strong cigarettes' with the cook, and were laughing raucously. 'Come in, Julie,' Jeff encouraged, 'Gelaal [the Pakistani policeman/guard with the expedition] says he wants to f . . . you' . . . 'Well, what do you say?' Jeff, our supposedly responsible doctor, giggled. 'I would say that it was typical of you and your friends, you all seem to keep your brains in your balls,' I retorted and walked out. (Tullis 1986: 150)

And finally there was a question of "paternalism," which was a particularly thorny issue among women mountaineers. There was the sense that, in climbing as in other areas of life, men will tend to take over and this must be resisted. Thus many women argued against mixed-sex expeditions, taking the position that the only way to maintain leadership and independence for women in mountaineering is by not climbing with men altogether.

This was by no means a fully shared position. Many women who were in other ways gender-radical continued to climb in mixed groups and/or with a strong male climbing partner. Julie Tullis, the English climber who told off a bunch of men on Nanga Parbat in the text quoted just above, nonetheless identified single-sex women's expeditions with a kind of "feminism" that she was not interested in. She always climbed in mixed groups, often as the only woman on the expedition, and she commented about an all-women Polish expedition on K2:

The four girls [*sic*] got on well together and were very strong and extremely determined in their climbing, but I could never see myself as
part of a "feminist" expedition. (Tullis 1986: 227)[17]

And Junko Tabei, one of the first two women to reach the summit of Everest,
had no qualms about acknowledging that she relied heavily on her male
Sherpa climbing partner, Ang Tshering. Ang Tshering led the whole way on
the final summit assault, keeping up the momentum (if one can talk about
"momentum" at that altitude) for the effort (Unsworth 1981: 463; Birkett
and Peascod 1989: 99–111).

Yet for many of the women, climbing without men is an exhilarating experience. They express a sense of "liberation," a sense of being independent,
grown-up, on one's own. As the great American climber and leader Arlene
Blum put it,

I had taken part in a previous all-woman expedition—an ascent of Mt.
McKinley in 1970—and it had been my most satisfying climb so
far. . . . We felt as though we were climbing our mountain "without the
grownups," and we successfully handled some difficult problems.
(Blum 1980: 9)

We hear similar sentiments from Stacy Allison, the first American woman
to reach the summit of Mt. Everest:

Being together gave Ev and me the energy to do whatever we wanted.
We had male friends, male teachers, male climbing companions. We
didn't avoid climbing with men, but climbing together meant we didn't
have to rely on them, to worry one might question our strength or our
ability to climb where only men had gone before. (Allison 1993: 46)[18]

In these cases (see also Johnson, in Gardiner 1990: 91)., what is being resisted is not men as sexual partners, lovers, or husbands, but quite specifically men in the mode of "patriarchy," men-as-"fathers," men who take
over and make women feel childish.[19]

The question of whether to climb with men or not is relatively unproblematic if women climbers can simply choose between mixed-sex and all-
women's expeditions. But in the context of Himalayan mountaineering,
with its tradition of Sherpa support, the choice is not so simple, as we may
now consider.

FEMINISM, SHERPAS, AND THE
ANNAPURNA WOMEN'S EXPEDITION

Intercultural relations in borderlands are never gender neutral. Although Junko Tabei was happy to accept the Sherpa Ang Tshering's help, in fact one of the effects of the women's movement, combined with the sexual liberation movement, was to problematize relationships between memsahibs and Sherpas. Both movements brought to the fore—though in different ways— the fact that "the Sherpas," hitherto seen as a relatively sexless category of function-performing human beings, were actually MEN.

In the context of all-male expeditions, the fact that Sherpas were of the male persuasion was, as noted earlier, played upon by both Sherpas and sahibs for certain purposes.[20] At the same time, contradictorily, the Sherpas may well have been coded in some metaphorical sense as female. While this is probably true of many forms of Western otherizing—the Western self is male, the "Oriental" or "Primitive" Other, regardless of gender, is female— in the Sherpa case the linkages were perhaps more specific. The Sherpas' job could be seen as basically mothering the sahibs—cooking, cleaning, carrying their loads, and occasionally even carrying them. Indeed it may be in part for this reason—that Sherpas were coded female—as well as for their small size, that their physical strength, speed, stamina, and overall physical superiority were so disturbing to the sahibs (Ortner n.d. b).[21]

It took the women, then, to truly notice Sherpa male climbers' maleness. More precisely, one should say that it took this particular, historically shaped, cohort of women, producers and products of both sexual liberation and feminist politics, to construct Sherpas as "male." By "construct" I mean here not simply noticing that the Sherpas were physical men, but endowing this maleness with a range of meanings with practical and political implications. Thus on the one hand there was the pattern discussed earlier: constructing Sherpa men as sexual males and getting involved with them sexually. But on the other hand there was the amplification of feminist awareness: constructing Sherpa men as *political* males, in all the senses feminists were trying to get away from or change—men who would view themselves as superior to women, who would want to tell women what to do, who would not be willing to take orders from women leaders, and so on and so forth. Thus when explicitly "feminist" expeditions were put together in the 1970s, there was a real question for some women about whether such expeditions should take Sherpas at all. If the expedition was a success, but (Sherpa) men had assisted, would it still be a success as a *women's* expedition?

Both of these issues—sex with Sherpas, and the question of excluding men from the climb—came together in the 1978 Annapurna Women's Expedition, as described in probably one of the most extraordinary mountaineering books ever written, Arlene Blum's *Annapurna: A Woman's Place*. I want to trace some of the ways in which this expedition manifested—as both triumph and tragedy[22]—the points just discussed.

The expedition was organized by Arlene Blum, an experienced climber who had previously participated in the mixed-sex American Bicentennial Mount Everest Expedition, among other climbs. At the time she and some friends began to think about an all-women's climb, no woman had ever reached the top of an over-8,000-meter peak.[23] The Annapurna Women's Expedition received enormous publicity from the outset, at least in part because of its double-entendre slogan, "A Woman's Place Is on Top," which was printed on tens of thousands of T-shirts that were sold (very successfully) to raise money for the expedition (Blum 1980).

The party consisted of thirteen women, all American, ranging in ages from twenty-one (Annie Whitehouse) to fifty (Joan Firey). The group comprised the usual sociological mix discussed earlier. Most of the women had some, and some had a lot, of higher education. Blum herself has a Ph.D. in biochemistry, one of the women was a doctor, and so forth. There was also the usual mix of marital/relationship/sexual statuses—some were married, some in long-term relationships with men, one was a mother, and the sexual/marital statuses of others was unclear.

One aspect of the "feminism" of the expedition was that the group had asked to have it arranged that some Sherpa women be brought along to be trained as "sherpas" (here, a role term meaning skilled high-altitude porters). This was largely (though not completely—see below) unheard of at the time, and the Sherpa sardar (leader), Lopsang, was felt by the women to be resistant to the idea. He did, however, hire two of his female relatives to act as kitchen girls in the base camp. But this appeared to be just the opposite of what the American women wanted, and produced—like everything else about this star-crossed expedition—irresolution and conflict. It is not clear from the book what happened but, according to a Sherpa friend of mine, one of the Sherpa women got sexually involved with one of the Sherpa men. In any event Blum wound up firing the women, who in turn were very angry. There was an ugly confrontation which left Blum very shaken.

In addition, right from the beginning there was an incipient split in the expedition over whether to use Sherpas or not. Alison Chadwick-Onyszkiewicz and some others were in favor of not using Sherpas, echoing the theme of independence that we have heard from some other women climbers: The Sherpas "may turn out to be a bloody nuisance," Chadwick-Onyszkiewicz warned. "This is a women's climb, after all. We don't really need Sherpas. *We should do it on our own*" (Blum 1980: 27, emphasis added).

But they did take male Sherpas, and everything that everyone feared one way or another did come to pass. Although the expedition had a rule ("no romance during the climb" [1980: 38–39]) Annie Whitehouse, the youngest member of the group, fell in love with and began sleeping with the Sherpa kitchen boy.[24] This is not terrible in and of itself, but it did put the question of "sex with the memsahibs" on the table for the expedition as a whole.

> The Sherpas were very conscious of the relationship between Annie and Yeshi and apparently couldn't understand why the rest of us were not similarly inclined. Marie complained that the Sherpas kept looking at her in a way that made her feel very uncomfortable. (1980: 179)

Evidently another member of the expedition later got involved with a Kami (blacksmith/untouchable) porter, which the Sherpa telling me the story (in 1990) found to be completely beyond his comprehension. The collective take on the expedition among large sectors of the Sherpa community was that "the whole expedition was looking for husbands" (a polite Sherpa way of saying they were looking for sex).

The fallout of this came later, when the expedition began to break down in various ways. Some of the women were clearly hostile to the Sherpas, and some of the Sherpas in turn began to engage in a form of sexual harassment:

> "Besides, they're getting awfully obnoxious," Liz added. "They keep pointing at us and giggling all the time. I know they're making obscene comments."
>
> . . .
>
> "How do you know?" I [Blum] asked.
>
> "Well, for one thing, they keep drawing phallic symbols in the snow," Liz said. "And when Vera W. asked them to stop, they just said, '*Yeti* [the "abominable snowman"] make pictures in snow—not Sherpas.'" (1980: 110)

More generally the women felt either disrespected (as in this and other [less sexualized] incidents) or patronized (e.g., 1980: 111, 169, 171). And while all the women felt to some degree these problems with the Sherpas as men, there was still the split between those who thought it would be enough of an achievement for women if they reached the top of Annapurna, even with Sherpa support, and those who did not. In the end the bitter conditions on the upper reaches of the mountain, combined with Sherpa insistence, produced a first summit party composed of two memsahibs and two Sherpas. They were successful.

Normally if one party reaches the top the entire expedition is deemed a success. However, on most expeditions, male or female, other members would like a shot at the top, and this was no exception. Remaining in the second party were Alison Chadwick-Onyszkiewicz and Vera Watson. Chadwick-Onyszkiewicz, it will be recalled, was one of the most vociferous in arguing that if one goes to the summit with Sherpa support, it virtually does not count as a success for women. There was one remaining Sherpa who might have accompanied this group to the summit, but he came down with altitude sickness on the final day (Blum had had doubts about him all along) and went down. Blum tried to talk Chadwick-Onyszkiewicz and Watson out of shooting for the summit with no Sherpa support but they took off anyway. They never came back.

The deaths of Alison Chadwick-Onyszkiewicz and Vera Watson seem almost a parable of the pitfalls of the women's movement, a just-so story that concludes with some version of "you can't fool mother nature." At one level this is an absurd interpretation. Death on the mountains respects neither gender (hundreds of men die) nor ideology: Julie Tullis, who always climbed with men and who never thought of herself as a feminist, died of altitude sickness on K2. At another level, however, one must conclude that the deaths of both male *and* female climbers are the effect of what I earlier called bodily politics, a risking of the body in the name of (the honor of) the gendered self.

The Annapurna women's expedition is also a terrible and perfect example of a borderlands encounter. Two groups meet, coming from two cultures, two histories, two politics. American women come from a history of both Western privilege and Western sexism, riding (even making) a wave of liberatory political energy. Sherpa men come from a history of both gender privilege and "Third-World" domination, as well as many decades of participation in "macho" expeditions. The two groups—both in this case well meaning, though that is not always true in the borderlands—wind up in almost perpetual conflict, and the tragic deaths of two climbers appear as, and must to some extent be taken as, the product of this political conflict.

Sherpa Women in the Twentieth Century

I noted earlier that the feminist movement that began in the 1970s went global very quickly, so quickly in fact that one begins to wonder about seeing its origins as Euro-American in the first place. Thus despite the failure of the Annapurna Women's Expedition's attempt in 1978 to recruit Sherpa women as "sherpas," in fact by that year some number of Sherpa women had already entered the mountaineering stage. In order to understand where they were coming from, we need to return to questions of Sherpa gender culture and politics.

Sherpa gender culture is in many ways disadvantageous to women (much of the following is condensed from Ortner 1983, this volume). The ideology favors men as "higher"; men are viewed as capable of greater spirituality, and as less mired in selfish and worldly sorts of concerns. In addition, menstruation is said to be offensive to the gods, and harmful to male spirituality. Femalehood is thus a bad rebirth; a woman who works hard on her spiritual improvement will hope to be reborn as a man.

In the practical realm, girls were generally given less education than boys (Fisher 1990: 79), not only because of prejudice, but because mothers felt they needed their daughters' help at home. In addition, the structural rules of the society favored men—residence after marriage in the traditional village setting was virilocal, with the woman having to move to her husband's village or homestead, and men inherited and owned most of the real property in the society, land and herds. Men also did the trading, the source of major wealth, and men occupied such few political positions as existed in the society.

At the same time one would not describe this as a heavily sexist or male-dominant society. There is virtually no sex-segregation in secular life, no arenas in which men regularly congregate and participate simply as men. Virtually all economic production and social life takes place in households. The domestic group, normally coterminous with the nuclear family, is a very tight unit. Husbands are defined as having ultimate authority in the husband-wife relationship, but as economic producers, and as social actors (especially as co-hosts) vis-à-vis the rest of the community, husbands and wives are tightly interlocked partners (Ortner 1978; March 1979).

Within this cultural and institutional context, Sherpa women's own position was, not surprisingly, quite contradictory. On the one hand there is a bundle of ideology about women as weak, self-indulgent, unreliable, and so forth (Ortner 1983, this volume; March 1979). On the other hand there is no ideology or practice of special protection for women. Sherpa women are encouraged to be outgoing and independent actors who can take care of themselves and operate in almost any capacity in the world.[25] In particular they are seen as capable domestic managers who may be left to operate the household as an economic enterprise for long periods of time, while husbands are away on extended trading expeditions (a traditional part of the Sherpa economy) or climbing expeditions.

After the 1950s an increasing number of Sherpa families began settling permanently in Kathmandu. The moves had multiple effects on women. Because of the prevalence in the capital of Hindu models of family, and also because of the absence of agricultural work, Sherpa women found themselves more confined to the home than they would have been in the village. Contradictions about the independence and autonomy of women were thus heightened in this context.[26]

At the same time, daughters were much more likely to get a full education in the city than they were in the villages. My data suggest that, interestingly enough, it was often Sherpa fathers who pushed harder for educating daughters, partly because it would be useful to the family economy, but also because it would stand the daughter in good stead in her own life. But Sherpa mothers in the city also had fewer objections to their daughters going to school, as the work of a Kathmandu housewife is much less demanding than that of a village householder. In 1979 a village woman told me that she had to keep her terribly bright and lively daughter at home to help her, though her husband, an expedition Sherpa, really wanted the two daughters to go to school. And in the film "Sherpas," the mountaineering sardar Mingma Tenzing talks about educating all of his children, girls as well as boys. He says he does not know what they will do later on, but education will stand all of them in good stead (Ortner 1977). As of my last visit in 1990, one of his daughters was a nurse in a Kathmandu hospital, one was a bilingual secretary for the French embassy in Kathmandu,[27] and one was a student in a private school in Darjeeling.

One should also mention in this context a gender "equalization" law put on the books in Nepal in the mid-1970s: For every eight male district leaders, there had to be one woman.[28] In the village where I did my original fieldwork, the daughter of one of the big men of the village was appointed. As I wrote in my fieldnotes in 1976:

> C. F. [the father] stressed the woman's lib [*sic*] aspects of all this. So does he think it's a good thing? Yes. Why? Because before if he didn't have a son, and only daughters, who would inherit the property? Now, his daughters can inherit. . . . Before men were *che* (higher/senior) and women *tua* (lower/junior), but now they're *chikparang* (equal/identical).

And while it was and is hardly true that Sherpa men and women, or the male and female citizens of Nepal more generally, are *chikparang*, clearly a law like this did not go down without some impact.

Behind a number of these developments for Sherpa women is a broader kind of economic and cultural pragmatism among the Sherpas that links up with aspects of Sherpa gender ideology sketched above. While there are certain prejudices about women, most of them do not have implications for women's freedom of movement, or their assumed ability to learn, excel, and make money if they can. Thus when conditions opened up for various kinds of personal advancement for women, women themselves were predisposed to take advantage of them, and "their culture" (whether in the hands of husbands, parents, "men," or whatever) was not disposed to hold them back.

Sherpa Religion and Female Independence

There is one other major arena of Sherpa society in which women's independence was given a major boost over the course of the twentieth century: religion. The Sherpas are and always have been Tibetan Buddhists, but prior to the twentieth century there were no full-time monasteries in the region. A movement to upgrade Sherpa Buddhism began in the late nineteenth century; the first full-time residential celibate male monastery was founded in 1916, and the second was founded in 1924 (see Ortner 1989).

The monks in turn embarked on a campaign to clean up and raise the level of spirituality in popular religious practice. One aspect of this was the institution (or expansion) of a ritual called Nyungne, in which lay people embark on extended fasting, silence, and prayer, and become, as the Sherpas say, monks for a day. The Nyungne ritual is supposed to bring its practitioners an especially high level of religious merit, "points" toward a better rebirth.

The ritual in turn is said to have been brought to the world by a female bodhisattva called Gelungma Palma. The story of Gelungma Palma is told every year during the ritual, and is well known, at least in its general outlines, to most Sherpas. In the story, a young princess is unhappy with all the sins committed in her father's kingdom. She resolves not to marry, and when she learns of marriage arrangements being made on her behalf, she runs away from home and takes vows of celibacy. She becomes a brilliant and learned religious practitioner, and is appointed to the position of head of a male monastery. But she becomes ill and the monks, thinking she is having a baby, throw her out of the monastery. She wanders about for many years achieving greater and greater levels of spirituality, until finally she becomes a bodhisattva. She goes to the heaven of the god Cherenzi, who sends her back to the world with the text of the Nyungne ritual, to bring enlightenment to the ignorant and suffering creatures who remain in the world (see Ortner 1978: chap. 3).

The Gelungma Palma story was given a good bit of prominence in the course of the monastic clean-up campaign and the annual observance of Nyungne that was one of its manifestations. The story must be taken in turn as part of the context for the founding the first Sherpa nunnery, Devuche, in 1928. Devuche was founded by a group of young women from "big" or high-status families, who ran away from home without parental consent, took vows at a monastery across the border (and across the Himalayas!) in Tibet, and then returned to study and eventually found the nunnery in their home Sherpa region (Ortner 1983, this volume). The women knew that their parents would not be happy about their running away from home and, in at least some cases, foiling marriage arrangements already in the works. But they hoped as well that the legitimacy and cultural value of the act was such that the parents would accept it as a fait accompli and back them up in the end; this is indeed what happened (Ortner 1989: chap. 9).

Other nunneries (like other monasteries) were subsequently founded. Female monasticism in turn apparently had a consciousness-raising effect for some women about the privileges of men and the constraints on women in Sherpa society. For example, one nun commented:

"As a woman one is always inferior . . . however much one learns one is never given as much respect as a lama [the Buddhist religious specialist]. Even corrupt lamas are still treated with some respect; a man can lead a sinful life, and yet later become a lama and be considered superior to any woman." (quoted in von Fürer-Haimendorf 1976: 148)

Other young women of my acquaintance at least toyed with the idea of becoming nuns; the idea that there were alternatives to marriage gave them a sense of options. They might get married in the end but this no longer had the status of inevitability and naturalness it otherwise would have had.

In much the same period, opportunities for wage labor opened up in Darjeeling, under the "development" efforts of the British raj in India. Here again, women ran away from home to take up these opportunities. They did so in smaller numbers than the men, but there is no question that they did so. The general framing of the process was similar to that of becoming a nun: that one's parents would not let one do it if they knew, but that they would ratify it and go along after the fact. Whereas running away to join a nunnery was something largely engaged in by women from wealthier families, running away to work in Darjeeling or Kathmandu was done more by women from poorer (but also quite middling) families.

Finally, then, we return to the entry of Sherpa women into mountaineering in the 1970s and thereafter. The changing culture and politics of Sherpa gender relations just discussed will enter into this story in a number of ways.

Sherpa Women Mountaineers

There was (and still is) resistance on the part of many Sherpa men to having Sherpa women join expeditions. The question of women menstruating on the mountain (this applies to memsahibs as well) is worrisome, as offending the gods whose favor many Sherpas still believe is important to the success of the expedition. (The status of this "belief" among contemporary Sherpas will be discussed in another context, but there is no doubt that for many individuals it is phenomenologically real.) One sardar in the early 1990s told me the story of the 1979 French Dhaulagiri expedition on which one Sherpa died and the French leader lost both hands and feet to frostbite. The leader and his girlfriend, according to this account, stayed too long at high altitude because the woman was "personally sick."[29] This sardar felt that the woman should not have been climbing with her period and that she caused much misfortune as a result. Many Sherpa sardars also feel that women as "sherpas" among the male "sherpas" will cause discord and conflict among the men. Most still say they would not hire women, and it is the sardar who is in charge of the hiring.

As early as 1977 a Sherpa woman joked in the film "Sherpas" that her husband has had many chances to go on mountaineering expeditions and now it's her turn. Next year, she says with a twinkle in her eye, she's going to Everest (Ortner 1977). In 1990 I asked this woman—who never did go climbing—what she thought of Sherpa women climbing:

> She said many women want to go but they don't get the chance. Her second daughter would like to climb, but probably sardars won't give her jobs. Sardars feel that women are weak, won't carry, and also if you mix boys and girls you'll have problems.

Yet there were always exceptions to these points, and the exceptions multiplied over time. From early on, as Sherpas wished to keep mountaineering jobs within the Sherpa community in general and their own families in particular, it became the practice to use Sherpa women, and even children and old people, as "local porters" (who carried supplies to the base of the mountain) if not actual climbers. Somewhat later, women began moving into the kitchen jobs—cooks and kitchen helpers. We saw that Lopsang recruited some of his female relatives into these jobs, and although the Annapurna memsahibs evidently took this to be "traditional" women's work, and essentially non-liberatory, in fact expedition cooking had been, like all expedition jobs, men's work. It is a step up from local portering—it pays a bit more, it gets one onto the mountain proper, and for many men it was and is the route to more skilled "sherpa" work in mountaineering. For women, too, as we shall see, it could serve this function.

Starting in the 1970s, then, some women did indeed seek to get involved in the more difficult, dangerous, but also more highly paid and prestigious role of "sherpa," involving high-altitude portering and expedition support. And most recently some women, as well as some Sherpa men, sought simply to be mountaineers in their own right, with or without sahib partners.

How shall we understand this history? We cannot assume that Sherpa women enter high-altitude mountaineering for the same motives as "first world" women (Mohanty 1991a, b). But we also cannot assume that their motives are entirely different; that would simply reinscribe the hard self/other boundary. Rather we need, as I said earlier, a sense of "culture" without Otherness, and a sense that difference comes as much from different histories and politics as from different "cultures." In order to see this I will examine the only material currently available on Sherpa women mountaineers: interviews with two of them that I conducted in 1990, as well as various second-hand accounts about a third woman, who became the subject of intense public debate in Nepal following her success and death on Mt. Everest in 1993.[30]

ANG HRITA

The first of the women I interviewed is called Ang Hrita, from Pangboche village in Khumbu (the upper Sherpa valley). In 1976 or so she and two other Sherpa women went for a training course at the Nepal Mountaineering Association. All three of them passed the course, and thus began her career.

One of her early expeditions was the joint Italian-Nepali Everest expedition in 1980. She had conflict with the Nepali co-leader of the expedition:

> She and [one of the other women] wanted to go all the way to the summit but the Nepali [leader] didn't support her. The leader was an officer in the Nepal army. She got to Camp 2 but the men wouldn't support them. They went as far as just below Camp 3 without the leader's authorization. The leader got very angry, said why did you go without permission? He didn't give her a chance.

In 1981, she climbed with a Japanese expedition to Langtang Ri, and reached camp 3. She had a chance to go to the summit but at that time received word that her brother had been killed on Annapurna, and the Liaison Officer told her not to go because she was upset about her brother. She participated in at least four more climbs, of which the last was the Japanese women's expedition to Changla Himal in 1983. She concluded the interview by saying that she would still like to climb but apparently had no other chances.

Ang Hrita was quite shy throughout the interview, and did not offer any general reflections on women climbing. However, a few points may be noted here. First, although she never mentioned it, I know from other sources that she was married to a sardar, or Sherpa expedition leader, in her younger years, and all of her climbs were on expeditions on which he was the sardar.[31] In fact, in all three cases I will discuss, the women climbed with their husbands. Partly this was because, as noted earlier, men as sardars would not take unrelated women on climbs. But there may be something else at work, to which I will return shortly.

Second, it is worth noting that Ang Hrita's confrontation with the Nepali co-leader of the expedition took a distinctive form: She did not argue or talk back; she simply pushed the limits with her behavior (climbing to camp 3 without permission) and hoped to create a fait accompli. This is perhaps another variant of running away to a nunnery or to Darjeeling, and hoping or assuming that others will go along with it after the fact.

NYIMI

The second woman climber I interviewed is called Ang Nyimi (or just Nyimi),[32] from Zhung village in Solu (the lower Sherpa valley). Her husband, Hlakpa Norbu, is a sardar. They met in 1977 when she was sixteen, and were married shortly thereafter. She began trekking with him and enjoyed it very much, and they have operated pretty much as a team ever since. Her first real expedition was the French expedition to Ama Dablam in 1979. This was Hlakpa Norbu's first expedition as a sardar. She was the second cook, which was a bit daunting as there were twenty-one French members, but she did it. The expedition was successful and she is still friends with some of the French women of the group. She was the cook again on the French/Nepal Police joint expedition to Dhaulagiri, and again on the 1983 French expedition to Ama Dablam. In the interim she also led many trekking groups, and was in those contexts herself the sardar.

In 1984 she joined a French expedition to Nuptse, and in this case for the first time she actually reached the summit. Here's how she tells the story.[33]

> At first she was not a sherpa. But the French offered some training and then chose four boys and her. (The leader had asked her if she was interested and she had said yes.) After about four days of training she asked the leader and the Liaison Officer [if she could go], and they said, we'll see how you do, if you do well you can go to the summit. At that time there was no insurance for her because she wasn't supposed to be a sherpa. And she didn't really become a sherpa, they just let her go.

> She said the climbing was not bad until after about 7,000 meters (the mountain is 7,865 meters high). They were climbing without supplementary oxygen, which makes it much more difficult. Sometimes she became afraid when it was very steep. It took twelve days round-trip from Base Camp to the summit and back.

> There were four people in the first group—one member and three Sherpas including herself and her husband Hlakpa Norbu. Her husband kept telling her to go down, she only had single boots, he said her parents would be angry with him if she had an accident. Even just below

the summit he said go down—she got a little angry with him. But each time he said go down she said, "just a little more."

And she made it to the top.

Nyimi had obviously thought a great deal about the implications of what she had done and why. When I asked her why she began climbing, she said that because she isn't educated, she isn't equipped to do much else, and it's important to do *something* with one's life.[34] She said other women are equally strong—if they wanted to they could do it too, but they don't try, or their families won't let them. She repeated this dual theme of how others hold women back, but also women themselves are too timid:

> There's a problem for Sherpa women because if they go out and do things people think badly of them. People are "very conservative." Also women's psychology is a problem—they are too retiring. She doesn't care what other people think—she lets it go in one ear and out the other (which she illustrated graphically with a gesture). Otherwise you'll never do anything.

Nyimi's story illustrates a number of things. We hear in it the same kind of independence that we heard from Ang Hrita—a sense of capability and autonomy that I think is characteristic of Sherpa women in general. We also see in Nyimi's story the same silent but active resistance that we have come to recognize as something like a cultural script for Sherpa women: she didn't argue with her husband when he told her to go back, but she just kept climbing.

But let us focus here for a moment on Nyimi's partnership with her husband. It will be recalled that there were a variety of ways in which mountaineering was destabilizing the Sherpa gender system. Young men were being encouraged in a kind of machismo that had not been common in the culture. "Memsahibs" offered many attractions up to and including marriage and long-term residence in Europe and the United States. At the very least there was a tendency for at least some men to stay away, both on expeditions and in Kathmandu, for longer and longer periods of time, and to have very attenuated ties with their families back in the villages.

Nyimi's very committed partnership with her husband then could be read as an active move against these developments in Sherpa gender relations. We will see in the next case too that Pasang Lhamu and her husband worked in a literal partnership with one another. Not only did they climb together, they were partners with some other relatives in the ownership of a trekking agency. All of this contrasts rather sharply with the sense for some Western feminists of the need to climb without men in order to feel independent. Yet far from being "traditional," as it might appear in the Western context, Sherpa women's pattern of climbing with their husbands may be read as gender-radical in this historical moment; that is, it may be read as an attempt to work against some of the creeping machismo of the young generation of men, and to (re-)establish more mutually respectful gender relations.

Nyimi was probably the most famous of the small number of Sherpa women mountaineers in the 1970s and 1980s. She was invited to Europe where she climbed Mont Blanc, and she and her husband made a film about Sherpas and Himalayan mountaineering with a French filmmaker. But as she told me in the interview, she still wanted to climb Mt. Everest. If she were to do so—although she didn't say this—she would be the first Sherpa woman to achieve that distinction, and equally important from the point of view of ethnic and national politics, the first Nepali (in the sense of citizenship) woman to do so. But that was not to be. Instead the woman called Pasang Lhamu reached the top in 1993 as part of an expedition which she herself organized and led. She also died, along with another Sherpa, on the way down from the summit.

THE PASANG LHAMU STORY

The story of these events—the narrative of what happened and of people's motivations—is tremendously contested. The following version, which is also consistent with most published accounts, comes from a conversation with some Sherpa friends—a husband and wife—who were visiting with me in Ann Arbor shortly after Pasang Lhamu's funeral.

Pasang Lhamu, a native of Pankongma village in the Pharak region of Solu-Khumbu,[35] had climbed as a "sherpa" on a number of previous expeditions with the French. In 1991 she had been on a French Everest expedition, and had reached the south col, but then the leader did not choose her for the summit party and she had been angry. She subsequently went on another Everest expedition but it was cancelled because of bad weather. So she was determined to make it to the top.

In 1993, an Indian women's expedition was being planned. The organizers contacted Pasang Lhamu, but she wanted to be named co-leader (with the Indian leader) with a guaranteed shot at the top. The Indians would not agree, so Pasang Lhamu refused. They then asked Nyimi, who agreed. According to this informant, as well as to a number of published sources, Pasang Lhamu and Nyimi were very *chana*, competitive.[36]

Meanwhile Pasang Lhamu determined to go ahead. She formed a Nepal Women's Expedition with herself as the leader, and two other women, Lhakputi Sherpa and Nanda Rai, as members. She applied to the government for a waiver of fee (as a citizen of Nepal) but for complex reasons which became the subject of debate later, the government refused. So she went about fund-raising herself. She needed $50,000,[37] which is now the fee for Everest. She got San Miguel Beer/Nepal to put up half, and she raised the other half by the sale of T-shirts and the like.

So they went. She took five male Sherpas, including her husband, an experienced climbing Sherpa. She and four men reached the summit, not including her husband. (Her husband wanted to go, but they agreed that it was better for their three small children if they not go together.) Then bad weather started coming in. They all bivouacked[38] at the south summit one night. Then two Sherpas came down to get help, but the weather totally closed in. They had no radios and no way to get back up. Within a day or two she sent down another Sherpa for help. She died with one male Sherpa (Sonam Tsering), whose body was never found, only his rucksack. There were no further communications. They think he stayed with her till she died, then tried to get down but fell. Her body wasn't found for twenty-one days.

Pasang Lhamu became a tremendous heroine. While she was missing, the situation was a front-page story in the papers, day after day. Appeals were put out to pray for her safety. When it was confirmed that she had died, the government announced that it was awarding her the Nepal Tara award, of which only two had been given before, one to the first ethnic Sherpa and Nepali citizen[39] to reach the top of Everest, Tenzing Norgay. Her body was brought all the way back from just below the summit of Everest to Kathmandu (itself a very difficult and completely unprecedented feat), and she was cremated in the national stadium, with a national flag over her coffin, and tens of thousands of people in attendance.

Pasdang Lhamu's intentions, motives, and self-representations are almost impossible to recover, at least from the kinds of reporting that have appeared thus far. Several reporters portray her as highly competitive and self-promoting, while others respond not so much with a counter-portrait as with charges that this description is sexist and ethnically or nationally prejudiced.[40] She certainly must have been a person of impressive drive, energy, and persuasiveness. And it is important to remember that she not only died on Mt. Everest; she raised the money, organized the expedition, and climbed to the top of it first.

There are many things going on in the Pasang Lhamu story that cannot be explored in detail here. There is the (alleged) rivalry with Nyimi, which connects with certain Sherpa cultural schemas of competition usually involving men (Ortner 1989).[41] There are the echoes of the Annapurna Women's Expedition, involving everything from the entrepreneurial sale of T-shirts to the excessively risky bodily politics. There are divisions of opinion and feeling over whether Pasang Lhamu as a mother of three small children should have been taking such risks.[42] And there is the play of transnational capital in the background, with the sponsorship of San Miguel Beer/ Nepal.

Again, I can only attend to a small number of points. The first concerns a question that arises here more clearly than it did in the other women's stories: the intertwining of gender and ethnic/national issues. This issue deserves more attention than I can give it here. The intertwining of gender with other political issues and identities is a major point of difference between various forms of "first world" feminism on the one hand, and various forms of minority and/or "third world" feminism on the other (Mohanty 1991a, b; Johnson-Odim 1991). In any event it is clear in the Pasang Lhamu case that questions of gender were from the very beginning tied up with questions of Sherpa ethnic politics vis-à-vis the dominant Nepali state, and with questions of Sherpa-Nepali nationalist solidarity vis-à-vis larger/ stronger/more "modern" nations.

In some contexts, Pasang Lhamu would join the two discourses. Thus, for example, when she had the falling out with the French climber in 1990, she "went public accusing [him of] discrimination against a woman and a native climber" (Risal 1993: 43). But in contexts where the gender issue was equalized, for example in her conflict with the Indian Women's Expedition, Pasang Lhamu framed the issue purely as a national one: "She felt that since the joint venture was envisioned at a national level and patronised by the Prime Ministers of the two countries, the question of co-leadership was very important" (Sangroula 1993: 7). The counterpoint between frames of gender and of nation continued in the journalism following her death. When a Nepali journalist suggested that the heroization of Pasang Lhamu had been greatly blown out of proportion (Risal 1993), the angry responses from letter writers switched back and forth between charges of "sexism" (Acharya 1993) and charges of national divisiveness (Sharma 1993).

The second point on which I will comment briefly here is that, as in the other two cases, Pasang Lhamu climbed with her husband. Not only did they climb together, they were business partners as well. I suggested earlier that it would be at least plausible to suggest that Sherpa women climb with their husbands not only because they cannot get climbing jobs without them, but because it is part of a more active and intentionalized move to re-establish some solidarity and relative equality with Sherpa men. This of course may seem to beg the question of why they want to climb in the first place, to which several answers have already been suggested: that they come from a tradition of independence that had been enhanced by various religious changes over the course of the twentieth century; that they had been chafing in the more housewifely role they were forced to take up in Kathmandu; that climbing is both well paying and charismatic in Nepal; that, given the role of tourism and climbing in the Nepal economy, for young people without formal education (and even to some extent with it) climbing is virtually the only game in town; and so forth.

None of these points, of course, exclude the possibility of the one I am suggesting here: that climbing with one's husband is an act of gender-radical politics in this context, an attempt to intervene in, and counteract, a situation of growing inequality. And in fact it is my impression, though only at this point an impression, that the various aspects of Sherpa women's gender politics seem to be paying off. Following a period in which Sherpa society seemed to be splitting between men in the cities getting caught up in the national and transnational swirl, and women in the villages remaining "backward" and "traditional," the number of husband/wife teams in this story is at least suggestive of a shift.[43] Along with this shift may come a certain self-awareness. For example, at the conclusion of the conversation in Ann Arbor, the discussion moved from Pasang Lhamu's death to gender politics more generally:

> I asked, do you think more Sherpa women will climb, because in my interviews with sardars most of them said they wouldn't take a woman, it causes trouble on the expedition. And Rinzi [not his real name] said yes, most people do not feel comfortable taking someone else's wife on an expedition.

And he also said, you know, we Sherpas are still kind of "male dominant." I said well yes, but the Sherpas seem to me relatively egalitarian compared to some of the Hindu groups. And he said yes, our wives don't have to wait till we finish eating. And I said, or wash their husbands' feet. And he said yeah, a Sherpa wife would just say, wash them yourself! And we all cracked up.

Brief Conclusions:
Politics and Meaning in and Beyond the Borderlands

This paper has told several different, but interrelated, stories. The first is a historical narrative about gender radicalism and borderland encounters in a particular corner of the world over much of the twentieth century. It has traced out what I called earlier a "dialectics of sex," in which "first-world" women, Sherpa men, and Sherpa women have come together in different ways at different times, bringing with them their own histories, politics, and cultures.[44] They have caused one another pleasure and pain, they have probably changed one another as persons, and they have shared in and contributed to a transnational gender revolution that is still going on.

The second story is methodological and theoretical. It joins a line of discussion in anthropology that asks how the ethnographic enterprise is refigured when one focuses on borderlands rather than on "cultures." Borderland analysis has some powerful advantages over earlier kinds of ethnographic work. First, it gets around some of the problems of the classic ethnography—the treatment of cultures as timeless integrated wholes. In addition, it emphasizes relations of difference, power and struggle, an emphasis that is both important in itself, and that produces a much more dramatic story. Further, it places "us" and "them" within the same frame, and subjects all parties to the same analytic scrutiny. And finally (though there are no doubt other reasons) in its complex intertwining of multiple and continuing histories it comes closer to capturing the complexity and the never-finished nature of the real world.

But the pitfalls of a borderlands perspective must also be noted. We lose many things that were valuable in earlier kinds of ethnographic work. In particular, we lose a sense that people have their own worlds beyond the borderlands, worlds of shared (even if partially so) meanings, worlds of local invention and creativity, local politics (good and bad), shared history, and so on and so forth. Much of this is produced and reproduced, in turn, through the small and routine practices and struggles of everyday life, accounts of which were also more prominent in classic ethnographies, and which tend to get lost in the heightened drama of borderlands narratives.

This is not to try to reinvent "culture" as we knew it—it is by now perhaps a spoiled category. And the Himalayan case represents a relatively "easy" kind of borderland, one where people get to go home after the expeditions (although they do not thereby leave it entirely behind—but that is another story). But I would argue that there is *always* a home beyond the borderland, even for people who are forced to live with dominant Others every day of their lives. For even in these situations, the making and keeping of some kind of cultural space, some kind of world of shared forms of relationship and shared meanings, is precisely one of the things that is at stake in the struggle. The most powerful of the new ethnographies will be those that can move between, and recognize the authenticity of, both kinds of worlds.

Notes

One: Making Gender

Many thanks to Nancy Chodorow, Louise Lamphere, Judith Stacey, Abigail Stewart, Timothy D. Taylor, and Marya Van't Hul for excellent and productive readings of a much earlier and very different (because of them!) version of this introduction. I presented a version of this essay to the Finnish Anthropological Society as the Edward Westermarck Memorial Lecture; I had lively and useful conversations about it with Finnish students and colleagues, and especially with Professor Jukka Siikala. Special mention must also be made of the excellent discussions in my graduate seminar on "Practice Theory" at the University of California, Berkeley (Spring 1996) where the students pushed me to think harder at every turn. And finally, thanks to Tim Taylor again for yet more readings and, as ever, for ongoing support.

1. It was not until 1987 that R. W. Connell published *Gender and Power*, linking practice theory and feminist theory. I regret not doing more with Connell's book in the present essay. I found it in many ways insightful and useful. But although it claims to be working within a practice theory perspective, it is largely "objectivist," and does not sustain the commitment to moving between objective and subjective perspectives that is the strength of full-fledged practice theories.

2. For feminist anthropology see, e.g., Linnekin 1990, Ong 1987, Povinelli 1993, Stacey 1990, Tsing 1993.

3. Without engaging in any kind of deep self-analysis here, I will say that I have found this strange myself, after the fact. It is doubly strange in that it

was precisely through feminist scholarship that I came to move away from my earlier training and to try to work out, first on my own, and then through the discovery of the likes of Bourdieu et al., some kind of practice perspective.

4. For extensive discussions of power and practice, see Dirks, Eley, and Ortner 1994.

5. De Certeau is an apparent exception to this point. I do not deal with him much in this essay because, despite the title of his book (*The Practice of Everyday Life*), I do not see him as a theorist of practice in the broad sense defined by the work of Bourdieu, Giddens, and Sahlins. While I like his work, I see him largely as a "resistance" theorist, not particularly interested in the ways in which practice either reproduces or transforms enduring "structures."

6. In his appendix titled "On the Wrath of Cook," Sahlins focuses on the events surrounding the removal of a wooden fence from a temple compound by some of Cook's sailors. Obeyesekere uses sources that show that some Hawaiians were quite upset by this event and took it as sacrilegious, and Sahlins spends most of the appendix dismissing Obeyesekere's key sources. Aside from the fact that I found Sahlins's discussion in this context relatively unpersuasive, it does not actually address the larger portrait of the growing "wrath of Cook" constructed by Obeyesekere from other sources that Sahlins elsewhere treats as reliable.

7. The issue of gender in *Grimms' Fairy Tales* is now the subject of a lively and growing body of literature. See Barzelai 1990, Zipes 1993, and especially Bottigheimer 1987.

8. In one version of "Little Red Riding Hood," the girl and her grandmother get up on the roof and successfully kill the wolf and turn him into sausage. In "The Seven Ravens," the girl goes to seek her brothers, and finds and rescues them with great resourcefulness, virtually unassisted. In "Hansel and Gretel," as noted, it is Gretel who kills the witch. In "The Robber Bridegroom," the girl is helped by an old woman and between the two of them they bring about the execution of the robber and his band. And in "Fundevogel," the girl actively and resourcefully saves her brother from a wicked old woman.

9. "Sweetheart Roland" is a variant of a tale called "Fundevogel." Other examples in this pattern would include "The Twelve Brothers" and "The Six Swans" (variants of each other and of "The Seven Ravens"). In all of these, the heroine sets out on a quest to rescue her brothers. But despite her good intentions, she causes her brothers damage as a result of her activities to save them, and goes through a seven-year period of complete silence and solemnity (including in one case making shirts for her brothers and in the

other case simply spinning for seven years) before getting married at the end.

10. See Ahearn (1995) and Kratz (n.d.) on the negativity of female agency in a Nepalese and an African case respectively.

11. I cannot resist a footnote about what appears to be a cultural configuration often found among French intellectuals: an unshakable opposition to theoretical notions of intentionality and agency on the one hand, combined with a tendency toward extraordinary authorial agency on the other.

12. Geertz used the phrase "serious games" in "Blurred Genres" (1983: 23) as part of a discussion that overlaps in some ways with the one developed in this paper. One is reminded as well of his phrase "deep play" in the cockfight paper (1973).

13. Sahlins (1981) gets in trouble with Obeyesekere for his "cosmological dramas," although I did not in fact read him as Obeyesekere did, as implying a rigid pre-scripting of life. I used a similar notion in *High Religion* (1989), which I called "cultural schemas." But I also discussed in that context the variability of ways in which actors may hold, or be held by, such schemas (1989: 126–29).

14. I find the idea of narrative to be a very powerful intellectual tool, and have tentatively explored some of its theoretical implications in an unpublished paper (Ortner 1990b). Pieces of the discussion about the rupturing of agency in the present essay come from that paper, but the rest of it seemed too unworked out to be published.

15. My later work on Polynesian gender data indicated that the emergence of any kind of "stratification," institutionalized inequality, was enough of a factor, and one did not need the full apparatus of the "state" to make the argument.

16. The original title was "Gender and Sexuality in Hierarchical Societies: The Case of Polynesia and Some Comparative Implications."

17. Originally entitled "The Founding of the First Sherpa Nunnery, and the Problem of 'Women' as an Analytic Category."

18. See for example Trinh T. Minh-ha's demonization of "anthropology" (1989). Trinh's discussion is unfortunately both excessive and out of date (her main target is Malinowski), but I cannot discuss it in any detail here.

Two: Is Female to Male as Nature Is to Culture?

Preface 1996: In about 1971, Michelle Zimbalist Rosaldo and Louise Lamphere sent out a note to a number of women anthropologists, inviting them to write something for a contemplated volume on—I'm not sure what they called it—(maybe) "the anthropology of women." They also called a meeting in one of their rooms at the next American Anthropological Association meetings, and I can still picture the scene—people sitting on beds and on the floor and standing around along the walls. And I said it sounds like a good idea, but I don't know anything about women, and Shelly said, neither does anyone else. I can't remember how the rest of the conversation unfolded but although I had been meaning to refuse I wound up agreeing. Shelley was very persuasive.

This paper was one part response to early feminists inside and outside of academia hunting for examples of "matriarchal" or "egalitarian" cultures; one part appropriation of the hot theory of the day, the structuralism of Claude Lévi-Strauss; and one part personal meditation on the pitfalls of inhabiting a female body. It came together almost full-blown in my head, and most of it was written quite feverishly in one sitting.

The paper was first published in 1972 (*Feminist Studies* 1(2): 5–31) and then again in 1974 in the Rosaldo and Lamphere volume. Over time, it took on a life of its own, something that was at first gratifying, and subsequently both fascinating and problematic. I address some of the criticisms the paper has attracted in "So, *Is* Female to Male as Nature is to Culture?" and "Gender Hegemonies" later in this volume.

Preface 1974: The first version of this paper was presented in October 1972 as a lecture in the course "Women: Myth and Reality" at Sarah Lawrence College. I received helpful comments from the students and from my co-teachers in the course: Joan Kelly Gadol, Eva Kollisch, and Gerda Lerner. A short account was delivered at the American Anthropological Association meetings in Toronto, November 1972. Meanwhile, I received excellent critical comments from Karen Blu, Robert Paul, Michelle Rosaldo, David Schneider, and Terence Turner, and the present version of the paper, in which the thrust of the argument has been rather significantly changed, was written in response to those comments. I, of course, retain responsibility for its final form. The paper is dedicated to Simone de Beauvoir, whose book *The Second Sex* (1953), first published in French in 1949, remains in my opinion the best single comprehensive understanding of "the woman problem."

1. It is true of course that *yin*, the female principle, has a negative valence. Nonetheless, there is an absolute complementarity of *yin* and *yang* in Taoism, a recognition that the world requires the equal operation and interaction of both principles for its survival.

2. Some anthropologists might consider this type of evidence (social-structural arrangements that exclude women, explicitly or de facto, from certain groups, roles, or statuses) to be a subtype of the second type of evi-

dence (symbolic formulations of inferiority). I would not disagree with this view, although most social anthropologists would probably separate the two types.

3. While we are on the subject of injustices of various kinds, we might note that Lowie secretly bought this doll, the most sacred object in the tribal repertoire, from its custodian, the widow of Wrinkled-face. She asked $400 for it, but this price was "far beyond [Lowie's] means," and he finally got it for $80 (Lowie 1956: 300).

4. With all due respect to Lévi-Strauss (1969a, b, and passim).

5. Semantic theory uses the concept of motivation of meaning, which encompasses various ways in which a meaning may be assigned to a symbol because of certain objective properties of that symbol, rather than by arbitrary association. In a sense, this entire paper is an inquiry into the motivation of the meaning of woman as a symbol, asking why woman may be unconsciously assigned the significance of being closer to nature. For a concise statement on the various types of motivation of meaning, see Ullman (1963).

6. A situation that often serves to make her more childlike herself.

7. David M. Schneider (personal communication) is prepared to argue that the incest taboo is not universal, on the basis of material from Oceania. Let us say at this point, then, that it is virtually universal.

8. I remember having my first male teacher in the fifth grade, and I remember being excited about that—it was somehow more grown-up.

9. Nobody seems to care much about sororicide—a point that ought to be investigated.

10. Ingham's discussion is rather ambiguous itself, since women are also associated with animals: "The contrasts man/animal and man/woman are evidently similar... hunting is the means of acquiring women as well as animals" (1971: 1095). A careful reading of the data suggests that both women and animals are mediators between nature and culture in this tradition.

Three: The Virgin and the State

Preface 1996: I did my graduate training at the University of Chicago in the 1960s, with Clifford Geertz as my advisor. My intellectual interests were deeply shaped by this background, in the sense that I was committed (and still am) to a humanistic, interpretive anthropology concerned with elucidating questions of culture, meaning, and value. "The Virgin and the State" was written as a job talk for the University of Michigan, which had been a hotbed of "materialist" anthropology in the sixties. Sixties materialist anthropology was both extremely hostile to "culture," and heavily invested in "scientific" explanation as opposed to "humanistic" interpretation.

By the mid-1970s, however, materialist anthropology had changed quite a bit. It had become both more interested in issues of "culture," and more Marxist, in a critical/political rather than economistic sense. At the same time, through my feminist work I had become more broadly politicized. I also became dissatisfied with purely "cultural" interpretations, and felt the need to "ground" them in some kind of social/political/historical reality. This paper was my first effort to take a more "materialist," or at least more socially and historically grounded, point of view. The fact that it is done within a framework of social evolution—"the rise of the state"—I think must have been influenced by the fact that I was writing it for a University of Michigan audience, still imagined from my graduate school years at Chicago as the techno/ecomaterialist evil empire of Leslie White et al. I never did anything quite like it again. But I did get the job.

The paper was first published in *Michigan Discussions in Anthropology* in 1976, and subsequently in *Feminist Studies* in October 1978.

Preface 1978: This paper was written as an informal talk. It was my first stab in thinking about the problem and is highly speculative. It is really designed to generate and orient further thought and research—my own and others'.

1. For a Latin American example, see Watson 1972. For the Mediterranean, see Campbell 1974; Peristiany 1966; and J. Schneider 1971. For the Middle East and South Asia, see Hayes 1975; Papanek 1973, Gough 1955, Yalman 1963. For classical Athens, see Slater 1968. For China, see Stacey 1975. The ethnographic references for this paper are in no way definitive or comprehensive. They are taken from the sources that were at hand during writing. For most areas mentioned in the paper, there is a large body of literature concerning sexual ideology and female sociosexual control.

2. For some general considerations, see also Freud 1957 and Nemecek 1958.

3. For an even more gruesome case, see Hayes 1975 on infibulation, or Pharaonic circumcision, in the Sudan.

4. I am referring primarily to what anthropologists call "primary" (or "archaic") states, manifesting the novel social-evolutionary development of specialized centralized decision making and bureaucratized administration. See Wright 1977 and Rapp 1977.

5. Shore (1981) describes a similar pattern for Samoa, which would perhaps be characterized as a "pre-state" society, but not by much: It has a highly developed system of hierarchical social differentiation. [1996 note:

Shore's example is representative of many other parts of Polynesia—see "Rank and Gender" (this volume). It became clear to me later that the issue was stratification, institutionalized inequality, as such, with or without state-type administrative and military structures.]

6. Engels of course related the "defeat" of women to the rise of the state (1972), but my interpretation of this relationship is quite different from his. See also Reich 1971 for a rather bizarre, if provocative, discussion of these issues.

7. The pattern is also found throughout most of Latin America, presumably imported by the Iberian empires.

8. It seems that the Incas had celibate male and female priesthoods (von Hagen 1957), but we do not know whether an ideal of chastity for women was general. As for the Aztecs, Vaillant (1950) states that women were supposed to be chaste at marriage, but he does not elaborate on this point.

9. I must tack on here one of the more interesting points raised in discussion after I presented this paper as a talk. In many "tribal" societies, sexual activity begins at a very early age (for example, Tiwi men of Australia stretch the vaginas of their child wives with their fingers until the wives are grown enough to engage in full-scale sexual intercourse [see Goodale 1971].) It is conceivable then that females in such societies never really develop hymens at all. As premarital chastity is enforced for women to a later age, however, the hymen would have a chance to grow and harden, and would have to be broken more dramatically at first intercourse. The suggestion is, then, that the hymen itself emerges physiologically with the development of sexual purity codes, and thus presumably with the rise of the state.

Four: Rank and Gender

Preface 1996: This paper was originally entitled "Gender and Sexuality in Hierarchical Societies: The Case of Polynesia and Some Comparative Implications," and was written for inclusion in the volume that Harriet Whitehead and I co-edited, *Sexual Meanings: The Cultural Construction of Gender and Sexuality* (1981). It was directly inspired by Jane Collier and Michelle Rosaldo's paper, "Politics and Gender in Simple Societies," also written for that volume. Although I was then and still am committed to an interpretive approach to culture, that is, to a sense of culture as a set of symbolic constructs or "representations," I was looking for a way out of the relatively aesthetic approach to interpretation I had acquired to that point. Jane and Shelly's paper was written first, drawing on the French "structural Marxists" of that era—Godelier, Terray, Meillassoux. I was impressed with their ability to make sense of cultural representations not just as meaningful components of a people's "worldview" and "value system," but as emerging from the micro-politics of life in a particular culture. I basically took their approach, made some modifications, and tried it out myself on a body of data from traditional Polynesia. I acknowledge my debt to them now, more than I did in *Sexual Meanings*.

I also realize now, in retrospect, that it was my first real move into "practice theory." I had no name for it and was not yet reading any of the literature we now associate with it: Bourdieu, de Certeau, Giddens, Sahlins. But in setting up the analysis in terms of the question, "what do actors (in this kind of system) want?" and in defining people's desires and the limitations on their desires as essentially political, I was launched. The basic frame of the analysis is not really very different from what I later develop, with much more theoretical trimming, in my historical monograph on the Sherpas, *High Religion* (1989).

1. On the basis of an earlier draft of this essay, I solicited and benefited enormously from the generous criticism of Polynesianists: Irving Goldman, Bradd Shore, and Vern Carroll, to all of whom I am extremely grateful. I hope that the most egregious errors have been weeded out. Although it is conventional to assume responsibility for all errors that remain, I do so more than conventionally. I have never done fieldwork in the area, and I remain acutely aware of my own novicehood in relation to this fascinating body of data.

I also wish to thank the following friends for their very detailed suggestions and criticisms: Jane Collier, Salvatore Cucchiari, Raymond Kelly, John Kirkpatrick, Michelle Rosaldo, David Schneider and Harriet Whitehead. Finally, I am also most appreciative of the comments and reactions of Aletta Biersack, Nancy Chodorow, Keith Hart, Leslee Nadelson, Niara Sudarkasa, and Susan Contratto. Marshall Sahlins kindly sent me the manuscript of his forthcoming work [1981], *Historical Metaphors*.

This paper is dedicated to the memory of Margaret Mead.

2. The rank system throughout Polynesia is by now virtually defunct. I will however use the "ethnographic present" tense in the essay as if it were still operating.

3. The terms are from Goldman's (1970) classification of Polynesian societies, according to an evolutionary scheme that will not be central to the present essay, and that I will thus not discuss here. It need only be understood that the "traditional" societies are the least complex in terms of organization of the rank system, the "stratified" are the most complex, and the "open" societies form a middle category.

Sahlins (1958) also works with an evolutionary scheme, although he does not label the levels (Chapter I, passim). Although his theoretical presuppositions and interests are radically different from Goldman's, the outcome of his classification is similar. I present here the two schemes for the reader's reference.

Goldman (1970: 21): *"Traditional"*—Pukapuka, Ontong Java, Tokelau, Tikopia, Futuna, Tongareva, Uvea, Maori, Manihiki-Rakahanga. *"Open"*—Mangaia, Easter Island, Marquesas, Samoa, Niue; *"Stratified"*—Hawaii, Tonga, Society Islands (Tahiti), Mangareva.

Sahlins (1958: 11–12): *Group III*—Pukapuka, Ontong Java, Tokelau; *Group IIb*—Tikopia, Futuna, Marquesas; *Group IIa*—Mangaia, Easter Island, Uvea, Mangareva; *Group I*—Hawaii, Tonga, Tahiti, Samoa.

4. The discussion in this section is drawn primarily from Goldman (1970) and Sahlins (1958), further informed by the general ethnographic literature on Polynesia as listed in the Literature Cited. The description of the social organization, as well as of the sex/gender system that follows, is a composite, an "ideal type," to which probably no single Polynesian society perfectly conforms. I am aware of the wide range of variations throughout the area, but I have chosen to ignore them in the interest of establishing a general set of relations between rank and gender over the area as a whole. The merit of this approach must be judged not only by the persuasiveness of the present essay, but by the degree to which it proves valuable for future analysts in constructing hypotheses to account for the variations.

5. The patterns are clearer if one keeps in mind that the kin group ultimately owns the land, rather than individuals. Individual ownership thus depends on the kinship affiliation of the individual.

6. In some cases (see note 10) the head of the unit has exclusive or predominant control over the disposition of the unit's property. Hence one could run the analysis of sibling rivalry in terms of economic competition or conflict, rather than in terms of prestige and succession. The results would be similar, but in cultural terms less accurate, because property "ownership" (or control), like political power, is a by-product of status position. It is not in any meaningful sense a source of status (apart from the fact that more land can support more kin/followers) and it is certainly not a culturally valued end in itself.

7. Variations between Western and Eastern Polynesia with respect to kinship, marriage, and gender patterns are extremely interesting. In this essay, however, I have limited discussion to patterns that appear over the area as a whole, with only minor exceptions. For the reader's reference on this point, here is Goldman's classification of Eastern and Western societies (1970: xxvii; see also Burrows 1940): *Eastern*: Maori, Manihiki-Rakahanga,

Tongareva, Mangaia, Easter, the Marquesas, Mangareva, the Society Islands (Tahiti), the Hawaiian Islands; *Western*: the Samoan Islands, Tonga, Uvea, Futuna, the Tokelaus, Tikopia, Pukapuka, Niue, Ontong Java.

8. Brother-sister marriage is also noted for Rarotonga (Suggs 1966: 177).

9. Parallel cousin marriage, between children of same-sex siblings, is reported for the aristocracy in Mangareva (Buck 1938: 132). Several other accounts report marriage with "cousins," without distinguishing between cross and parallel: Suggs 1966: 110; Oliver 1974: 764; Handy and Pukui 1958: 109.

10. In the Marquesas only the senior child inherits (Linton 1939: 154); in Mangareva (Buck 1938: 163) and in Tonga (Kaeppler 1971: 178) only the senior son inherits. Note however that in none of these cases are women categorically disinherited as against men; the category of noninheritors includes junior males as well as females.

11. There are two additional means of intentionally and controllably enlarging the group: adoption and polygyny. Both are widely practiced, the latter mainly by the aristocracy. Space limitations prohibit discussing the differential advantages and disadvantages of each here.

12. Sisters' daughters would be especially powerful symbols in the process under discussion. They represent the "hold" on kinswomen across two generations. Most sacred maids, as well as the *tamaha* (the "favored" and highest ranking kinswoman of the Tongan chief) are supposed to be sisters' daughters, although as in Samoa they are often daughters, and sometimes even sisters.

13. Except for the very highest wife of the Tui Manua, the highest chief (Mead 1930: 184).

14. A Samoan man who is caught and branded as a sleep crawler, however, appears as shameful, and "no girls will ever take [him] seriously" (Mead 1930: 62).

15. It appears that in Tahiti women may have also occasionally done it to men (Oliver 1974: 365).

16. Because virginity is more strongly enforced for chiefly daughters—Goldman calls it a "privilege of rank" (1970: 564)—it has special aristocratic associations as well. This probably gives added spice to deflowering virgins, in that a man would be symbolically asserting chiefly status in getting to any virgin.

17. The argument has clear Freudian overtones. They seem to me wholly appropriate to the case at hand, which is quite "patriarchal" in the classical sense. Gough's Freudian interpretation of Nayar girls' puberty rites (1955)

seems to me similarly appropriate to the Nayar case, Yalman's pointed comments on it notwithstanding (1963).

18. I omit from the discussion chiefly rape of lower-status women, which is also not uncommon, especially in the "stratified" societies (e.g., Gifford 1929: 72, 184; Mariner I 1827: 231; Malo 1903: 255). Essentially it is parallel to (though not exactly legitimately part of) chiefly rights of appropriation and/or disposition of goods and services in his domain.

19. The exception is rape of high-status women by low-status men. This is everywhere severely penalized.

20. Bradd Shore (1981) suggests that much of Samoan rape may be explained by the fact that all women are seen primarily as "sisters," and there is difficulty in transforming a nonsexual into a sexual relationship. I agree that Polynesian women are seen primarily as "sisters," and Shore's suggestion would not be incompatible with many of the interpretations of the present essay.

Vern Carroll (1976) has suggested that rape is "no big deal" to women of Nukuoro, a Polynesian outlier in Micronesia where Carroll did research. Given the discussion just presented in the text, it would make sense that even Polynesian women might find rape less psychologically traumatic, though not necessarily more morally acceptable, than in our own culture.

[1996 addendum. Ever since the publication of this article, I wish I had written this section on rape differently. The way in which the conclusion to the section is written may sound (I fear) as if I am blaming girls and women for transmitting inflammatory sexual messages to men, and hence for getting raped. I certainly meant no such thing; just the opposite. I was arguing that girls and women within this cultural framework have been culturally "set up."

Moreover, the way in which the 1981 footnote is written may sound as if I am suggesting that Polynesian women do not mind being raped. I am not in any way whatsoever suggesting this, but I do suppose that the cultural context might affect the degree to which, and the way in which, the girl or woman might be psychologically traumatized or suffer long-term emotional damage from the experience.]

21. It does occasionally happen that a lower man marries a higher woman, probably when a chief intentionally marries a daughter downward in order to forge a clientship. This is not allowed to interfere with the normative superiority and authority of the husband within the household (see, e.g., Gifford 1929: 16).

22. Institutionalized "bond friendships," found in many Polynesian societies, perform many of the same functions (Firth 1967: 108–15 passim;

Suggs 1966:131; Handy 1923:89; Mead 1949:48; Oliver 1974:825, 844).

23. In Samoa this "tabu" on public interaction between people in a sexual relationship applies to married couples, but not to adolescents. The tabu against public interaction between husbands and wives is said to be almost as strong as that against brother–sister interaction (Mead 1949:83).

24. Much of the following account is drawn from Handy's *Polynesian Religion* (1927). Handy presents an account of an ideal-type Polynesian religion for which he draws heavily on the Maori case, and it appears that he makes many unfounded generalizations for the area as a whole. But Polynesian religion is by and large not well documented. A careful survey of the available fragments, as well as a specification of variations, is beyond the scope of the present essay.

25. The Hawaiians had an Earth Mother goddess; they were apparently the only people in the area who did (Handy and Pukui 1958:22).

26. But a Tongan wife of a high chief does bring in many of her kin as dependents and helpers in her husband's household (Gifford 1929:17, 36). She may also bring her younger sisters as secondary wives or concubines for her husband.

27. Among the Maori only wives could cut their husbands' hair (Best II 1924:533). It is not clear what an unmarried man would do for a haircut.

28. Firth reports little adultery for Tikopia (1963:118). Adultery in modern Mangaia is said to be "relatively rare" but also "heavily folklorized" (Marshall 1971:146). Adultery in Tonga is also reported as "rare" (Goldman 1970:565), but here and there throughout Mariner's marvelous first-hand account of eighteenth-century Tongan society, largely of high-ranking people, both men and women allude to and joke about their extramarital love affairs (see I: 116, II: 49).

29. Oliver (1974:804) reports "uxoriousness" for Tahiti, which is stronger than "amiability." Marshall says that Mangaian husbands and wives are not very social or conversational with one another, and that the husband–wife relationship is mostly sexual and economic (1971:140). He later says however that "over the long term husbands and wives develop emotional attachment" (1971:159).

30. Throughout the area there are no formal "divorce" mechanisms. Divorce is effected simply by separation.

31. Mead reports jealousy to be rare in both sexes in Samoa (1949:68, 97).

32. Married women get general "deference" in Tikopia (Firth 1963:122) and are "respected" as a category in Tonga (Mariner 1827: passim).

This does not negate their subordination to their husbands in the domestic context.

33. Firth says that Tikopian girls want to marry more than boys, to get out from under the heavy control of their fathers (1957: 434). This motive would clearly be possible for girls throughout the area, although it is not reported elsewhere.

At any rate, given the relatively low presumed motivation of girls to marry, it is clear that a girl's best bet when she does marry would be to reside uxorilocally, where she would retain on a day-to-day basis her status and prerogatives as a kinswoman. Thus her interests would coincide with her kinsmen's interest in keeping her (and her children) with the group.

34. In the context of these suggestions, intense wifely jealousy is less explicable than the jealousy of husbands. It is reported rare in Tahiti (Oliver 1974: 826) and also in Samoa (where, however, jealousy in general is rare—see note 31). But in some places it is reported to be intense (e.g., Firth 1963: 120), sometimes leading to suicide (Best I 1924: 475; Buck 1938: 472) or to fatal neglect of children (Marshall 1971: 148). The solution to this puzzle would lie in assuming that women have quite as much pride as men in Polynesian societies, partly because they are raised as valuable persons, and partly because pride is a very generally cultivated emotion in these status-conscious systems. Women's jealousy may thus be parallel to men's at the level of personal feeling, even if it is not culturally supported and encouraged as men's is.

35. In Samoa, too, only high-rank women had birth feasts, but these were described as being for the mother (Mead 1949: 113).

36. Despite the high rates of abortion and infanticide, and of giving children up to others in fosterage and adoption, Polynesians are generally reported to be fond of children (see Loeb 1926: 85; Henry 1928: 274; Handy and Pukui 1958: 46, 71, 164–66). It may be suggested that, because children's independence of parents is culturally encouraged, their loyalty and love must be courted and wooed. This perhaps accounts for the great indulgence and affection they are evidently shown.

37. Goldman considers that the status of women in Polynesia was higher in the more complex societies than in the "traditional" ones (1970: 554).

38. Pollution beliefs and practices surrounding women vary significantly between Western and Eastern Polynesia. Comparative analysis on this point would be extremely important.

39. This means among other things that some women, like some men, are in all hierarchies of *very* high status, and occasionally (though far less often than men) succeed to highest offices. The "queens" and other female para-

mounts that surface here and there in the ethnographic literature are not products of "matriarchies," but of systems organized along the lines discussed in this essay.

40. There are presumed historical links between Polynesia and Southeast Asia. Their languages belong to the same macro-family (Goldman 1970: xxv).

41. Virginity also expresses continuing male dominance *within* the (nongender-defined) "strata," because it is largely maintained by male control of kinswomen.

42. I am hardly suggesting that Christian and Buddhist monasticism evolved *in order to fulfill* this function. Normally I give religion rather more serious treatment in its own terms. See, e.g., my monograph on Sherpa ritual and religion (1978).

Five: The Problem of "Women" as an Analytic Category

Preface 1996: This paper was originally entitled "The Founding of the First Sherpa Nunnery, and the Problem of 'Women' as an Analytic Category." It was written for an anniversary volume commemorating the founding of the Women's Studies Program at the University of Michigan, and was never really published except in an in-house production of the Women's Studies Program (V. Patraka and L. Tilly, eds., *Feminist Re-Visions: What Has Been and Might Be*, 1983).

The paper contains a number of intellectual firsts for me. First, as noted at the opening of the paper, it was my first attempt to combine feminist theorizing with my own Sherpa ethnography. I had begun fieldwork among the Sherpas in the mid 1960s with a focus on religion. Questions of gender were not for the most part on the table in academia; the feminist revolution had yet to break. Thus at that stage of my young, pre-professional life I was determined to get the respect of my professors by studying the "big (implicitly male) issues" (religion was very big at that point) and not "female issues" (women and domestic life were often studied in that era by the male anthropologist's wife). Nonetheless, as a result of obeying the rule of writing everything down in the field; and as a result too of working with Robert Paul who, because of his Freudian interests, did in fact study childrearing and other "female issues," I had built up a small stock of observations on women and gender among the Sherpas that I was able to use for this paper.

The second first in the paper is the focus on women. I had always been concerned with "gender as a cultural system." I could never understand how one could study women without understanding first the overarching set of meanings that defined female and male, women and men, in the first place. I would still strongly argue for that position. But with my growing interest in practice theory, it seemed that one needed to look at real gendered agents in relation to the cultural order—at the ways in which the cultural categories both facilitated and constrained agency, and at the ways in which agents faithfully enacted or radically stretched the cultural categories. This was the beginning of such an effort.

Yet even as I tried to see women as agents in this paper, I argued for the importance of realizing that "women" did not constitute a unified subject. The paper thus linked up with various emerging positions in feminist theory—with a poststructuralist argument against the notion of the unified subject, with the argument against interpretations grounded in binary (gender) oppositions, and with the more general shift to insisting on the linkage between gender and other forms of inequality.

Preface 1983: The fieldwork for the larger project on the history of Sherpa monastic institutions (of which the founding of Devuche is one part) was conducted in 1979, supported by the National Science Foundation and the University of Michigan. This paper was written at the Center for Advanced Study in the Behavioral Sciences (Stanford, California), with support from the Center (NSF Grant #BN8206304) and from the Guggenheim Foundation. I am grateful to all these agencies. I also wish to thank Barbara Aziz, Nancy Chodorow, Raymond Kelly, Kathryn March, and Louise Tilly for critical comments and suggestions.

1. I mean no disrespect in talking of "religious empire building." To spread and improve Buddhist practices by—among other things—building monasteries, is to perform acts of great merit and virtue.

2. The *korwa* are either widowed or divorced laywomen, or former nuns who had broken their vows by getting sexually involved with men—often, in the case of the Devuche *korwa*, with Tengboche monks. The nuns and the *korwa* divide all donations equally among themselves, except that on one holiday (Nyungne) the nuns do more extensive ritual work, and so keep a larger share. In addition, there is a ritual that was endowed by the high reincarnate lama involved in the founding of Tengboche monastery, that should only be performed by the fully ordained nuns; therefore only they are fed by the nunnery on that occasion.

The general term for nun, both in address and reference, is *ani*. However in both monasteries and nunneries, the fully ordained members (*tsowa*) are contrasted with the "peripheral ones" (*korwa*).

3. There is an important myth about a female *gelung* "long ago," that is known to all Sherpas, and that serves as a precedent for Nyungne, an important ascetic ritual for lay people (March 1979: 277–78; Ortner 1978: 51).

4. Lands owned by the nunnery as a whole are rented out to tenants, who

work the land and give back a share of the produce. The transactions are handled by the *nyermu*.

5. The house is private property, and may be passed on to another member of the nun's family who may enter the nunnery at a later date. Should the nun die with no family member to replace her, the house reverts to her nearest male kin who may sell it, or hold it for a future nun in the family if they wish. If the nun breaks her vows, however, the house is—in theory—confiscated by the nunnery as a corporation, which may then sell it to a new nun.

6. Each nun contributes some *tso* foods for the ritual, paying for her contributions from interest on an endowment provided by the previous head lama of Tengboche monastery. Tengboche monks do the same ritual on the twenty-fifth of each month. (The dates are based on the Tibetan calendar.)

7. The endowment for the annual observance of *yerne* was provided by a sister-in-law (?) of one of the wealthy sponsors of both Tengboche and Devuche, Karma Lama. The endowment was in the form of cash, to be lent out at interest, and the interest was to support the ritual. But now the principal is gone. People borrowed, nobody paid back; the nun telling me this added ruefully that she still has all the promissory notes. Now each *ani* supports herself for the *yerne* period, reduced to about seven days.

8. Ngawang Samden was on her seventh husband in 1954 (von Fürer-Haimendorf 1964: 283). This number of spouses is quite high for any Sherpa, male or female. The fact that Ngawang Samden broke her vows, however, is not unusual. The vows are taken for life, but there is an estimated 50 percent rate of "falling" for both nuns and monks.

9. They were described to me as *ongchermu*, a term meaning powerful, but in an illegitimate, strong-man sort of way. The informant on this point said that "they took everyone's money."

10. Polygyny is relatively rare in Sherpa society—around 2 percent (Lang and Lang 1971: 3; von Fürer-Haimendorf 1964: 68; Oppitz 1968: 122).

11. Rumbu monastery is (usually) spelled Rong-phug in Tibetan. In general, I am spelling native terms throughout the paper more or less as they are pronounced by the Sherpas. Most of the terms have Tibetan spellings, which I am not providing, as the primary audience is not assumed to be area specialists.

12. There were ten altogether: Ama Digi, Ngawang Samden, Ani Zhinba (the elder), Ani Zepa, Ngawang Konjok, and Ngawang Diki, all of Khumjung village; Ngawang Ongmu and Ngawang Chokar of Nauje; Ani Tarchin of Zhung; and Ani Ngawang Zangmu from a village in the Pharak area.

13. The letter of authorization from the higher religious authority is a standard part of the process of launching any religious institution.

14. "Zatul Rimpoche" is one of several names for the head lama of Rumbu monastery. He is also referred to as the Rimbi Sangye, the Dzarong Lama, or the Dzarong *tulku* (reincarnate). His personal religious name was Ngawang Tenzing Norbu. Again I will not provide Tibetan spellings here, although they will be provided in the monograph (Ortner 1989).

15. People traditionally bring the clothes of a newly deceased family member to a monastery as gifts, and the head lama redistributes them as he sees fit.

16. The main expense of any construction project is the cost of feeding all the workers who, as in this case, volunteer, or in the case of private house-building, contribute labor as part of reciprocal kinship obligations. The workers do not get paid (or perhaps only a token amount) but they must be fed throughout their time on the project.

17. Indeed, one Devuche nun did suggest that the impetus for building the nunnery had come from Lama Gulu, the head of Tengboche monastery: "Lama Gulu said the nuns needed a place."

18. For a few sources on the position of women in classical Buddhism, see D. Paul 1979; Horner 1930; and March n.d. For a few sources on women in Tibetan Buddhism, see March 1979; and Miller 1980.

19. There are certain labor exchange mechanisms between families, and wealthy families may also have access to (non-Sherpa) wage laborers. By and large, however, most families do their own work.

20. Occasionally, in a wealthy family, a daughter will be given a field and/ or an animal or two. March (personal communication) says that cattle are quite commonly part of Solu dowries; my impression is that the giving of an occasional field seems only to take place in Khumbu, where local endogamy is much more frequent. Nonetheless, girls are not normatively entitled to such productive resources, and whether any given girl gets them or not is up to her father.

21. In rare cases, a woman may choose to remain single, and yet not to become a nun. Then her father may set her up with a small house and some land to form an independent household. But again, such an arrangement depends on the disposition of the individual father.

22. Nowadays, this pattern is changing. Even in the past, however, the young people—especially sons—often had *some* veto power over an ar-ranged marriage. Indeed, in some cases the parents' "arrangements" were merely ratifications of a relationship already initiated by the girl and boy. Nonetheless, the general norm and practice was for the parents to arrange children's marriages.

23. March (1971: 181) found that 25 percent of Solu women marry into their mothers' natal villages, and another 23 percent marry sons of women who had been born in, but married out of, their own natal villages. But

(a) no girl can be assured of such a marriage in advance, and (b) even if, as in these cases, the girl has kin where she marries, the new village is still a new social system to which she must adapt.

24. In established marriages, Sherpa women do not appear to mind their husbands' long absences. In newer marriages, however, these absences seem more problematic, partly—one may interpret—because the wife is insecure in the new village, and partly because (in several cases that I knew more directly) the wife was uncertain about the husband's commitment to come back.

25. She is probably, however, still *gamchu*, although perhaps less so than laywomen. (There is another form of pollution—called *thip*—which I have not emphasized in this paper. Certain female secretions—menstrual and childbirth blood—create *thip*, but then so do certain male exuviae, and many generically human ones. On balance, *thip*, unlike *gamchu*, is not especially sex-linked [see Ortner 1973a].)

26. The founding nun, Ngawang Samden, was apparently able to maintain some sort of economic independence even after breaking her vows, since she continued to give religious donations in her own name. Possibly her parents and/or her brothers allowed her to keep the resources she had been allotted at the time she became a nun, even after she left the nunnery. It would be interesting to know whether this was/is possible for other former nuns.

27. Despite her seven husbands (see note 8) Ngawang Samden apparently remained, *and continued to be considered by others*, a devoutly religious and highly meritorious individual. With one of her husbands, she worked out an arrangement for exchanging periods of religious retreat, wherein each would provide for the needs of the other while the other was in seclusion. As noted above, she also continued to make substantial donations to religious institutions (von Fürer-Haimendorf 1964: 282–83).

28. In some cases, where the wife has no brothers, a man may move at marriage to her house and take over her father's property.

29. Many of the apparent exceptions can be accounted for. Some of the "only sons" are illegitimate sons of nuns. Some of the other exceptions are from poor families where there is little or no property to divide. (They are likely to become servants of the head lama or of another monk.) Finally, even in better-off families, an eldest or youngest son may insist upon a monastic calling and eventually get his way, or alternatively may be considered by the parents to be too stupid or impractical for worldly affairs and thus be sent to the monastery.

30. The arguments here are drastically over-simplified. The full account may be found in Ortner 1989.

Six: Gender Hegemonies

Preface 1996: This paper was my first major attempt to look back at some of the debates generated by my own and Michelle Rosaldo's papers in *Woman, Culture, and Society*, including the debate over whether or not "male dominance" is universal, and the debate over Michelle Rosaldo's use of the domestic/public opposition to explain universal male dominance. By this time some of the nastier tones in the debate had faded back, as feminist anthropology and feminist scholarship shifted to new terrains. At the same time, new theoretical tools had become available—Raymond Williams's adaptation of Gramsci's notion of "hegemony," the further development of practice-based approaches, the greater anthropological use of historical perspectives—that allowed me to reopen the question in what seemed to be useful ways.

Preface 1990: This paper has had a very long history. An early version was drafted jointly by Harriet Whitehead and me for a symposium on the occasion of the Bryn Mawr College centennial in 1985 (we were once upon a time classmates at Bryn Mawr). There were several joint revised drafts, and then several individually authored drafts. The present version, while individually authored by me, builds heavily on all those earlier efforts. It is no exaggeration to say that without Harriet's contributions, at many levels, this paper would not exist. In addition, I wish to thank Ruth Behar, Nancy Chodorow, Sal Cucchiari, Carol Delaney, Raymond Kelly, Bruce Knauft, Richard Leppert, Bruce Lincoln, Jocelyn Linnekin, Michael Peletz, and Abby Stewart for extremely helpful comments and criticisms. Michael Peletz also provided me with an extended briefing, and several reprints, on the women-centered gender systems of Malaysia and Sumatra, for which I am extremely grateful. Rachael Cohen was kind enough to redo the references for me, in addition to doing her usual expert job of technical production of the manuscript. I thank her.

1. Karla Poewe (1980) has recently used the term matriarchy as a synonym for matrifocality, but this is not common usage.

2. Every author tends to have his or her favorite vocabulary for these things. For various reasons, "status" might have been preferable to "prestige," if only because prestige tends to lend itself to an image of accumulation—as in Bourdieu's notion of "symbolic capital" (1977, 1984)—which is often inappropriate to particular cases. But because *Sexual Meanings* began with "prestige," and because this paper was presented at a conference on prestige, I have stuck with the term. For a useful overview of various approaches to prestige, see Hatch (1989).

3. The issue of female autonomy has been emphasized by Eleanor Leacock in *Myths of Male Dominance* (1981).

4. See Ortner (1984) for a discussion of "practice theory," an umbrella term for a range of work in various disciplines that focuses on the relationship between the actions of actors and the ordering of society and culture.

5. In an earlier draft of this paper, I examined the case of Atjeh as a case of a "female-centered" hegemony. The general shape of the argument was similar to the Andaman discussion (below), and since there were space restrictions, I decided to leave it out. Readers interested in this case may consult Siegel (1969), Tanner (1974), and Jayawardena (1977a, b). An even stronger "female-centered" hegemony has been described recently by Michael Peletz for Negeri Sembilan (in the same general region as Atjeh)—see Peletz (1987a, b; 1988).

6. A nice example of this approach may be seen in a recent article (1989) by Rena Lederman.

7. The overall logic of the argument here is similar in some ways to Kelly's arguments about structural contradictions in Etoro social structure (Kelly 1977).

8. Raymond Kelly has brought to my attention the fact that Robert Lowie (1920) mentioned the Andaman Islanders as one of two examples of egalitarian societies in the ethnographic record (the other was the Toda). Lowie was jousting with the earlier generation of evolutionists (e.g., Bachofen 1967 [1861]), who had postulated (among other things) an evolutionary stage of "primitive matriarchy."

9. Radcliffe-Brown discusses these (1922: 172–74).

10. Lest this change of perspective be misunderstood, it is worth stating that I am not accepting the view that all simple societies were once egalitarian. I assume that simple societies have always exhibited, as they continue to exhibit, a range of gender status patterns, from extreme male dominance to relative egalitarianism.

11. I have also adopted the strategy of not citing specific pages in the two sources. I am not entirely comfortable with this choice, but the alternative was to have one or more citations attached to every sentence. Direct quotations are of course provided with full citations.

12. Man reports both male and female bachelor residences (Man 1883: 108), but the female residences had disappeared by Radcliffe-Brown's time (Radcliffe-Brown 1922: 34).

13. Radcliffe-Brown makes an ambiguous statement about husbands having had the right to "punish" their wives for adultery (Radcliffe-Brown 1922: 50), with the wife not being described as having the same right. This would seem to indicate a more asymmetrical situation, but Radcliffe-Brown also notes that a man was constrained from punishing his wife too severely, because of fear of retribution from the wife's kin, so that the pun-

ishment generally amounted to no more than "violent words" (1922: 50). In another place he says that "very often the husband seems to condone the adultery of his wife" (1922: 70), seemingly canceling out his other comments.

14. See also Radcliffe-Brown 1922: 78.

15. Cucchiari has suggested that patterns of child exchange tend to be associated with greater gender egalitarianism, insofar as they stand in, as it were, for exchange of women (Cucchiari 1981). For the larger theoretical arguments on "the exchange of women," see Rubin (1975).

16. Without directly addressing the Rosaldo article, Joan Scott (1988) makes similar comments about the analytic use of binary oppositions in gender analysis (e.g., 1988: 43).

17. Anna Yeatman, in a very interesting essay (1984), makes similar arguments about the generality of the universalism/particularism distinction and about the intrinsically greater social and cultural value of universalistic orientations. My position parallels hers quite closely on this point. But she chooses to continue to use the domestic/public terminology, whereas I have chosen to subordinate it to the encompassing/encompassed terminology, for the reasons explained.

18. Man 1883: 96. Radcliffe-Brown says that his informants claimed that women might occasionally take up the role but that shamans normally were men (Radcliffe-Brown 1922: 176).

19. Birth does not appear to have been ritualized. This does not, however, establish anything one way or another, since even in the initiation rites the rebirthing was not represented as an imitation of the physical act of birth but as feeding the "newborn" initiate.

20. By the 1970s, almost none of the indigenous population was left (Singh 1978: 27).

21. In the case of households headed by females, the domestic rituals were presumably performed by the woman's brother.

22. Collier and Yanagisako (1989) have recently critiqued the sacred/profane distinction in terms similar to the earlier critique of the domestic/public opposition. While it is indeed the case that these terms may carry certain kinds of problematic cultural baggage, the analytic effort here is to deconstruct them—to uncover the ways in which they play a role in constituting a given order of gender relations, and the ways in which their gender claims may be culturally subverted over time.

23. Goldman 1970: 212. Goldman seems to link the emergence of a more purely seniority-based system of succession to the shift from a so-called "traditional" rank system based on various forms of sanctity to a so-called "stratified" system more akin to a class structure. This would suggest then

that women's status *improved* with a shift from rank to class, something that would not have been predicted by many theories of women's status. The whole question would have to be investigated much more closely on a comparative basis, but it illustrates well the complexities of the relationship that may obtain between gender asymmetry and other forms of asymmetry.

24. Another theoretically predicted correlate of the relative equality of Hawaiian men and women relates to the relative hegemony of kinship-centered definitions of gender over marital ones. The arguments were developed in Ortner 1981 (this volume), but are too complex to be summarized here.

25. I am aware of the debates over Valeri's account (Charlot 1987; Valeri 1987). I am not competent to evaluate all the details, but Valeri's account does not seem to me wildly out of line with other literature on ancient Hawaii.

26. In a very interesting article, but one which is occasionally difficult to follow, Stephanie Seto Levin makes a similar argument (1968). Valeri also indicates some lines of historical analysis in his 1982 article.

27. The information on these events appears to be of very high quality—it is extremely detailed, and there is significant agreement about what happened among the various chroniclers. I rely here on secondary sources, as cited throughout this section.

28. Liholiho's deep discomfort was still evident to observers: "After the guests were seated and had begun to eat the king took two or three turns around each table as if to see what passed at each and then suddenly, and without any previous warning to any but those in the secret, seated himself in a vacant chair at the women's table, and began to eat voraciously, but was evidently much perturbed" (Kuykendall 1938: 68).

29. Kroeber (1948: 404) was an exception. He argued that the overthrow of the *kapu* system in Hawaii was a case of "cultural fatigue." His position did not gain many supporters.

30. Although I lumped together Susan Carol Rogers (1975) and Peggy Sanday (1981) in the earlier discussion, Rogers does tend to take a more historically dynamic view, at least for part of her argument.

Seven: So, *Is* Female to Male as Nature Is to Culture?

Prepared for the panel, "From the Anthropology of Women to the Gendering of Anthropology," organized by Louise Lamphere and Rayna Rapp at the American Anthropological Association annual meetings, November 1995, Washington, D.C.

1. Many thanks for excellent comments to Nancy Chodorow, Louise

Lamphere, Judith Stacey, Abigail Stewart, Marilyn Strathern, Timothy D. Taylor, Marya Van't Hul, and Harriet Whitehead.

2. There was another line of argument against the universal male dominance position, represented in part by Sanday (1981). The various positions are discussed relatively fully in "Gender Hegemonies" (this volume).

3. When I was in graduate school at the University of Chicago, for example, the introductory graduate core course was called "Systems." I think it still is, but in the 1960s the title was genuinely descriptive of the content of the course.

4. Maria Lepowsky (1993) has published a full-length monographic study of the people of Vanatinai, whom she shows to have a very similar configuration.

5. These points of cultural variation were at the heart of Ortner and Whitehead 1981.

6. Marilyn Strathern's brilliant essay, "No Nature, No Culture . . ." (1980), was a major exception to these charges against *Nature, Culture and Gender* as a whole. Among other things, Strathern specifically recognized that the structure could be present without cultural labeling, and interrogated a range of cultural data for this kind of indirect structural presence. Her conclusion that the linkage did not hold for the Hagen case was quite persuasive.

7. The problem of binary oppositions in relation to the nature, culture, and gender debate has been discussed by Rosaldo (1980) and more recently by Tsing (1990). Both argue that analysis based on binary oppositions produces essentialized views of the categories; both use this argument to launch an alternative, politics-of-meaning, kind of approach.

8. See again *Sexual Meanings* (Ortner and Whitehead 1981), as well as the papers in this volume.

Eight: Borderland Politics and Erotics

This paper is based on reading large amounts of expedition literature, as well as long-term ethnographic and oral history fieldwork among the Sherpas. The most recent stint of fieldwork was in August 1990, involving intensive interviewing of mountaineering Sherpas, male and female, in Kathmandu. Support for that trip came from the Horace Rackham School of Graduate Studies at the University of Michigan, to which I am very grateful. For valuable comments on this paper I wish to thank Vincanne Adams, Laura Ahearn, Nancy Chodorow, Coralynn Davis, Jim Fisher, Peter H. Hansen, Liisa Malkki, Abigail Stewart, and Tim Taylor. I am also indebted to an excellent discussion at the Department of Anthropology, Princeton

University, where Vincanne Adams, Hildred Geertz, Rena Lederman, and many others made important points.

1. In a broad sense, much of the recent work by historians and anthropologists on the intercultural dynamics of colonialism and post-colonialism, as well as about such world historical cultural encounters as the European "discovery"/invasion of the Western hemisphere (e.g., Greenblatt 1993) or the Pacific (e.g., Sahlins 1981), is part of this trend toward a borderlands perspective.

2. Starting in the 1970s, the Sherpas generally stopped using the hierarchical term "sahib" for the international mountaineers. But the term is handy for various reasons, including the fact of signalling the continuing inequality of the relationship, and I will continue to use it here.

3. The international mountaineers' view of this relationship is chronicled in a vast and fascinating expedition literature which is my main source for the "sahib" side of this paper. With the exception of Tenzing Norgay's very valuable autobiographies (1955, 1977), the Sherpas have thus far not written books describing expeditions from their own perspectives. The Sherpa side is thus assembled from my own interviews and other ethnographic work, as well as representations of Sherpas' words and views as found in other ethnographies, journalistic accounts, and the expedition literature.

4. In that same era, an American named Elizabeth Knowlton went along as a non-climbing member with the all-male German-American expedition to Nanga Parbat. Knowlton was an experienced climber who had "made many ascents," but joined this expedition "to handle the English-speaking newspaper work" (Knowlton 1933: 15).

5. According to the flap of her book, Jennifer Bourdillon "spent many weeks entirely alone among the Sherpas—the first white woman ever to do so." Her husband Tom was at that time climbing on Cho Oyu.

6. Kogan was killed along with three male Sherpas in an avalanche on this expedition.

7. Women from other parts of Europe, and virtually all of Asia, have become strong presences in Himalayan mountaineering since the 1970s. Some of them will make appearances later in this paper.

8. Explicit statements about sexual orientation are not made until very recently, and then only in passing, in the mainstream literature (see da Silva 1992: "Introduction"; O'Neill 1992).

9. For a very bohemian example, see Moffatt 1961. Gwen Moffatt climbed in Europe in the late 1940s and the 1950s.

10. For more on "big people" and "small people" in Sherpa society, see Ortner 1978 and 1989. For more on nunneries, see Ortner 1983 (this volume) and 1989: chap. 9.

11. Some of these were recorded by the writer and long-time Nepal resident Tom Laird, who was kind enough to send me some of his unpublished materials on this.

12. I was also part of a married couple the first time I was in the field. This certainly had an effect. When I went back as an unmarried woman on my second trip, there was a definite rise in the level of flirtation. Nonetheless I still felt completely physically safe. My biggest fears were of being bitten by a dog (which did happen once), and of falling off some of the more terrifying bridges.

13. James Fisher, personal communication. As far as I know, Laird has not published this account. I have tried to contact him for confirmation but have been unable to do so.

14. I have been unable to get firm information on the legal developments in Nepal relating to marijuana and hashish. According to one informant, who answered my query on the Web (1996), "hashish and marijuana were outlawed in Nepal in the spring of 1973." According to another informant, "only the sale of marijuana and hashish is outlawed, not possession or consumption."

15. For a remarkable first-person account of one of these marriages, see Donna M. Sherpa (1994).

16. Nineteen seventy-five was in fact International Women's Year. Junko Tabei later said she did not realize it at the time. The invention of things like "International Women's Year" by global agencies like the United Nations clearly has, at least in a case like this, more effect than might cynically be expected.

17. Jim Curran is very uncharitable about Tullis: he calls her a "housewife" who "hero-worshipped" her male climbing partner, and sees her as having been ambitious beyond her abilities (1987: 51).

18. I went to a women's college, and in retrospect I think it was for essentially these kinds of reasons. Perhaps this is the place to thank Bryn Mawr College, without which I am quite sure I would not be doing what I am doing today.

19. In some cases there are more disturbing issues involved than personal independence and freedom to be the best. Two major women climbers, Cherie Bremer-Kamp and Stacy Allison, describe leading lives of outward gender radicalism (including, in Allison's case, getting to the top of Mt. Everest), yet enduring deeply abusive relationships with men in their private lives (Bremer-Kamp 1987; Allison 1993).

20. There was no doubt a certain amount of male homoeroticism, if not actual homosexual relations, between sahibs and Sherpas, but none of this is written about. Most of the cases I am aware of—all at the level of gos-

sip—are from the older generation of British army officers who stayed in Nepal after World War II. Homosexual relations seem not to be practiced among Sherpa men, as far as Robert Paul (1970) or I could ascertain in earlier fieldwork. But there is fairly well-documented male homosexuality in some Tibetan monasteries (Goldstein 1964).

21. On "orientalism," see of course Said (1978) and the now vast literature on this subject. Although many non-Western Others are coded "female," many others are—as Nandy (1983) has discussed—hypermasculinized. In the Nepal context, the Gurkhas stand in this position, typed as disciplined soldiers and ferocious warriors. The issues here are very complex, and will be discussed more fully in Ortner n.d. b.

22. "Triumph and tragedy" is a standard combination in mountaineering. See Curran 1987.

23. By the time the expedition took place in 1978, however, Everest would have been twice climbed by women, as noted earlier.

24. They eventually got married.

25. James Fisher (1990: 154) reported a problem of getting Sherpa women to give "serious responses" to a questionnaire administered by a Sherpa research assistant. At issue here, I think, beyond *ngotza* or "shame," is the question of who "has knowledge," and especially the kind of knowledge being asked for in a questionnaire. At issue too may be the gender of the research assistant and other matters. One would need to know more to evaluate this observation.

26. Thanks to Vincanne Adams for emphasizing this point to me.

27. She now spends part of each year in Switzerland, where her Sherpa husband is a climbing and ski instructor.

28. This according to a Sherpa villager. I have tried to learn more precisely what the law actually says, but have been unable to do so. And by now, in fact, it has been changed again.

29. The words he used in Sherpa were *metsenga ten*, which translates literally as being "dirty." Another individual present translated it into English as "personally sick."

30. There are other Sherpa women who climbed in this period as well, but about whom little is known. There was, for example, Ang Maya, described as the younger sister of an expedition Sherpa, and another unnamed woman, both of whom passed the mountaineering course with Ang Hrita (mentioned in Ang Hrita's interview below). For a more recent, and fairly fully developed, account of a Sherpa woman trek leader, see Mitten 1992: 205ff.

31. At the time of the interview she and the sardar husband were di-

vorced. She had remarried, and was running a tea shop on the road between Kathmandu and Baudha.

32. "Ang" is a diminutive marker (meaning "child" or "young"). It gets attached to most children's names, and with some people it sticks for the rest of their lives. It should also be noted that Nyimi, as a member of the Lama clan, would be called "Nyimi Lama" rather than Nyimi Sherpa. For more on the distinctiveness of the Lama clan, see Ortner 1978.

33. There was no taped transcript. The indented texts are verbatim quotes from the fieldnotes, while the rest of the story is summarized from the fieldnotes.

34. Nyimi may not be "educated," but she speaks at least four languages fluently—Sherpa, Nepali, French, and English. The interview was in English.

35. Pasang Lhamu's village of origin did not appear in any of the published accounts. This information came from Vincanne Adams (personal communication): Adams discusses Pasang Lhamu as a personal friend, and as a public-cultural phenomenon, extensively (Adams 1996 passim).

36. It appears that the Indian Women's Expedition, and Nyimi Lama, did reach the summit of Everest. This went virtually unreported.

37. Adams gives the figure as $38,000 (1996: 5). Either way it is not a negligible amount of money.

38. Slept out in the open, or in a snow cave. Climbing on the upper reaches of Everest is so difficult that most climbers leave anything they can spare behind, including tents.

39. Tenzing's citizenship was contested. He actually lived in Darjeeling, India, and both Nepal and India claimed him. He himself was upset by demands that he declare his citizenship for one or the other country exclusively (Tenzing 1955).

40. See the debates in *Himal*: Risal 1993; Sharma 1993; Acharya 1993; Lieberman 1993a, b; Sherpa-Padgett 1993; and Sangroula 1993.

41. According to Vincanne Adams (personal communication), Pasang Lhamu and Lhakputi Sherpa were said to have been very competitive as well.

42. Laura Ahearn, then a doctoral candidate in anthropology at the University of Michigan, was in the field in a Magar village at the time of the Nepal Women's Expedition. She wrote in a letter to me: "It's been interesting for me to talk to Nepali women about Pasang's death: all the (educated) Kathmandu women I've spoken with strongly support Pasang's efforts and seem inspired by her achievement, despite the tragedy that followed it. Women in my own Nepali family (educated as well as uneducated), how-

ever, consider Pasang's desire to climb mountains at best folly, and at worst, especially when considering her three children, criminal" (letter dated 25 May, 1993).

43. A famous historical husband-wife business partnership is that of Sangye, the founder of Chiwong monastery, and his wife, in the early decades of the twentieth century (Ortner 1989). For an example of a Sherpa husband who supported his wife climbing, written from a male point of view, see Tenzing Norgay about his relationship with his third wife (Tenzing 1977: 39).

44. Needless to say, "first-world" men are a large part of the story too, but that is a different essay. See Ortner n.d. a.

Literature Cited

Abu-Lughod, Lila. 1992. "Writing against Culture." In *Recapturing Anthropology: Working in the Present*, edited by R. G. Fox. Santa Fe: School of American Research Press.

Acharya, Mamta. 1993. "A True Heroine." *Himal* 6(4) (July/August): 5.

Adams, Vincanne. 1996. *Tigers of the Snow (and other Virtual Sherpas): An Ethnography of Himalayan Encounters*. Princeton: Princeton University Press.

Ahearn, Laura. 1995. "Altering Agency: Changing Conceptions of Agentive Forces in Marriage among Magars in Nepal." Panel on "Agency," AAA meetings, Washington, D.C.

Alcoff, Linda. 1994 [1988]. "Cultural Feminism vs. Post-Structuralism: The Identity Crisis in Feminist Theory." In Dirks, Eley, and Ortner, op. cit.

Allison, Stacy, with Peter Carlin. 1993. *Beyond the Limits: A Woman's Triumph on Everest*. Boston: Little, Brown.

Another Ascent to the World's Highest Peak—Qomolangma. 1975. Peking: Foreign Languages Press.

Anzaldua, Gloria. 1987. *Borderlands/La Frontera*. San Francisco: Spinsters/Aunt Lute.

Appadurai, Arjun. 1991. "Global Ethnoscapes: Notes and Queries for a Transnational Anthropology." In *Recapturing Anthropology: Working in the Present*, edited by R. G. Fox. Santa Fe: School of American Research Press.

Atkinson, Jane. 1990. "How Gender Makes a Difference in Wana Society." In Atkinson and Errington, op. cit.

Atkinson, Jane, and Shelly Errington, eds. 1990. *Power and Difference: Gender in Island Southeast Asia*. Stanford: Stanford University Press.

Aziz, Barbara N. 1976. "Ani Chodon: Portrait of a Buddhist Nun." *Loka* 2:43–46.
———. 1978. *Tibetan Frontier Families.* Durham, N.C.: Carolina Academic Press.
Bachofen, J. J. 1967 [1861]. *Myth, Religion, and Mother Right.* Translated by Ralph Mannheim. Princeton: Princeton University Press.
Bakan, David. 1966. *The Duality of Human Existence.* Boston: Beacon Press.
Barzelai, Shuli. 1990. "Reading 'Snow White': The Mother's Story." *Signs* 15(1):515–34.
Baudrillard, Jean. 1988. *Selected Writings.* Edited by Mark Poster. Stanford: Stanford University Press.
Beaglehole, Ernest. 1941. *Pangai, a Village in Tonga.* Wellington, New Zealand: Polynesian Society.
Beaglehole, Ernest, and Pearl Beaglehole. 1938. *Ethnology of Pukapuka.* Bernice P. Bishop Museum Bulletin 150. Honolulu: Bishop Museum.
Behar, Ruth. 1993. *Translated Woman: Crossing the Border with Esperanza's Story.* Boston: Beacon Press.
Best, Elsdon. 1924. *The Maori.* 2 vols. Wellington, New Zealand: Board of Maori Ethnological Research.
Biersack, Aletta. 1974. "Matrilaterality in Patrilineal Systems: The Tongan Case." Curl Bequest Prize Essay 1974, unpublished.
Birkett, Bill, and Bill Peascod. 1989. *Women Climbing: 200 Years of Achievement.* Seattle: The Mountaineers.
Bloch, Maurice, and Jean H. Bloch. 1980. "Woman and the Dialectics of Nature in Eighteenth-Century French Thought." In MacCormack and Strathern, op. cit.
Bloom, Lisa. 1993. *Gender on Ice: American Ideologies of Polar Expeditions.* Minneapolis: University of Minnesota Press.
Blum, Arlene. 1980. *Annapurna: A Woman's Place.* San Francisco: Sierra Club Books.
Bonington, Chris. 1976. *Everest the Hard Way.* New York: Random House.
Bottigheimer, Ruth B. 1987. *Grimms' Bad Girls and Bold Boys: The Moral and Social Vision of the Tales.* New Haven: Yale University Press.
Bourdieu, Pierre. 1978 [1972]. *Outline of a Theory of Practice.* Translated by Richard Nice. Cambridge: Cambridge University Press.
———. 1984. *Distinction: A Social Critique of the Judgement of Taste.* Translated by Richard Nice. Cambridge, Mass.: Harvard University Press.
———. 1990. *The Logic of Practice.* Translated by Richard Nice. Stanford: Stanford University Press.
Bourdillon, Jennifer. 1956. *Visit to the Sherpas.* London: Collins.
Bremer-Kamp, Cherie. 1987. *Living on the Edge.* Layton, Utah: Gibbs M. Smith.
Brightman, Robert. 1995. "Forget Culture: Replacement, Transcendence, Relexification." *Cultural Anthropology* 10(4):509–46.
Brook, Elaine. 1985. "Sherpas: The Other Mountaineers." *Mountain* 101:36–39.
———. 1987. *The Windhorse.* New York: Dodd, Mead & Company.
Brown, Beverley. 1983. "Displacing the Difference." *m/f* 8:79–89.
Brownmiller, Susan. 1975. *Against Our Will: Men, Women, and Rape.* New York: Simon and Schuster.

Buck, Peter. 1932. *Ethnology of Tongareva*. Bernice P. Bishop Museum Bulletin 92. Honolulu: Bishop Museum.

———. 1938. *Ethnology of Mangareva*. Bernice P. Bishop Museum Bulletin 157. Honolulu: Bishop Museum.

———. 1939. *Anthropology and Religion*. New Haven: Yale University Press.

Burrows, Edwin G. 1940. "Culture Areas in Polynesia." *Journal of the Polynesian Society* 49:349–63.

Butler, Judith, and Joan W. Scott. 1992. *Feminists Theorize the Political*. New York and London: Routledge.

Campbell, Joseph K. 1974. *Honour, Family, and Patronage*. Oxford: Oxford University Press.

Carlson, Rae. 1971. "Sex Differences in Ego Functioning: Exploratory Studies of Agency and Communion," *Journal of Consulting and Clinical Psychology*, 37:267–77.

Carroll, Vern, ed. 1970. *Adoption in Eastern Oceania*. Honolulu: University of Hawaii Press.

———. 1976. "Rape on Nukuoro: A Cultural Analysis." *Michigan Discussions in Anthropology* 1 (Winter): 134–47.

Chambers, Iain. 1990. *Border Dialogues: Journeys in Postmodernity*. London: Routledge.

Charlot, John. 1987. Review of V. Valeri, *Kingship and Sacrifice*. *Pacific Studies* 10(2):107–47.

Chodorow, Nancy J. 1974. "Family Structure and Feminine Personality." In Rosaldo and Lamphere, op. cit.

Cipriani, Lidio. 1966. *The Andaman Islanders*. Translated by D. T. Cox and L. Cole. London: Weidenfeld and Nicolson.

Clifford, James. 1992. "Traveling Cultures." In *Cultural Studies*, edited by L. Grossberg, C. Nelson, and P. Treichler. London: Routledge.

Collier, Jane F., and Michelle Z. Rosaldo. 1981. "Politics and Gender in Simple Societies." In Ortner and Whitehead, op. cit.

Collier, Jane F., and Sylvia Yanagisako. 1989. "Theory in Anthropology since Feminist Practice." *Critique of Anthropology* 9(2):27–37.

Collins, Patricia Hill, 1990. *Black Feminist Thought: Knowledge, Consciousness, and the Politics of Empowerment*. New York and London: Routledge.

Connell, R. W. 1987. *Gender and Power: Society, the Person and Sexual Politics*. Stanford: Stanford University Press.

Cucchiari, Salvatore. 1981. "The Gender Revolution and the Transition from Bisexual Horde to Patrilocal Band: The Origins of Gender Hierarchy." In Ortner and Whitehead, op. cit.

Curran, Jim. 1987. *K2: Triumph and Tragedy*. Boston: Houghton Mifflin.

Danielsson, Bengt. 1956. *Love in the South Seas*. New York: Reynal.

da Silva, Rachel, ed. 1992. *Leading Out: Women Climbers Reaching for the Top*. Seattle: Seal Press.

Davenport, William. 1969. "The 'Hawaiian Cultural Revolution': Some Political and Economic Considerations." *American Anthropologist* 71(1):1–20.

Davis, Coralynn. 1994. "Cross-Cultural Encounters: Borderland Selves and Ethnographic Homes." Manuscript.

de Beauvoir, Simone. 1953 [1949]. *The Second Sex*. Translated by H. M. Parshley. New York: Knopf.

de Certeau, Michel. 1984. *The Practice of Everyday Life*. Translated by S. Rendall. Berkeley: University of California Press.

Dirks, Nicholas B., Geoff Eley, and Sherry B. Ortner, eds. 1994. *Culture/Power/History: A Reader in Contemporary Social Theory*. Princeton: Princeton University Press.

Douglas, Mary. 1966. *Purity and Danger*. New York and Washington, D.C.: Praeger.

Dumont, Louis. 1970. *Homo Hierarchicus: The Caste System and Its Implications*. Translated by Mark Sainsbury. Chicago: University of Chicago Press.

Encyclopaedia Britannica. 1974. "Harem." 15th ed. 4:907.

Engels, Friedrich. 1972 [1942]. *The Origin of the Family, Private Property, and the State*. Edited by Eleanor Leacock. New York: International Publishers.

Ferguson, James, and Akhil Gupta, eds. 1992. *Space, Identity, and the Politics of Difference*. Theme issue, *Cultural Anthropology* 7(1) (February).

Firestone, Shulamith. 1972. *The Dialectic of Sex: The Case for Feminist Revolution*. New York: Bantam Books.

Firth, Raymond. 1940. "The Analysis of *Mana*: An Empirical Approach." *Journal of the Polynesian Society* 49:483–510.

———. 1957. *We, the Tikopia*. 2d ed. London: George Allen and Unwin.

———. 1963. *We, the Tikopia*. Abridged. Boston: Beacon Press.

———. 1967. *Tikopia Ritual and Belief*. Boston: Beacon Press.

———. 1970. "Sibling Terms in Polynesia." *Journal of the Polynesian Society* 79:272–87.

———. 1975. *Primitive Polynesian Economy*. New York: Norton.

Fischer, J. L. 1970. "Political Factors in the Overthrow of the Hawaiian Taboo System." *Acta Ethnographica Academiae Scientiarum Hungaricae* 19:161–67.

Fisher, James F. 1990. *Sherpas: Reflections on Change in Himalayan Nepal*. Berkeley: University of California Press.

Foley, Douglas E. 1995. *The Heartland Chronicles*. Philadelphia: University of Pennsylvania Press.

Forster, John. 1960. "The Hawaiian Family System of Hana, Maui, 1957." *Journal of the Polynesian Society* 69:92–103.

Freud, Sigmund. 1957. "The Taboo of Virginity." *Standard Edition* 11: 193–208. London: Hogarth Press.

Gardiner, Steve. 1990. *Why I Climb: Personal Insight of Top Climbers*. Harrisburg, Pa.: Stackpole Books.

Geertz, Clifford. 1973. "Deep Play: Notes on the Balinese Cockfight." In his *The Interpretation of Cultures*. New York: Basic Books.

———. 1983. "Blurred Genres: The Refiguration of Social Thought." In his *Local Knowledge: Further Essays in Interpretive Anthropology*. New York: Basic Books.

Giddens, Anthony. 1979. *Central Problems in Social Theory: Action, Structure and Contradiction in Social Analysis*. Berkeley: University of California Press.

Gifford, Edward W. 1929. *Tongan Society*. Bernice P. Bishop Museum Bulletin 61. Honolulu: Bishop Museum.

Gillette, Ned, and Jan Reynolds. 1985. *Everest Grand Circle: A Climbing and Skiing Adventure through Nepal and Tibet*. Seattle: The Mountaineers.

Goldman, Irving. 1955. "Status Rivalry and Cultural Evolution in Polynesia." *American Anthropologist* 57:680–97.

———. 1970. *Ancient Polynesian Society*. Chicago: University of Chicago Press.

Goldstein, Melvin C. 1964. "A Study of the *Ldab Ldab*." *Central Asiatic Journal* 9:123–41.

Goodale, Jane. 1971. *Tiwi Wives*. Seattle and London: University of Washington Press.

Goody, Jack. 1973. "Bridewealth and Dowry in Africa and Eurasia." In *Bridewealth and Dowry*, edited by J. Goody and S. J. Tambiah. Cambridge: Cambridge University Press.

Gough, Kathleen. 1955. "Female Initiation Rites on the Malabar Coast." *Journal of the Royal Anthropological Institute* 85:45–80.

———. 1961. "Nayar: Central Kerala," and "Nayar: North Kerala." In *Matrilineal Kinship*, edited by D. Schneider and K. Gough. Berkeley and Los Angeles: University of California Press.

Greenblatt, Stephen, ed. 1993. *New World Encounters*. Berkeley: University of California Press.

Grimms' Fairy Tales. 1945. Translated by Mrs. E. V. Lucas, L. Crane, and M. Edwards. New York: Grosset and Dunlap.

Gupta, Akhil, and James Ferguson. 1992. "Beyond 'Culture': Space, Identity, and the Politics of Difference." *Cultural Anthropology* 7(1):6–23.

Handy, E. S. Craighill. 1923. *The Native Culture in the Marquesas*. Bernice P. Bishop Museum Bulletin 9. Honolulu: Bishop Museum.

———. 1927. *Polynesian Religion*. Bernice P. Bishop Museum Bulletin 34. Honolulu: Bishop Museum.

Handy, E. S. Craighill and Mary Kawena Pukui. 1958. *The Polynesian Family System in Ka-'u Hawai'i*. Wellington, New Zealand: The Polynesian Society.

Hannerz, Ulf. 1992. "The Global Ecumene." In his *Cultural Complexity: Studies in the Social Organization of Meaning*. New York: Columbia University Press.

Hatch, Elvin. 1989. "Theories of Social Honor." *American Anthropologist* 91(2):341–53.

Hayes, Rose Oldfield. 1975. "Female Genital Mutilation, Fertility Control, Women's Roles, and the Patrilineage in Modern Sudan." *American Ethnologist* 2:617–33.

Hecht, Julia. 1977. "The Culture of Gender in Pukapuka: Male, Female, and the *Mayakitanga* 'Sacred Maid.'" *Journal of the Polynesian Society* 86:183–206.

Henry, Teuira. 1928. *Ancient Tahiti*. Bernice P. Bishop Museum Bulletin 48. Honolulu: Bishop Museum.

Hocart, A. M. 1915. "Chieftainship and the Sister's Son in the Pacific." *American Anthropologist* 17:631–46.

Hogbin, H. I. 1931. "The Sexual Life of the Natives of Ontong Java." *Journal of the Polynesian Society* 40:23–34.

Hooper, Antony. 1976. "'Eating Blood': Tahitian Concepts of Incest." *Journal of the Polynesian Society* 85:227–41.

Horner, Isaline Blew. 1930. *Women under Primitive Buddhism: Laywomen and Almswomen.* London: G. Routledge and Sons.

Hoskins, Janet. 1990. "Doubling Deities, Descent, and Personhood: An Exploration of Kodi Gender Categories." In Atkinson and Errington, op. cit.

Huntsman, Judith, and Antony Hooper. 1975. "Male and Female in Tokelau Culture." *Journal of the Polynesian Society* 84:415–30.

―――. 1976. "The 'Desecration' of Tokelau Kinship." *Journal of the Polynesian Society* 85: 257–73.

Ingham, John M. 1971. "Are the Sirionó Raw or Cooked?" *American Anthropologist,* 73:1092–99.

Jackson, Monica, and Elizabeth Stark. 1956. *Tents in the Clouds: The First Women's Himalayan Expedition.* London: Collins.

Jameson, Fredric. 1984. "Postmodernism, or the Cultural Logic of Late Capitalism." *New Left Review* 146:53–93.

JanMohamed, Abdul R., and David Lloyd. 1987. "Introduction: Minority Discourse—What Is to Be Done?" *Cultural Critique* 7 (Fall): 5–18.

Jayawardena, Chandra. 1977a. "Women and Kinship in Acheh Besar, Northern Sumatra." *Ethnology* 16(1):21–38.

―――. 1977b. "Achenese Marriage Customs." *Indonesia* 23:157–73.

Johnson-Odim, Cheryl. 1991. "Common Themes, Different Contexts: Third World Women and Feminism." In *Third World Women and the Politics of Feminism,* edited by C. T. Mohanty et al. Bloomington, Ind.: Indiana University Press.

Kaeppler, Adrienne. 1971. "Rank in Tonga." *Ethnology* 10:174–93.

Kearney, Michael. 1991. "Borders and Boundaries of State and Self at the End of Empire." *Journal of Historical Sociology* 4(1):52–74.

Kelly, Raymond C. 1977. *Etoro Social Structure: A Study in Structural Contradiction.* Ann Arbor: University of Michigan Press.

Kirkpatrick, John T. 1979. "The Marquesan Notion of the Person." Unpublished Ph.D. dissertation, Department of Anthropology, University of Chicago.

Klages, Mary. 1980. "Pyro-Feminism: Thoughts on the Cultural Control of Fire and Women." B.A. thesis, Dartmouth College.

Knowlton, Elizabeth. 1933. *The Naked Mountain.* New York: G. P. Putnam's Sons.

―――. 1989. "The Final Attack." In *Mountain Journeys: Stories of Climbers and Their Climbs,* edited by James P. Vermeulen. Woodstock, N.Y.: Overlook Press.

Kratz, Corinne A. n.d. "Forging Unions and Negotiating Ambivalence: Personhood and Complex Agency in Okiek Marriage Arrangement." Forthcoming in *African Philosophy and Cultural Inquiry,* edited by D. Masolo and I. Karp. Bloomington: Indiana University Press.

Kroeber, A. L. 1948. *Anthropology*. New York: Harcourt, Brace, and Co.

Kuykendall, Ralph S. 1938. *The Hawaiian Kingdom*, vol. 1: *1778–1859*. Honolulu: University of Hawaii Press.

Laird, Thomas. 1981. "Mountains as Gods, Mountains as Goals." *Co-Evolution Quarterly* 31:116–29.

Lambert, Raymond, and Claude Kogan. 1956. *White Fury*. Translated by S. Styles. London: Hurst and Blackett.

Lang, S. D. R., and Ann Lang. 1971. "The Kunde Hospital and a Demographic Survey of the Upper Khumbu, Nepal." *New Zealand Medical Journal* 74(470) (July): 1–7.

Leach, Edmund. 1970. "A Critique of Yalman's Interpretation of Sinhalese Girl's Puberty Ceremony." In *Échanges et Communications*, edited by J. Pouillon and P. Maranda. The Hague: Mouton.

Leacock, Eleanor. 1980. "Montagnais Women and the Jesuit Program for Colonization." In *Women and Colonization: Anthropological Perspectives*, edited by M. Etienne and E. Leacock. New York: Praeger.

———. 1981. *Myths of Male Dominance: Collected Articles on Women Cross-Culturally*. New York: Monthly Review Press.

Lederman, Rena. 1989. "Contested Order: Gender and Society in the Southern New Guinea Highlands." *American Ethnologist* 16(2):230–47.

Lepowsky, Maria. 1993. *Fruit of the Motherland: Gender in an Egalitarian Society*. New York: Columbia University Press.

Levin, Stephanie Seto. 1968. "The Overthrow of the *Kapu* System in Hawaii." *Journal of the Polynesian Society* 77(4):402–30.

Lévi-Strauss, Claude. 1960. "The Family." In *Man, Culture and Society*, edited by H. Shapiro. New York: Oxford University Press.

———. 1963a. *Structural Anthropology*. Translated by C. Jacobson and B. G. Schoepf. New York: Basic Books.

———. 1963b. *Totemism*. Translated by R. Needham. Boston: Beacon Press.

———. 1969a. *The Elementary Structures of Kinship*. Translated by J. H. Bell and J. R. von Sturmer. Edited by R. Needham. Boston: Beacon Press.

———. 1969b. *The Raw and the Cooked*. Translated by J. and D. Weightman. New York: Harper & Row.

Levy, Robert I. 1973. *Tahitians: Mind and Experience in the Society Islands*. Chicago: University of Chicago Press.

Lieberman, Marcia R. 1991. "A Trek of One's Own in Nepal." Travel section, *New York Times*, Sunday, July 28.

———. 1993a. "Scott, Amundsen, and Pasang Lhamu." *Himal* 6(4) (July/August): 76.

———. 1993b. "Marcia Lieberman Responds." *Himal* 6(5) (September/October): 7.

Limón, José. 1991. "Representation, Ethnicity, and the Precursory Ethnography: Notes of a Native Anthropologist." In Richard G. Fox, ed., *Recapturing Anthropology: Working in the Present*. Santa Fe: School of American Research Press.

Linnekin, Jocelyn. 1985. *Children of the Land: Exchange and Status in a Hawaiian Community*. New Brunswick, N.J.: Rutgers University Press.

———. 1990. *Sacred Queens and Women of Consequence: Rank, Gender, and Colonialism in the Hawaiian Islands*. Ann Arbor: University of Michigan Press.

Linton, Ralph. 1939. "Marquesan Culture." In *The Individual and His Society*, edited by A. Kardiner. New York: Columbia University Press.

Loeb, E. M. 1926. *History and Traditions of Niue*. Bernice P. Bishop Museum Bulletin 32. Honolulu: Bishop Museum.

Lowie, Robert H. 1920. *Primitive Society*. New York: Boni and Liveright.

———. 1956 [1935]. *The Crow Indians*. New York: Holt, Rinehart, and Winston.

Lutz, Catherine. 1990. "The Erasure of Women's Writing in Sociocultural Anthropology." *American Ethnologist* 17(4): 611–27.

Lyotard, Jean-François. 1984. *The Postmodern Condition*. Minneapolis: University of Minnesota Press.

MacCormack, Carol, and Marilyn Strathern, eds. 1980. *Nature, Culture and Gender*. Cambridge: Cambridge University Press.

MacKinnon, Catharine A. 1987. *Feminism Unmodified: Discourses on Life and Law*. Cambridge, Mass.: Harvard University Press.

Malo, David. 1903 [1898]. *Hawaiian Antiquities*. Translated by N. B. Emerson. Honolulu: Hawaiian Gazette.

Man, E. H. 1883. "On the Aboriginal Inhabitants of the Andaman Islands." *Journal of the Anthropological Institute* 12: Part 1: 69–116; Part 2: 117–75; Part 3: 327–434.

March, Kathryn S. 1979. "The Intermediacy of Women: Female Gender Symbolism and the Social Position of Women among Tamangs and Sherpas of Highland Nepal." Unpublished Ph.D. dissertation, Department of Anthropology, Cornell University.

———. n.d. "Theriigaathaa and Theragaathaa: A Comparison of Imagery Used by Women and Men Recluses in Their Early Buddhist Poetry." Manuscript.

Mariner, William. 1827. *An Account of the Natives of the Tonga Islands*. 2 vols. Compiled by John Martin. Edinburgh: Constable.

Marshall, Donald S. 1971. "Sexual Behavior on Mangaia." In *Human Sexual Behavior*, edited by D. S. Marshall and R. C. Suggs. New York and London: Basic Books.

Mead, Margaret. 1930. *The Social Organization of Manu'a*. Bernice P. Bishop Museum Bulletin 76. Honolulu: Bishop Museum.

———. 1949. *Coming of Age in Samoa*. New York: New American Library.

Miller, Beatrice D. 1980. "Views of Women's Roles in Buddhist Tibet." In *Studies in the History of Buddhism*, edited by A. K. Narain. Delhi: B. R. Publishing Corp.

Mishkin, Bernard. 1961. "The Maori of New Zealand." In *Cooperation and Competition among Primitive Peoples*, edited by M. Mead. Boston: Beacon Press.

Mitten, Denise. 1992. "The American Team." In da Silva, op. cit.

Moffatt, Gwen. 1961. *Space Below My Feet*. Cambridge, Mass.: Houghton Mifflin.

Mohanty, Chandra T. 1991a [1984]. "Under Western Eyes: Feminist Scholarship and Colonial Discourses." In *Third World Women and the Politics of Feminism*, edited by C. T. Mohanty et al. Bloomington, Ind.: Indiana University Press.

———. 1991b. "Introduction: Cartographies of Struggle: Third World Women and the Politics of Feminism." In *Third World Women and the Politics of Feminism*, edited by C. T. Mohanty et al. Bloomington, Ind.: Indiana University Press.

Nandy, Ashis. 1983. *The Intimate Enemy: Loss and Recovery of the Self under Colonialism*. New Delhi: Oxford University Press.

Nemecek, Ottokar. 1958. *Virginity: Pre-Nuptial Rites and Rituals*. New York: Philosophical Library.

Obeyesekere, Gananath. 1992. *The Apotheosis of Captain Cook: European Mythmaking in the Pacific*. Princeton: Princeton University Press.

Oliver, Douglas. 1974. *Ancient Tahitian Society*. 3 vols. Honolulu: University Press of Hawaii.

O'Neill, Maureen. 1992. "Queen of All She Surveys." In da Silva, op. cit.

Ong, Aihwa. 1987. *Spirits of Resistance and Capitalist Discipline: Factory Women in Malaysia*. Albany: SUNY Press.

Oppitz, Michael. 1968. *Geschichte und Sozialordnung der Sherpa*. Innsbruck-Munich: Universitätsverlag Wagner.

Ortner, Sherry B. 1970. "Food for Thought: A Key Symbol in Sherpa Culture." Unpublished Ph.D. dissertation, Department of Anthropology, University of Chicago.

———. 1972. "Is Female to Male as Nature Is to Culture?" *Feminist Studies* 1(2):5–31. Revised and reprinted in Rosaldo and Lamphere, op. cit.

———. 1973a. "Sherpa Purity." *American Anthropologist* 75:49–63.

———. 1973b. "On Key Symbols." *American Anthropologist* 75:1338–46.

———. 1974. "Purification Beliefs and Practices," *Encyclopaedia Britannica*, 15th edition, 15:298–304.

———. 1976. "The Virgin and the State." *Michigan Discussions in Anthropology* 2:1–16; reprinted 1978 in *Feminist Studies* 4(3) (October): 19–37.

———. 1977. *Sherpas*. Produced by Leslie Woodhead. Manchester: Granada Television. Film.

———. 1978. *Sherpas through Their Rituals*. Cambridge and New York: Cambridge University Press.

———. 1981. "Gender and Sexuality in Hierarchical Societies: The Case of Polynesia and Some Comparative Implications." In Ortner and Whitehead, op. cit.

———. 1983. "The Founding of the First Sherpa Nunnery, and the Problem of 'Women' as an Analytic Category." In *Feminist Re-Visions: What Has Been and Might Be*, edited by V. Patraka and L. Tilly. Ann Arbor: University of Michigan Women's Studies Program.

———. 1984. "Theory in Anthropology since the Sixties." *Comparative Studies in Society and History* 26(1):126–66.

———. 1989. *High Religion: A Cultural and Political History of Sherpa Buddhism*. Princeton: Princeton University Press.

―――. 1990a. "Gender Hegemonies." *Cultural Critique* 14 (Winter):35–80.

―――. 1990b. "Narrativity in History, Culture, and Lives." Presented at the AAA meetings, New Orleans. Manuscript.

―――. 1995a. "Resistance and the Problem of Ethnographic Refusal." *Comparative Studies in Society and History* 37(1) (January): 173–93.

―――. 1995b. "So, *Is* Female to Male as Nature Is to Culture?" Presented at the AAA meetings, Washington, D.C.

―――. n.d. a. "Discourses of Masculinity: Sherpas and 'Sahibs' in Himalayan Mountaineering." Manuscript.

―――. n.d. b. *Sex and Death on Mount Everest.* Manuscript.

Ortner, Sherry B., and Harriet Whitehead, eds. 1981. *Sexual Meanings: The Cultural Construction of Gender and Sexuality.* Cambridge and New York: Cambridge University Press.

Papanek, Hannah. 1973. "Purdah: Separate Worlds and Symbolic Shelter," *Comparative Studies in Society and History* 15:298–325.

Paul, Diana Y. 1979. *Women in Buddhism.* Berkeley: Asian Humanities Press.

Paul, Robert A. 1970. "Sherpas and Their Religion." Unpublished Ph.D. dissertation, Department of Anthropology, University of Chicago.

Peletz, Michael. 1987a. "Female Heirship and the Autonomy of Women in Negeri Sembilan, West Malaysia." *Research in Economic Anthropology* 8:61–101.

―――. 1987b. "The Exchange of Men in 19th-Century Negeri Sembilan (Malaya)." *American Ethnologist* 14(3):449–69.

―――. 1988. *A Share of the Harvest: Kinship, Property, and Social History among the Malays of Rembau.* Berkeley: University of California Press.

―――. 1996. *Reason and Passion: Representations of Gender in a Malay Society.* Berkeley: University of California Press.

Peristiany, J. G., ed. 1966. *Honour and Shame: The Values of Mediterranean Society.* Chicago: University of Chicago Press.

Pitt-Rivers, Julian. 1961. *People of the Sierra.* Chicago: University of Chicago Press.

―――. 1966. "Honour and Social Status." In Peristiany, op. cit.

―――. 1977. *The Fate of Schechem or the Politics of Sex.* Cambridge: Cambridge University Press.

Poewe, Karla O. 1980. "Universal Male Dominance: An Ethnological Illusion." *Dialectical Anthropology* 5(2):111–25.

Povinelli, Elizabeth A. 1993. *Labor's Lot: The Power, History, and Culture of Aboriginal Action.* Chicago: University of Chicago Press.

Pratt, Mary Louise. 1992. *Imperial Eyes: Travel Writing and Transculturation.* London and New York: Routledge.

Propp, V. I. 1968. *Morphology of the Folktale.* Translated by L. Scott. Austin: University of Texas Press.

Radcliffe-Brown, A. R. 1922. *The Andaman Islanders.* Cambridge: Cambridge University Press.

Rafael, Vicente. n.d. "Colonial Domesticity: White Women and United States Rule in the Philippines." Manuscript.

Rapp, Rayna. 1977. "Gender and Class: An Archaeology of Knowledge Concerning the Origin of the State." *Dialectical Anthropology* 2:309–16.

Redfield, Robert. 1953. *The Primitive World and Its Transformations*. Ithaca, N.Y.: Cornell University Press.

Reich, Wilhelm. 1971. *The Invasion of Compulsory Sex-Morality*. New York: Farrar, Straus and Giroux.

Reiter, Rayna R., ed. 1975. *Toward an Anthropology of Women*. New York: Monthly Review Press.

Ridgeway, Rick. 1979. *The Boldest Dream: The Story of Twelve Who Climbed Mount Everest*. New York and London: Harcourt Brace Jovanovich.

Risal, Dipesh. 1993. "Pasang Lhamu." *Himal* 6(3) (May/June): 42–43.

Rogers, Garth. 1977. "The Father's Sister Is Black: A Consideration of Female Rank and Power in Tonga." *Journal of the Polynesian Society* 86:157–82.

Rogers, Susan Carol. 1975. "Female Forms of Power and the Myth of Male Dominance." *American Ethnologist* 2(4):727–57.

Rohrlich-Leavitt, Ruby, Barbara Sykes, and Elizabeth Weatherford. 1975. "Aboriginal Women: Male and Female Anthropological Perspectives." In Reiter, op. cit.

Rosaldo, Michelle Z. 1974. "Woman, Culture and Society: A Theoretical Overview." In Rosaldo and Lamphere, op. cit.

———. 1980. "The Use and Abuse of Anthropology: Reflections on Feminism and Cross-Cultural Understanding." *Signs* 5(3) (Spring): 389–417.

Rosaldo, Michelle Z., and Louise Lamphere, eds. 1974. *Woman, Culture and Society*. Stanford: Stanford University Press.

Rosaldo, Renato, 1989. "Border Crossings." In his *Culture and Truth: The Remaking of Social Analysis*. Boston: Beacon Press.

Rouse, Roger, 1991. "Mexican Migration and the Social Space of Postmodernism," *Diaspora* 1(1):8–23.

Rubin, Gayle. 1975. "The Traffic in Women: Notes on the 'Political Economy' of Sex." In Reiter, op. cit.

Sahlins, Marshall. 1958. *Social Stratification in Polynesia*. Seattle: University of Washington Press.

———. 1963. "Poor Man, Rich Man, Big-Man, Chief: Political Types in Melanesia and Polynesia." *Comparative Studies in Society and History* 5:285–303.

———. 1981. *Historical Metaphors and Mythical Realities: Structure in the Early History of the Sandwich Islands Kingdom*. Ann Arbor: University of Michigan Press.

———. 1985. *Islands of History*. Chicago: University of Chicago Press.

———. 1995. *How "Natives" Think. About Captain Cook, for Example*. Chicago: University of Chicago Press.

Said, Edward. 1978. *Orientalism*. New York: Pantheon Books.

Sanday, Peggy Reeves. 1981. *Female Power and Male Dominance: On the Origins of Sexual Inequality*. New York: Cambridge University Press.

———. 1990. *Fraternity Gang Rape: Sex, Brotherhood, and Privilege on Campus*. New York: New York University Press.

Sangroula, Yubaraj. 1993. "A National Heroine." *Himal* 6(5) (September/October): 7.

Sartre, Jean-Paul. 1968. *Search for a Method*. Translated by H. E. Barnes. New York: Vintage Books.

Scarr, Josephine. 1966. *Four Miles High*. London: Victor Gollancz.

Schneider, David M. 1968. *American Kinship: A Cultural Account*. Englewood Cliffs, New Jersey: Prentice-Hall.

———. 1976. "The Meaning of Incest." *Journal of the Polynesian Society* 85:149–69.

Schneider, Jane. 1971. "Of Vigilance and Virgins: Honor, Shame, and Access to Resources in Mediterranean Society," *Ethnology* 10(1):1–24.

Scott, Doug. 1984. "Himalayan Climbing: Part One of a Personal Review." *Mountain* 100:26–36.

———. 1985. "Himalayan Climbing: Part Two of a Personal Review." *Mountain* 101:26–32.

Scott, Joan W. 1986. "Gender: A Useful Category of Historical Analysis." *American Historical Review* 91(5):1053–75; reprinted in her *Gender and the Politics of History*. New York: Columbia University Press, 1988.

Sharma, Prayag Raj. 1993. "Don't Belittle Pasang Lhamu." *Himal* 6(4) (July/August): 5.

Sherpa, Donna M. 1994. *Living in the Middle: Sherpas of the Mid-Range Himalayas*. Prospect Heights, Ill.: Waveland Press.

Sherpa-Padgett, Linda M. 1993. "Devastating Words." *Himal* 6(5) (September/October): 5–6.

Shore, Bradd. 1976. "Incest Prohibitions and the Logic of Power in Samoa." *Journal of the Polynesian Society* 85:275–96.

———. 1981. "Sexuality and Gender in Samoa: Conceptions and Missed Conceptions." In Ortner and Whitehead, op. cit.

Siegel, James T. 1969. *The Rope of God*. Berkeley and Los Angeles: University of California Press.

Singh, N. Iqbal. 1978. *The Andaman Story*. New Delhi: Vikas.

Siu, R. G. H. 1968. *The Man of Many Qualities*. Cambridge, Mass.: MIT Press.

Slater, Philip. 1968. *The Glory of Hera*. Boston: Beacon Press.

Spivak, Gayatri Chakravorty. 1988. "Can the Subaltern Speak?" In *Marxism and the Interpretation of Culture*, edited by C. Nelson and L. Grossberg. Urbana, Ill.: University of Illinois Press.

Stacey, Judith. 1975. "When Patriarchy Kowtows: The Significance of the Chinese Family Revolution for Feminist Theory." *Feminist Studies* 2(2/3):64–112.

———. 1990. *Brave New Families: Stories of Domestic Upheaval in Late Twentieth-Century America*. New York: Basic Books.

Stein, R. A. 1972. *Tibetan Civilization*. Translated by J. E. S. Driver. Stanford: Stanford University Press.

Stoler, Ann. 1992. "Sexual Affronts and Racial Frontiers: European Identities and the Cultural Politics of Exclusion in Colonial Southeast Asia." *Comparative Studies in Society and History* 34(3):514–52.

Strathern, Marilyn. 1980. "No Nature, No Culture: The Hagen Case." In MacCormack and Strathern, op. cit.

———. 1981. "Self Interest and the Social Good: Some Implications of Hagen Gender Imagery." In Ortner and Whitehead, op. cit.

Suggs, Robert C. 1966. *Marquesan Sexual Behavior*. New York: Harcourt, Brace and World.

———. 1971. "Sex and Personality in the Marquesas: A Discussion of the Linton-Kardiner Report." In *Human Sexual Behavior*, edited by D. S. Marshall and R. C. Suggs. New York and London: Basic Books.

Sweet, Louise, ed. 1967. *Appearance and Reality: Status and Roles of Women in Mediterranean Societies*. Special Issue of *Anthropological Quarterly* 40(3).

Tambiah, Stanley J. 1973. "Dowry and Bridewealth and the Property Rights of Women in South Asia." In *Bridewealth and Dowry*, edited by J. Goody and S. J. Tambiah. Cambridge: Cambridge University Press.

Tanner, Nancy. 1974. "Matrifocality in Indonesia and Africa and among Black Americans." In Rosaldo and Lamphere, op. cit.

Tenzing Norgay. 1955. (Tenzing of Everest with James Ramsay Ullman). *Tiger of the Snows*. New York: G. P. Putnam's Sons.

———. 1977. (Tenzing Norgay Sherpa). *After Everest: An Autobiography*. As told to Malcolm Barnes. London: George Allen & Unwin.

Thompson, E. P. 1966. *The Making of the English Working Class*. New York: Vintage.

Trinh T. Minh-ha. 1989. "The Language of Nativism: Anthropology as a Scientific Conversation of Man with Man." In her *Woman, Native, Other: Writing Postcoloniality and Feminism*. Bloomington: Indiana University Press.

Tsing, Anna Lowenhaupt. 1990. "Gender and Performance in Meratus Dispute Settlement." In Atkinson and Errington, op. cit.

———. 1993. *In the Realm of the Diamond Queen: Marginality in an Out-of-the-Way Place*. Princeton: Princeton University Press.

Tullis, Julie. 1986. *Clouds from Both Sides*. London: Grafton Books.

Turner, Victor. 1967. *The Forest of Symbols*. Ithaca: Cornell University Press.

Ullman, Stephen. 1963. "Semantic Universals." In *Universals of Language*, edited by Joseph H. Greenberg. Cambridge, Mass.: MIT Press.

Unsworth, Walt. 1981. *Everest: A Mountaineering History*. Boston: Houghton Mifflin.

Vaillant, George. 1950. *The Aztecs of Mexico*. Baltimore: Penguin.

Valeri, Valerio. 1982. "The Transformation of a Transformation: A Structural Essay on an Aspect of Hawaiian History [1809–1819]." *Social Analysis* 10:3–41.

———. 1985. *Kingship and Sacrifice: Ritual and Society in Ancient Hawaii*. Translated by Paula Wissing. Chicago: University of Chicago Press.

———. 1987. "Response [to Charlot]." *Pacific Studies* 10(2):148–214.

———. 1990. "Both Nature and Culture: Reflections on Menstrual and Parturitional Taboos in Huaulu (Seram)." In Atkinson and Errington, op. cit.

van Gennep, Arnold. 1960. *Rites of Passage*. Translated by M. B. Vizedom and G. L. Caffee. Chicago: University of Chicago Press.

Vayda, A. P. 1961. "Love in the Polynesian Atolls." *Man* 61:204–5.

von Fürer-Haimendorf, Christoph. 1964. *The Sherpas of Nepal*. Berkeley and Los Angeles: University of California Press.

———. 1975. *Himalayan Traders*. New York: St. Martin's Press.

———. 1976. "A Nunnery in Nepal." *Kailash* 4:121–54.

———. 1984. *The Sherpas Transformed: Social Change in a Buddhist Society of Nepal*. New Delhi: Sterling Publishers.

von Hagen, Victor W. 1957. *The Realm of the Incas*. New York: New American Library.

Watson, Lawrence. 1972. "Sexual Socialization in Guajiro Society." *Ethnology* 11:150–56.

Webb, M. C. 1965. "The Abolition of the Taboo System in Hawaii." *Journal of the Polynesian Society* 74:21–39.

Weber, Max. 1958. *From Max Weber: Essays in Sociology*. Translated and edited by H. H. Gerth and C. Wright Mills. New York: Oxford University Press.

———. 1978. *Economy and Society: An Outline of Interpretive Sociology*. Edited by Guenther Roth and Claus Wittich. Translated by Ephraim Fischoff et al. Berkeley: University of California Press.

Williams, Raymond. 1977. *Marxism and Literature*. Oxford: Oxford University Press.

Willis, Paul. 1981. *Learning to Labor: How Working Class Kids Get Working Class Jobs*. New York: Columbia University Press.

Wright, Henry. 1977. "Recent Research on the Origin of the State." *Annual Review of Anthropology* 6:379–97.

Yalman, Nur. 1963. "On the Purity of Women in the Castes of Ceylon and Malabar." *Journal of the Royal Anthropological Institute* 93:25–58.

Yanagisako, Sylvia. 1979. "Family and Household: The Analysis of Domestic Groups." *Annual Review of Anthropology*. Palo Alto, Calif.: Annual Review Press.

Yeatman, Anna. 1984. "Gender and the Differentiation of Social Life into Public and Domestic Domains." *Social Analysis* 15:30–49.

Zipes, Jack. 1993. *The Trials and Tribulations of Little Red Riding Hood*. New York: Routledge.

Index